JACK SMITH

Jack Smith

a painter in pursuit of marvels

Norbert Lynton

momentum

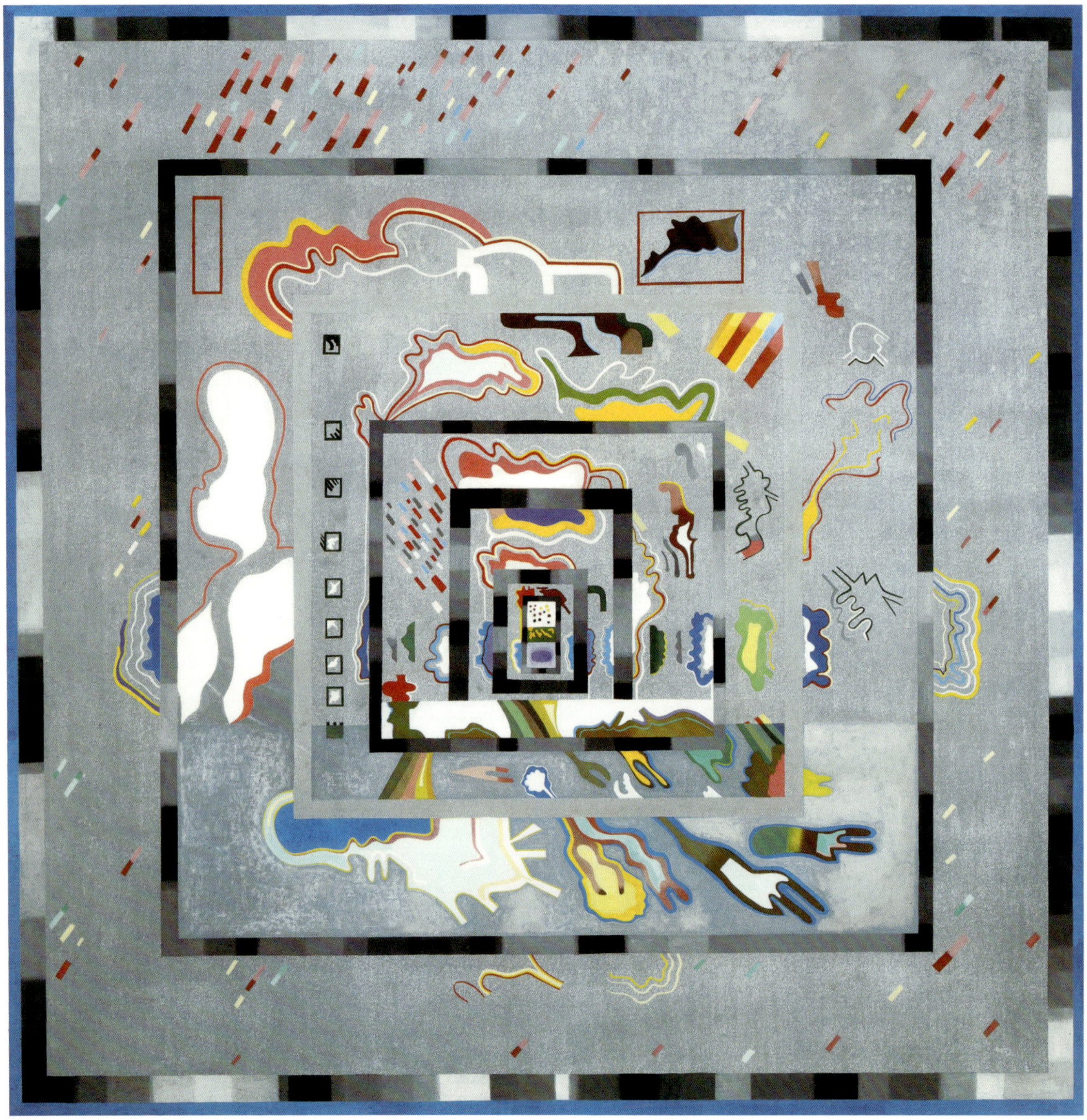

Inside. Outside. Roundabout (Blue Border) 1965

Oil on canvas

122 x 122 cm

Preface

Jack Smith
notes on painting

1965

I think of my paintings as diagrams of an experience or sensation. The subject is very important. The sound of the subject, its noise or its silence, its intervals and its activity. When I talk about the sound of the music of the subject, I'm not always thinking in terms of a symphony, but groups of single notes. The closer the painting is to a diagram or a graph, the nearer it is to my intention. I like every mark to establish a fact in the most precise, economical way.

This statement seems relevant to my work since 1960. The development from the 1952 snowscape to the figures in a room and then to the round diagrams of 1962/3 is to me absolutely logical. I have been consistently interested in light; between 1952/6 as an outside source and since then as a quality within the painting. Light as a subject no longer interests me, but it's still essential that each painting contains it.

This kind of remoteness I feel makes one more aware of certain aspects of a subject that cannot be visually explained without preconceived ideas getting in the way. There is silence in the earlier paintings, though that is not the subject. Later on that silence becomes the subject. Painting is full of contradictions; hence the necessity of not believing. If one set of paintings produces a belief, the next tends to cancel it out. I feel that this is as it should be if painting is to remain creative and not become a middle aged activity. One must move forward.

More and more do I find that activity of different kinds is essential in a painting. I want it to be as complex as a symphony. Keep the surface as flat as possible, letting it have visual space or eye dance, but no Impressionist, Cubist or continued space. I would like the surface to be as remote as Vermeers. Usually a painting is only a success when I am surprised at the final form the painting has taken. One discovers that certain things are real and that one's original idea was only a shadow of the finished object. Each work should be a visual celebration. There must be no compromise. An artist reaches maturity when he no longer has the need for heroes.

1995

I am not a practitioner of instant art, my paintings are objects of contemplation. I want to produce a truly modern painting. It doesn't need the prop of history to support it. One has not been there before: it is a unique experience. In much contemporary painting there is too much Wagner and not enough Stravinsky. This is not true of sculpture.

The only important quality eventually is the spirit within the painting. Painting must emanate light. I don't think of myself as an English artist at all; some of us are exiles in our own country. In England the academic mind always triumphs. Poetry is precision.

To produce work that stands outside the hysteria of our time. How difficult it is to produce the perfect painting. Nothing can be added to it, nothing can be subtracted from it. The perfect painting and a memorable image. I suppose we are fortunate if we can produce half a dozen such paintings in a lifetime. The painted image, its silence is beautiful.

If the work contains that important vein of creativity it will be controversial. External logic should be ignored. There is logic within the painting which needs to be discovered.

> *"He is the kind of man who would have told Vermeer to loosen up."*

> *"Everyone wants originality, as long as they are familiar with it." (Nathalie Sarraute)*

I've heard it said that painting is finished, not to my way of thinking. Abstract painting is still in its infancy; there is so much to explore.

> *Visual music. Visual invention. Visual celebration.*

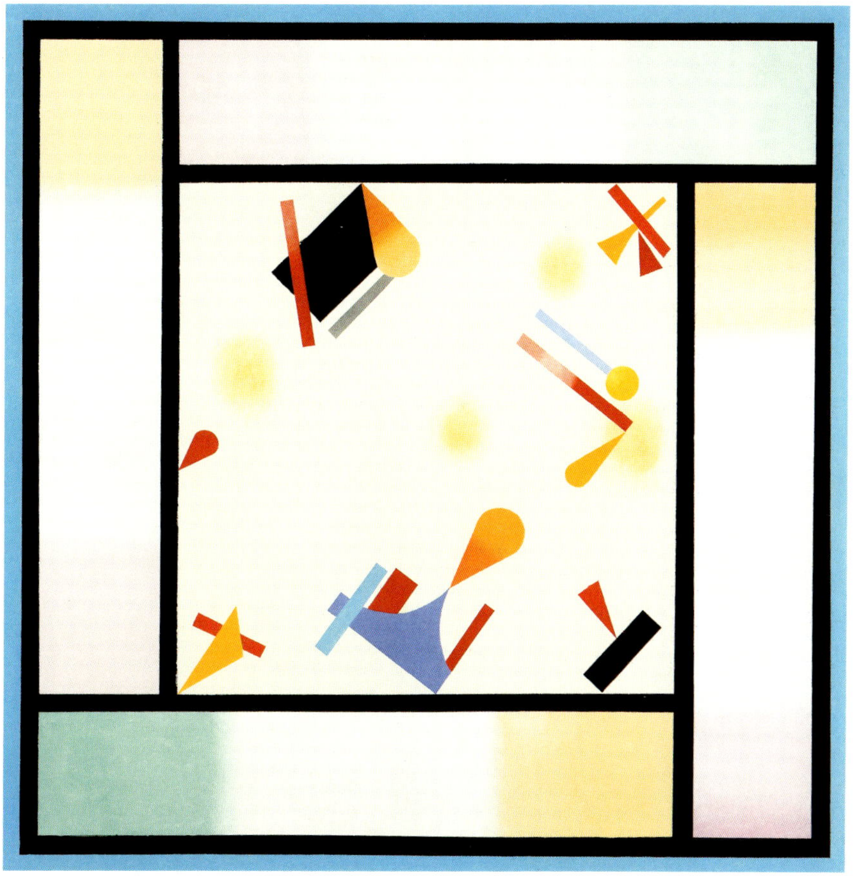

Musical Invention 1995

Oil on canvas

91 x 91 cm

Collection: Matthew and Huei Flowers

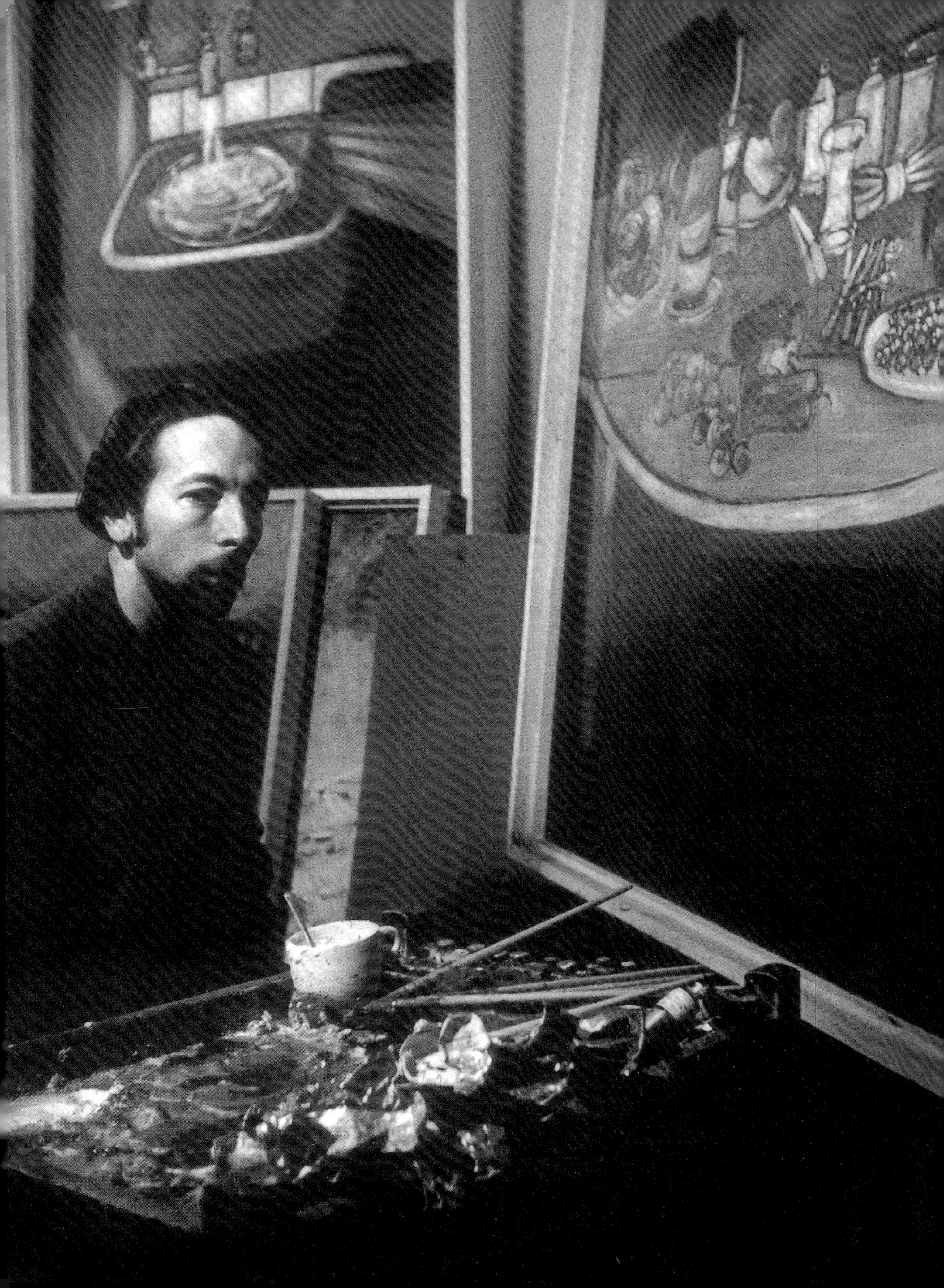

Jack Smith
a painter in pursuit of marvels

by Norbert Lynton

In 1952, while still a student at the Royal College of Art, Jack Smith had his first one-man exhibition. This was at the Beaux Arts Gallery, where he showed almost annually until 1958, and was associated with other painters from the RCA, brought in after himself. Together they were seen as a new generation of British realists, proving the gallery's dedication to art of this sort. In 1958 his connection with the gallery suddenly ended: his work had changed too much to be called realistic. When, in 1959, he had his early retrospective show at the Whitechapel Art Gallery, all the more recent work was about the transformations wrought by light and movement on, mostly, observed still life objects and on the sea; a group of drawings were of figures in a room, almost abstract and attending more to rhythms and rhymes discovered in the intervals than to physical presences. By 1962 Smith's work was not abstracted but wholly abstract: a celebration of making and seeing, a kind of visual music.

So Jack Smith has been an abstract painter for close on forty years. His early work, of 1952-1956, did include a number of domestic interiors, kitchens and living-dining rooms, with and without figures. They were ordinary, un-posh, and based on the house he shared with other artists and with his brother. They were neither sordid nor resentful. They stood at some distance from the often more pleasing or romantic art produced in England since the war, but they were dignified representations, honouring what they pictured. Yet they were received as images of protest. Contemporary realistic movements in France and Italy were more directly polemical. Jack Smith, John Bratby and the others were taken to be an English equivalent, and welcomed or disdained as such according to taste.

All Europe was in a post-war and Cold War mood, anxious and eager to see art signalling violence and vulnerability. British artists had generally shown little inclination to use art in this way. Smith himself met with much interest from the start, especially from two new and influential voices among the art critics of the time. John Berger, looking for art that would advance social reform, thought Smith might well be a genius. David Sylvester, less concerned with social purposes than aesthetic power, found his work wholly significant. Both watched his progress. Unfortunately, an article by Sylvester led the media to

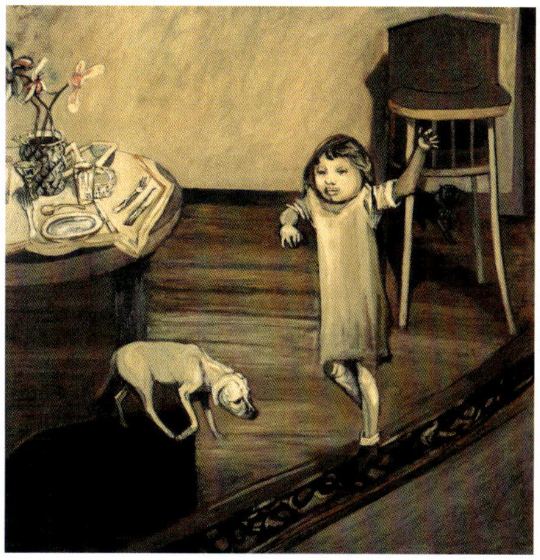

Interior with Child 1953

Oil on board
122 x 122 cm
Royal College of Art Collection

left:
Jack Smith, Kensington Studio, Pembroke Road, London 1953
Photograph: Brian Seed

attach the label 'Kitchen Sink School' to the group. This, including the expectation of images of seedy urban life, has stuck especially to Smith and his work. He is still thought of as a Kitchen Sink painter and blamed or ignored for not supplying Kitchen Sink pictures. Unlike baseball players, English artists are allowed just one strike, assuming they are admitted onto the playing field at all; that missed or somehow mismanaged and they're out.

The Beaux Arts Gallery was run by Helen Lessore, a painter herself and a woman of strong convictions. Her husband had set it up before his death in 1951; she now wanted to make it more youthful and purposeful. In January 1952 Berger reported on the annual *Young Contemporaries* show with unusual excitement. The six hundred paintings there revealed a common attitude: 'the deliberate acceptance of the importance of the everyday and the ordinary', and could 'help to reform a European tradition.' Its realism was akin to that of the

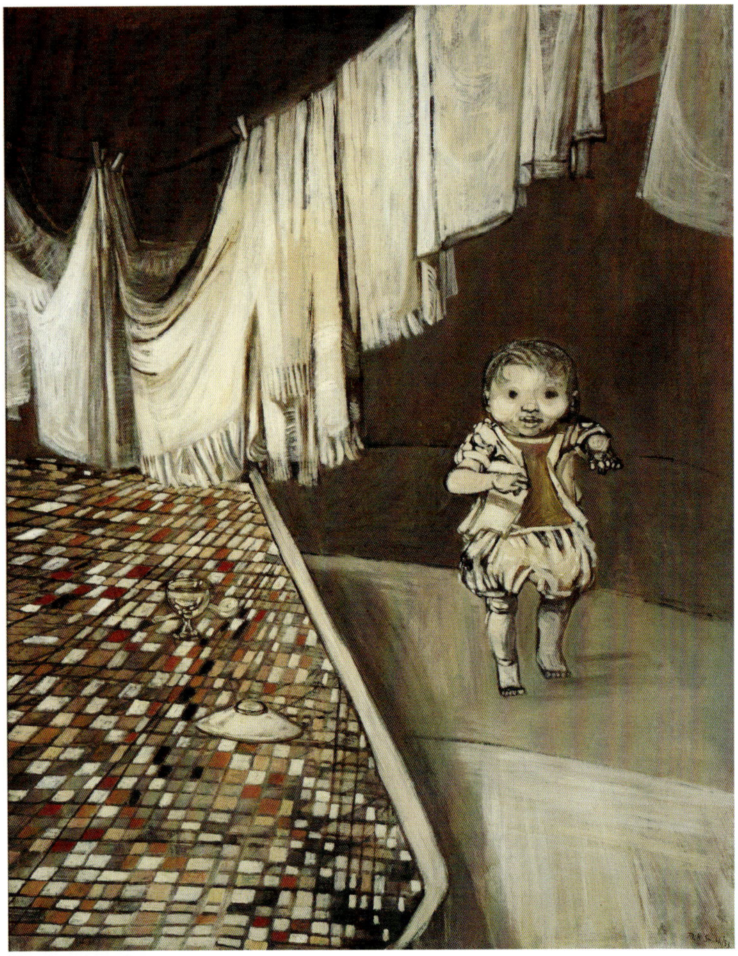

Child Walking with Check Tablecloth 1953

Oil on board
153 x 122 cm
The British Council

best post-war Italian films (Rosselini, de Sica, etc.). He mentioned Derrick Greaves and Edward Middleditch; Jack Smith was not in the show.[1] Both Sylvester and Berger curated exhibitions of a wide range of French and English 'realist painting' at the Whitechapel that year, and the question of realism loomed large in art debates. Early in 1953 Berger reflected on the previous year's art events. He thought little of most of them but pointed to two related moments of importance. One was that 1952 *Young Contemporaries*; the other was a show, at the Arcade Gallery, of 'the young Frenchman Rebeyrolle and his friends', evidence that 'a similar trend was making itself felt on the Continent'.[2] Rebeyrolle had had his first one-man show in Paris in 1951; his second was in London in 1954. In 1948 Rebeyrolle, Bernard Buffet and other French painters had been noticed in Paris, offering their art as *Témoignage*, witness to mankind's vulnerability and wretchedness. In Italy an older group of artists had formed the *Fronte Nuovo delle Arti* in 1946, dedicated to treating social realities in sympathy with the political left after years of Fascist culture. Some of its members were Communists. The most convincing among them, Renato Guttuso, was well known in London. At the Venice Biennale of 1952 a section was devoted to these Italian realists. Berger reported that these 'Italian Social Realists' were important but not good: it was just that 'all the others are pointless'. Only one painting on show was successful: Guttuso's large battle-scene of Garibaldi and his Thousand, 'a painting which connects instead of isolates'.[3] It seems that a substantial part of the London art world of the early 1950s was eager to 'join Europe', as we would say today, after a period of enforced insularity and Neo-Romanticism. Helen Lessore's assessment of what mattered coincided with Berger's.

Smith was in his last year at the Royal College of Art when she gave him his first exhibition. Solo exhibitions followed every year until 1958. She took on Derrick Greaves at Smith's suggestion, showing him in 1953 and 1958; then Edward Middleditch, showing him frequently from 1954 to 1962, and Bratby whom she showed almost every year from 1954 to 1959 after which he moved to the Zwemmer Gallery. The Beaux Arts Gallery closed in 1965. Before this Lessore had complemented what was seen as her Social Realist group with two additional ex-RCA students who appeared to be Expressionists: Frank Auerbach in 1956 and Leon Kossoff in 1957. The meaning then ascribed to their work was always negative: it spoke of Existentialist anxieties and Cold War fears.

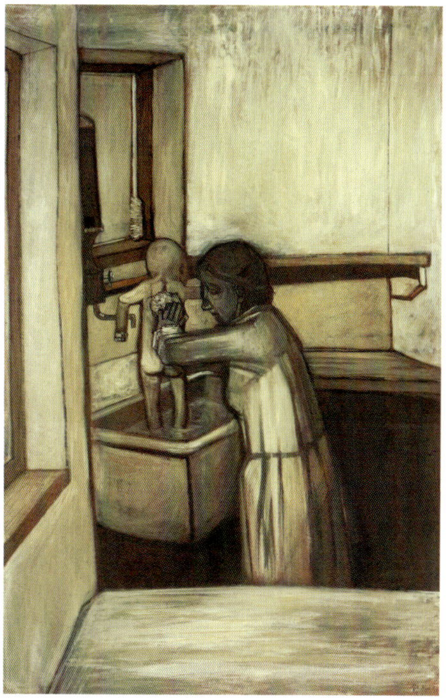

Mother Bathing Child 1953

Oil on board
183 x 122 cm
© Tate, London 2000

1. John Berger in The New Statesman [referred to below as NS], 19 January 1952.
2. NS, 29 March 1952.
3. NS, 5 July 1952.

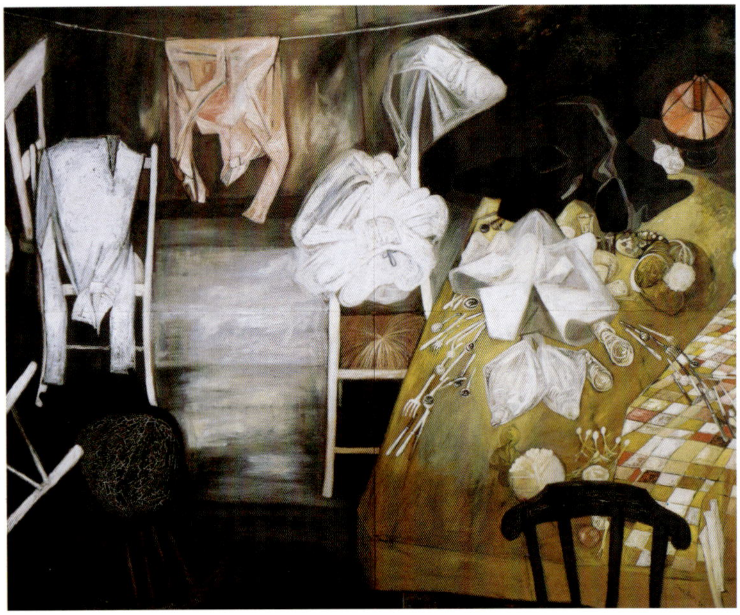

Creation and Crucifixion 1956

Oil on board
244 x 305 cm
Board of Trustees of the National Museums and Galleries on Merseyside (Walker Art Gallery, Liverpool)

Sylvester's article was published under the heading 'The Kitchen Sink' in 1954.[4] Painters had long rejoiced in the commonplace, such as 'the contents of humble kitchens', because these, would not be burdened with 'social implications'. He referred to French painters, mentioning particularly Buffet. Sylvester was telling the world that a new group with similar aims had emerged in Britain with Smith and Bratby 'and their followers'. In spite of his warning that no 'social implications' were to be read into this art, the tag Kitchen Sink was firmly attached to the four painters, and they were seen as campaigning Social Realists. Occasionally they were dubbed the Beaux Arts Quartet. Smith wrote later what he felt then: 'There was much talk at the time about "social or politically committed work", a phrase that always makes me check that my passport is in order.'[5] A burden from the start, the tag became a trap as critics learned to praise or criticize his work according to how far it matched the formula.

In 1955 Lessore showed her quartet of realists in Cambridge, at Heffer's bookshop. In 1956 the British Council exhibited them as 'Quattro Giovane Pittori Inglesi' in the British Pavilion at the Venice Biennale, and the work of two older artists, paintings by Ivon Hitchens and sculpture and drawings by Lynn Chadwick, in adjacent galleries. Whereas Chadwick was awarded the main prize for sculpture, the English realists were seen as contributors to a European trend

4. *Encounter*, December 1954, pages 61-64.
5. From Smith's statement of 1983, written for the catalogue of 'The Forgotten Fifties' exhibition, curated by John Spalding for the Graves Art Gallery in Sheffield in 1984 and then toured, page 49.

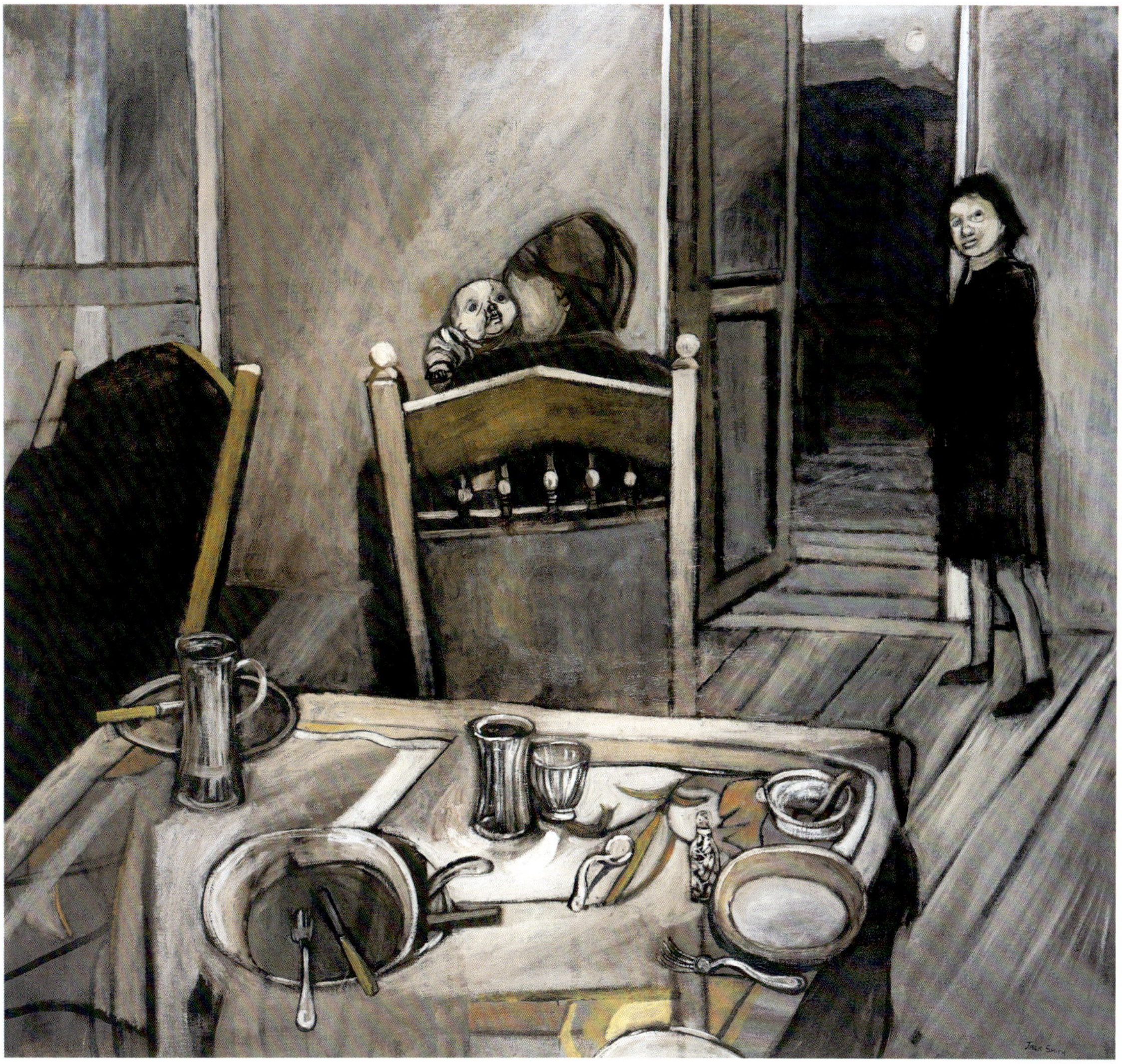

After the Meal 1952

Oil on canvas

112 x 121 cm

Arts Council Collection, Hayward Gallery, London

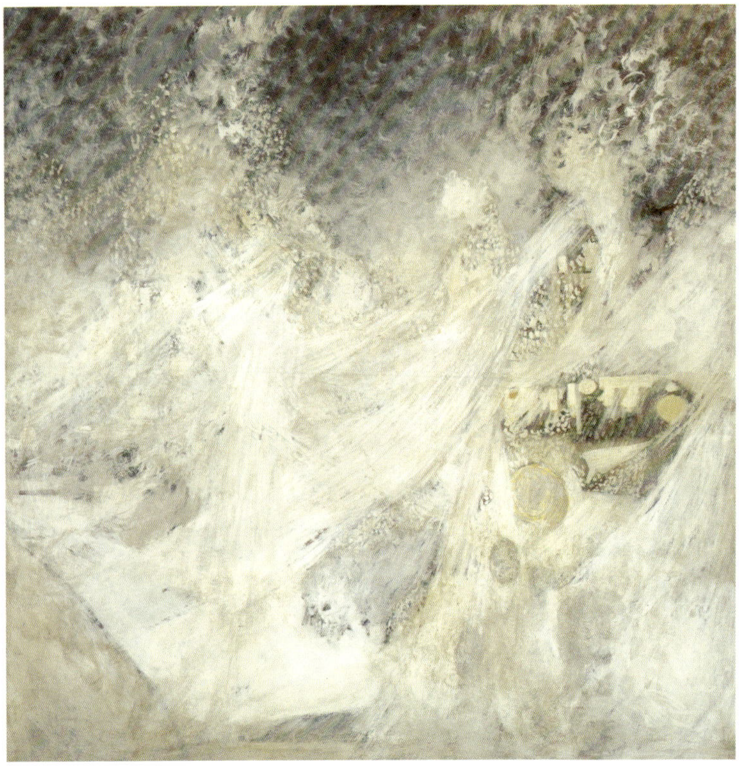

Snowstorm in a City 1952/53

Oil on canvas
122 x 122 cm

but less all-out – a standard complaint against English art.

This did not dishearten Lessore who believed deeply in what she called 'the Great Tradition of European Art', now threatened by abstraction. In 1958 she suddenly dropped Jack Smith. His latest work proved he was abandoning realism. It was now not *Child Walking with Check Tablecloth,* ill. p.10 or *Mother Bathing Child*, ill. p.11, but *Bottles in Light, Patch of Light over Cylinders* and, abstracted beyond legibility, *Figures in a Room*, ill. p.15. This made him a traitor to the cause: she announced she could no longer be his dealer. When another Beaux Arts painter, Michael Fussell, protested at this, she dropped him too.

Smith's dismissal coincided with a warmly supportive review of his show. Sylvester, who generally wrote with respect of the Beaux Arts' shows, in September 1958 had nothing but praise for Smith's way of dealing 'with increasing assurance with those problems of effects of light'.[6] The previous year he had responded negatively to changes he had noticed in Smith's new paintings, as we shall see.

6. *Encounter*, December 1954, pages 61-64.

Jack Smith and Derrick Greaves were both born in Sheffield, Jack on 18 June 1928, Greaves in 1927. They grew up in the same street, knew each other as boys, went to the same art school and remained good friends. Smith's parents were very supportive without sharing his developing interests. They were quiet people, holding the traditional, conservative views of the Yorkshire working class. Jack's brother Gordon, five years older, read and collected books. Gordon was away in the Royal Air Force for much of Jack's teen years, leaving Jack the run of his bookshelves; then he tried the almost infinite offerings of the Sheffield Public Library. He particularly remembers reading Theodor Dreiser's novels about poverty and power in early twentieth-century America, and the plays and prefaces of George Bernard Shaw. He liked *Titus Groan* more for Mervyn Peake's illustrations, in little black dots, than for the text; he bought himself a copy. Soon after, he embarked on D.H.Lawrence, Kafka, Zola, Lewellyn Powis, Dostoevsky — a whole range of solid stuff, at times romantic, more often tough.

He did not like Sheffield. It strikes him today that when he saw the damage caused by Hitler's bombs and incendiaries when he was fourteen and fifteen – the ravaged, collapsing buildings, the burnt-out tram on its side, the paint factory still on fire, they were to him amazing sights, not human disasters. (Much the same age, I responded the same way in London.) School was all right: Jack was generally competent and particularly enjoyed English Literature and Art. At sixteen he won a scholarship and left to study at the College of Art; the training there would prepare him to be a teacher and his family approved of that. What he found there was of some use technically but did little to stretch his imagination. He visited the Graves Art Gallery, above the Central Library, but nothing there held his attention. The Old Masters were too remote. He felt already that art's task was to break away, to change the world. There were art books supporting this view.

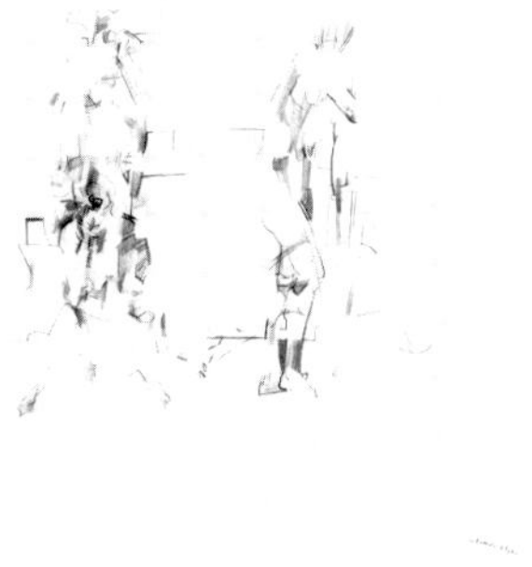

Figures in a Room 1959/60

Pencil on paper
54.5 x 71 cm

Figures in Light 1959/60

Pencil on paper
51 x 51 cm

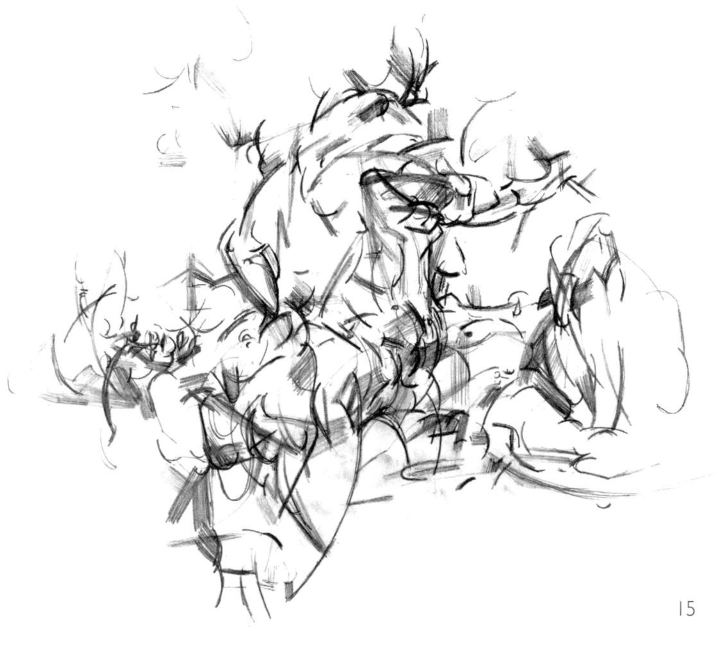

Of key importance to him, at this stage, was R.H.Wilenski's *Modern French Painters*, first published in 1940. For a while it was his Bible. Gauguin was especially stimulating because of the power of his often exotic figures shown in clear, essentially classical compositions, and also his bold grasp on colour. His message, Smith says, was 'to take every painting to an extreme position'. In other books he came across Mondrian and recognized in him a guide of another sort, mysterious though the Dutchman's work must have seemed at first. Again, it was the clarity that excited him. In the 1950s he told Lessore that he wanted 'one day to do a painting as well structured as a Mondrian'; she simply could not understand what he meant. In 1946 he went to Leeds to see the Matisse and Picasso exhibition that had scandalized London the previous winter at the Victoria and Albert Museum. Almost everyone denounced Picasso for the grossly distorted women of his wartime paintings and their crazy, surrealistic hats. Next to such paintings the Matisses looked reasonably benign even to suspicious English eyes. Smith found the exhibition exhilarating: Picasso was another painter who took 'every painting to an extreme position'.

That summer Smith turned eighteen, passed the Intermediate examination and finished at the College. National Service had to be done next. Like Gordon, he went into the RAF. He was trained to be a teleprinter operator, but found himself posted to Stranraer on the west coast of Scotland, where his job was to take re-usable radio equipment out of obsolete sea-planes, hundreds of them, stranded on the shore like whales, 'huge white shapes by a chocolate-coloured sea'. Often he reclaimed also their emergency stocks of chocolate. These sweetened existence quite measurably. Daily life was wet and cold. NAAFI food was basic; off-base everything was still rationed.

It was not an especially bad time, just an odd one and physically very uncomfortable. It worked against his tendency to keep himself apart. His friends know him to be an easy, outgoing and communicative man. He is also slim and rather good-looking in a distinguished, El Greco-ish way. But there is a touch of the hermit about him. He works; he reads; he listens to music; he observes the world and his experience of it, and works again. He lives simply in an enduring marriage and enjoys company but does not need much of it. At Stranraer life could not be like that, and he thinks there was some virtue in being taken out of himself for a while. After some months there, he was moved south to a signals centre near Bedford. London was only forty-odd miles away and in range for day and weekend visits. His 'demob' was delayed by the Berlin airlift of summer 1948. On one of his visits to the bookshops along Charing Cross Road, Smith noticed St Martin's School of Art, went in, requested to see the Principal and asked him whether he might join the painting school that autumn.

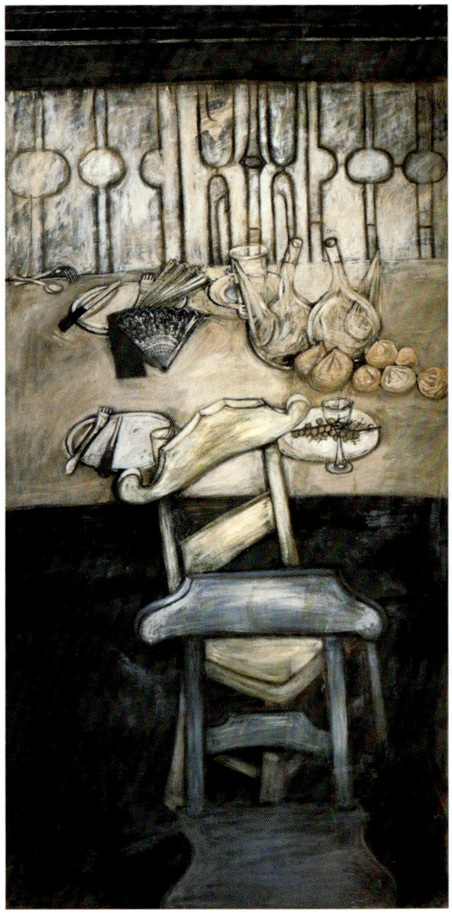

Spanish Still Life 1955

Oil on board
244 x 123 cm
Sheffield Galleries and Museums Trust

He was told to come again and bring some work. He did so and was accepted. He was demobbed in time, and studied at St Martin's for two years, from 1948 to 1950.

Separateness became his situation there too, a degree of remoteness from staff and most of the students. But one of these, Susan Craigie Halkett, was of a like mind and admired him from the start for his evident talent and seriousness. They became friends and found working space for themselves on a landing outside the studios where no one took much notice of them. They worked hard, drawing each other every day and painting a lot. In spite (or because?) of this Smith failed the National Diploma in Design (NDD). He recalls an interesting moment when he was painting a life model and the tutor asked him whether he intended to pass the exam, in which case the tutor would know how to help him, or whether he preferred to have his work seen as that of a serious artist; he should think about this and report back. A week later, Smith asked the tutor to look at his work as that of an artist, and so failed the exam.

None the less, he gained a place on the RCA's advanced course and an extension of his grant. In 1949 he had moved into a crowded house in Pembroke Road, West Kensington. Derrick Greaves lived there, as did another Sheffield-born artist, the sculptor George Fullard and his wife 'Corky', and also another sculptor, Geoffrey Dudley; in the basement were his brother Gordon, and his family. This household became the main subject of Smith's art for some time. 'I just painted the objects around me, I lived in that kind of house ... If one had lived in a palace, one might have painted chandeliers', he wrote in 1960, a shade disingenuously.[7]

In 1983 he made the same point more fully:

> *The art of the 1940s in France and England didn't excite me.*
> *I reacted against its lack of creative and inventive energy. So, like many artists before me, I turned to my own environment for subject matter.*
> *Out of that chaos I tried to establish visual order, to establish some kind of rapport between a person and the objects which surrounded him.*
> *The objects became part of the human struggle, reflecting anxieties and tribulations. I had wanted to make the ordinary miraculous. This had nothing to do with social comment. If I had lived in a palace I would have painted the chandeliers.*[8]

He would have agreed with the words Doris Lessing wrote for Tom Maschler's

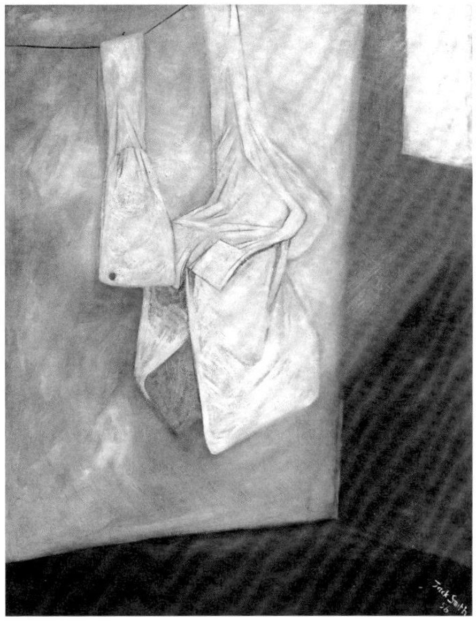

Shirt in Sunlight 1956

Oil on board
152.5 x 122 cm
Leicestershire Museums Arts and Records Service Artworks Collection

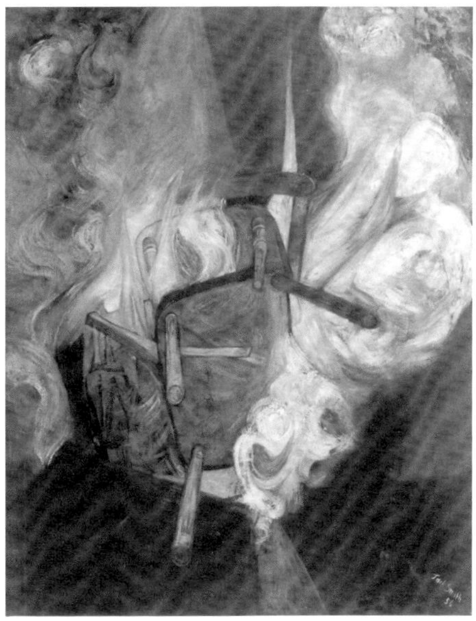

Two Chairs on Fire c.1952-56

Oil on board
152.5 x 152.5 cm

---

7. Statement in the catalogue of his exhibition at the Matthiesen Gallery, London, 1960.
8. From the artist's 1983 statement (see note 4 above).

collection *Declarations*, published in 1957: 'If there is one thing which distinguishes our literature, it is a confusion of standards and the uncertainty of values'.[9]

The RCA painting school was then headed by Rodrigo Moynihan as Professor. His staff included Carel Weight, John Minton and Ruskin Spear. Their teaching, like their painting, inclined to realism of some sort though each had his own style. Smith found Moynihan a little remote and characterless though widely experienced, Spear shallow and too eager to teach young painters how to seduce the public with paint, and Carel Weight (the oldest of them at forty in 1948) rather set in his idiosyncratic ways. John Minton, just into his thirties and widely admired for his portraits and illustrational drawings, cared deeply about art as construction as well as expression, and was to Smith more or less the ideal tutor at this stage. After the first year, Minton made it possible for Smith to work out of the College by recommending him for six-weekly permits to work at home and undertaking to visit him there regularly. Smith recalls Minton's amazement at the quantity of work he was producing and at the size of the paintings. In those days four by four feet was exceptional, and four by four, even six by four, were Smith's preferred sizes, painted on hardboard. This had fairly recently come into general use, imported from Sweden for all sorts of building and furnishing purposes. It came in eight by four foot sheets, made a good support for painting if properly rubbed down and sized, and was cheaper than canvas plus stretchers. The thin sheets were also more easily stacked than canvases, though heavier to handle.

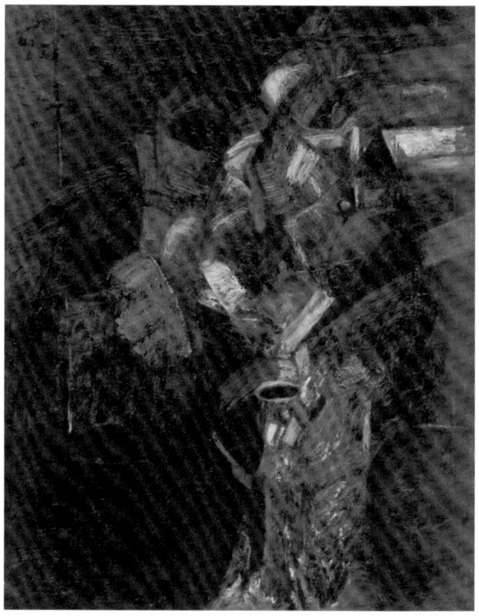

Talking Head 1957

Oil on board

152.5 x 122 cm

Private collection

In 1949 Smith had painted a series of paintings of the sea, recalling the Scottish coast. Then the Kensington interior became his prime subject, renewed by daily experience. The people appearing in them are the women and children, never the men. They are only slightly characterized: individuals but not quite portraits. He made pencil drawings, and sometimes pen-and-ink drawings, from life and from memory, and built his paintings from these. The paints he used were mostly earth colours — the cheapest available, he says. I suspect he would have armed himself with others had he felt the need; in fact, to some extent he did. In any case, he modulated his earth colours with others. His point is that we should not see his use of earth colours as declaring misery or protest.

Today we need not accept that Jack Smith's art of this period was an entirely innocent, disinterested account of his environment. In part, he was reacting against the middle-class, comfortable art that was his inheritance. In so

9. Quoted in the introduction in ibid., page 9, presumably written by John Spalding.

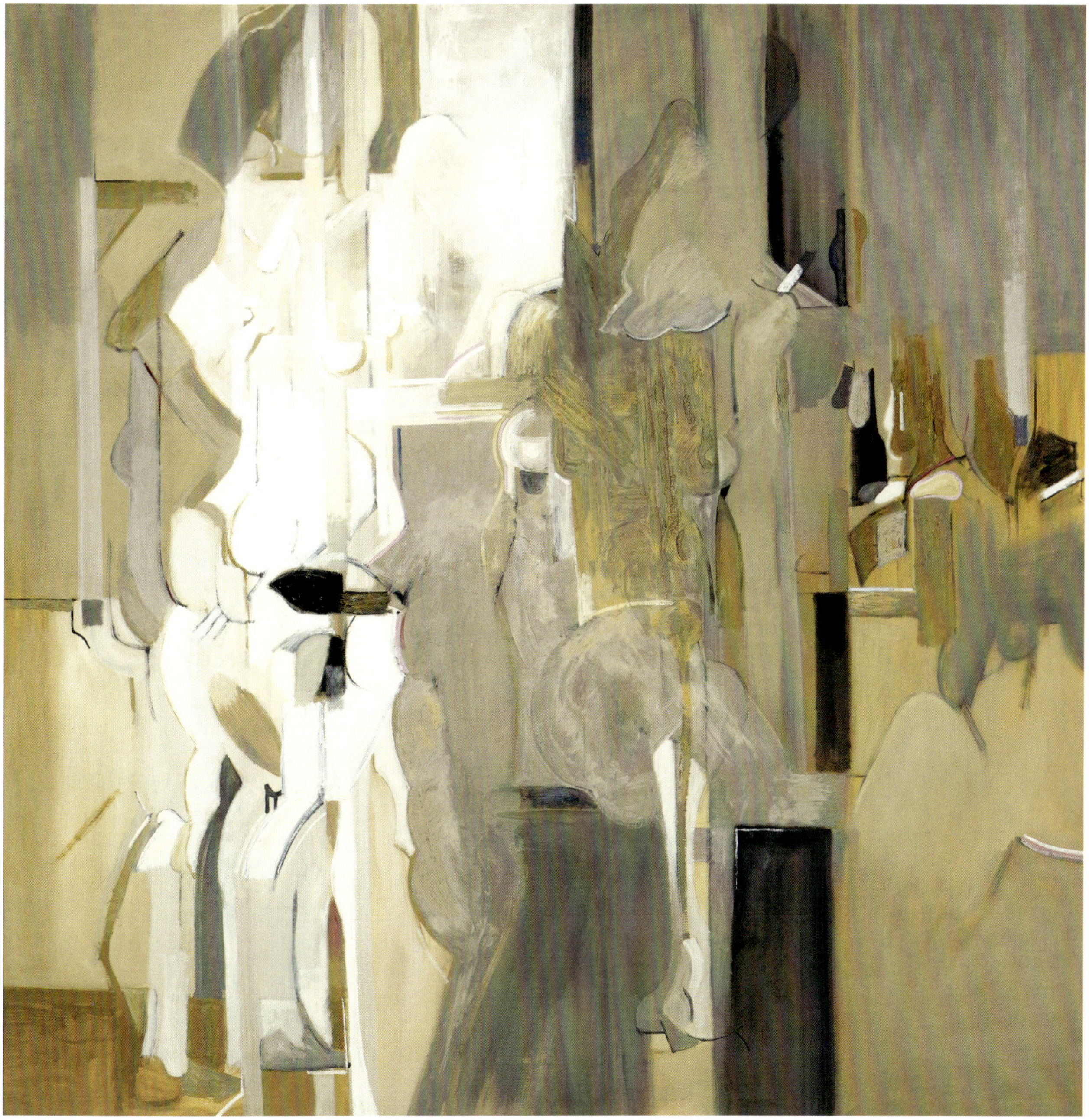

Figures and Objects in a Room 2 1960

Oil on canvas
152.5 x 152.5 cm

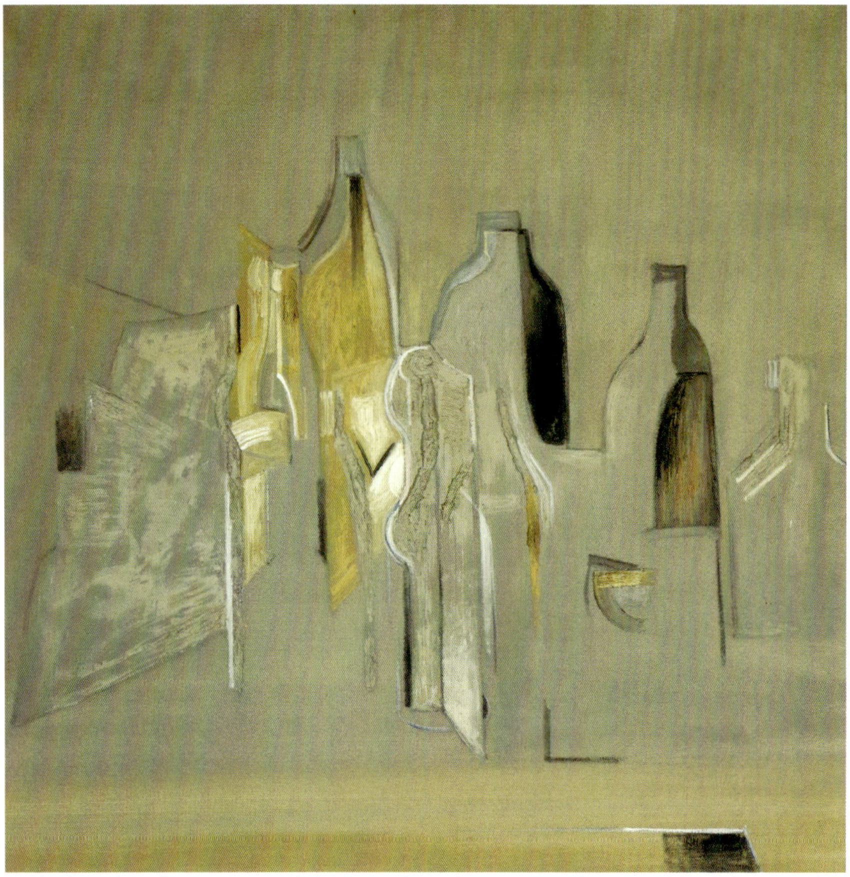

Still Life in Shadow 1959

Oil on canvas
91.5 x 91.5 cm

far as it reflected reality, art in England presented life as good and nature as a friend. The exceptions came from individuals who themselves were exceptions and not always very English: Bomberg, Gertler, Herman (a Pole in Glasgow and in Wales), Stanley Spencer, David Jones, etc., Epstein (American) in his monumental sculpture, Gill with his eccentric religiosity, Moore whose international status, (announced in Venice in 1948) removed him far from his Yorkshire working-class origins. The list could well go on and needs another alongside it, well nigh infinite. This would start with Sir Alfred Munnings, the fashionable painter of landed gentry and their horses, whose broadcast 1949 speech, delivered as president of the Royal Academy at its annual banquet, was a drunken assault on modern art in general and on its champions in Britain. Rejecting this inheritance meant not painting like any member of the RA, nor like many a well-known artist outside it like, say, Duncan Grant whose often charming portraits, interiors, garden scenes and landscapes spoke of the pleasure these yielded to the spirit as well as to the eye. It meant not adopting the rather suave naturalistic idiom the Euston Road painters had developed in the late 1930s to paint the industrial North or the un-smart streets and pubs of London; nor the almost sacramental charting process Coldstream and his associates used after the war. It also excluded the Neo-Romantic visions of life and nature that dominated during the war, as well as the poetic dialogue with nature which was the basis of the abstract and nearly abstract work of the leading St Ives painters. It found nothing of interest, at that stage, in the Constructive art movement instigated by Pasmore about 1948.

The loose grouping to which Smith belonged through his association with the Beaux Arts Gallery was not merely naturalistic, working from impartial observation of the visible world, but realistic in the selection each artist made within it. Selection reveals personal attachments. Staying with it, working with it in differing ways over time, carries a message. This applies even to Derrick Greaves whose subjects and idiom were generally more derivative than the others'. Greaves went to Italy in 1952-53 and again in 1953-54, and often pictured Italian rustic and urban subjects. Though not overtly political, his early painting had something of the tone of his Communist friend Renato Guttuso's, and in 1957 he was invited to exhibit at the Pushkin Museum in Moscow, a rare event for an English artist.

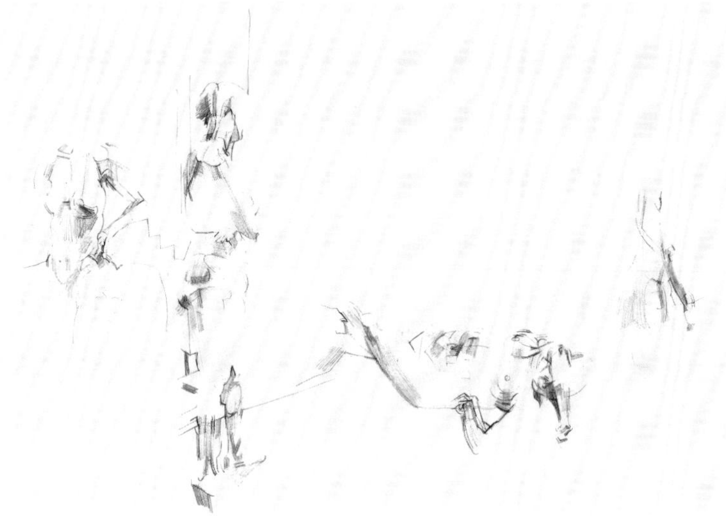

Figures in Light 2 1959/60

Pencil on paper
50 x 72 cm

Art is rarely unambiguous in its messages. Critics and the media tend to bring readings to art from other areas; the public is not encouraged to develop its own responses. The 1950s dwelt on memories of war and the dangers of the present world situation. Much European art, abstract and figurative, spoke of pain and fear. Britain had suffered deeply during the war and, though she had earned much respect, would never recover her power or status. The 1950s novels of Doris Lessing, John Wain, Alan Sillitoe and others had launched a movement of realistic writing, much of it with a polemical purpose, and in 1956 John Osborne's *Look Back in Anger*, produced at the Royal Court, initiated what was quickly called the 'theatre of anger'. It gave birth to the tag 'angry young men' although, Malcolm Bradbury reminds us, 'a lot of the authors were not angry, many were not young, and a lot of them were women'.[10]

Bratby's crowded and richly-painted scenes can be read as celebrating the visual complexity of daily life but were seen as gruff statements of protest. He himself emphasized the tensions and anxieties of those days. Helen Lessore would later write of Middleditch that he was 'purely a poet of appearances' who has 'never been interested in Realism, social or of any other kind', perhaps forgetting her own role in suggesting that her 'quartet' was playing realistic tunes.[11] The art of Greaves was never overtly passionate; it would soon

10. Malcolm Bradbury's account of tendencies in British writing during 1945-60 forms chapter five of his *The Modern British Novel*, first published 1993, enlarged edition Penguin 1994; see especially pages 316-20.
11. See her essay in the catalogue of the 1987-88 touring exhibition of Edward Middleditch's work, curated by Lynda Morris for the South Bank Centre.

Figures in a Room 1960

Pencil on paper
55 x 75 cm

become quasi-Oriental in its detachment and its decorative refinement.

The question of colour in English early-1950s painting warrants a separate study. Hardly anyone was aware of the range and power of Matisse's colour until his great posthumous exhibition of 1956 in Paris. Nicolas de Staël's lavish use of thick blocks of layered colours pleased Paris in the late 1940s and drew some British painters into emulation when he showed in London in and after 1952; others found it merely seductive. The weighted splendour of Rothko's and Newman's colour would not be revealed to London until 1959. Meanwhile we had, say, Sutherland's rather routine brightness and the much more subtle, landscape-derived colours of the St Ives painters. William Scott, who used colour richly by the end of the 1950s, in 1952-54 was using blacks and whites, and Roger Hilton echoed this concentration for a time. Prunella Clough had reduced her colour quite markedly, as Berger pointed out in reviewing her 1953 show: 'Those who expect colour to be an essentially exotic visual element will say that her work is drab. ... Her colour – within its greys, service browns and metal blues – is firmly and exquisitely organised.'[12]

From the autumn of 1953 on Jack Smith taught painting and drawing at the Bath Academy of Art located in Corsham Court. Corsham (as the art world called it) was then a strange, unique art school, run by the impressive,

12. *NS*, 18 April 1953. Robin Gibson has written that Bratby painted *Three People at a Table* (1955) in sombre Sickertian colours then in vogue at the Royal College. See R.Gibson, *John Bratby – Portraits*, catalogue of the 1991 exhibition at the National Portrait Gallery, page 54. Some other Bratby paintings of 1954-55 are more colourful but he tended to use colour for surface vigour, against Sickertian harmony.

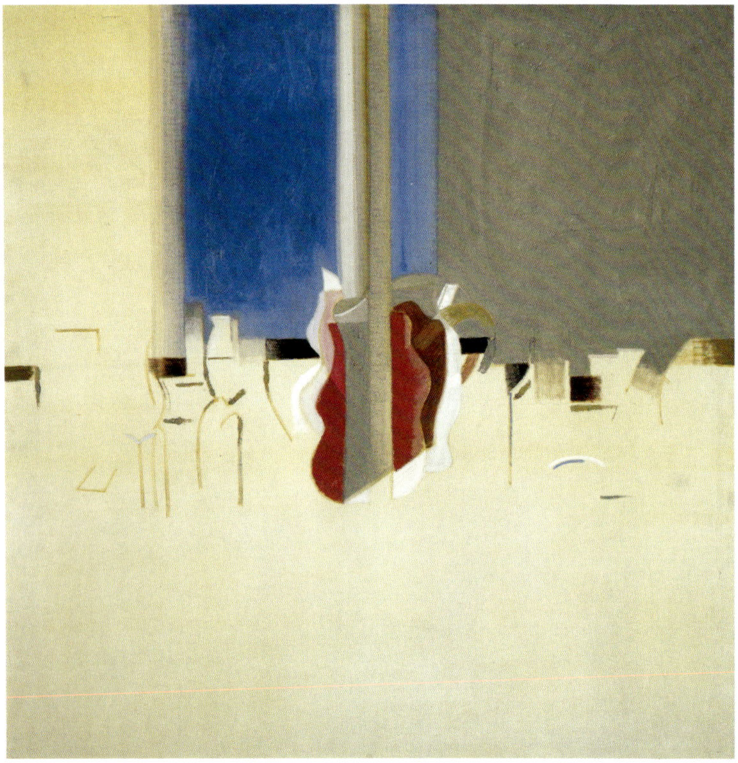

Jug and Other Objects 1959/60

Oil on canvas
107 x 107 cm

dictatorial painter Clifford Ellis. Smith encountered there a different range of fellow artists. William Scott was head of the painting school; Peter Lanyon, Bryan Wynter and Terry Frost taught in it, all associated with St Ives, as did the forceful Polish painter Peter Potworowski; Adrian Heath joined them in 1955, Martin Froy in 1956. These appointments, controlled by Ellis, were always precarious. But he wanted his staff to be working artists and encouraged them to plot their teaching commitments usefully, for instance by teaching for blocks of weeks as an alternative to so many hours and days throughout the academic year. Smith chose to do block teaching and then to paint without interruption in London. While at Corsham he experimented in his spare time outside his usual range by modelling sculpture in plaster, subsequently destroyed. Most British sculpture of the 1950s was worked in clay and/or plaster; traditionally this was also the process used in teaching. Smith recalls making heads, also a woman holding a child high above her head. Kenneth Armitage was head of sculpture at Corsham, himself modelling figures and groups of figures, and dramatising their silhouettes by contrasting lumpish torsos with stretched, stiff limbs. Herbert Read in 1952 had burdened Armitage's work, together with that of the other sculptors exhibiting with him at that year's Venice Biennale, with the phrase 'the geometry of fear'. It certainly helped to get them noticed on the European art stage of the time, but lingers misleadingly to the present. Armitage's art was more often humorous and affectionate than angst-ridden.

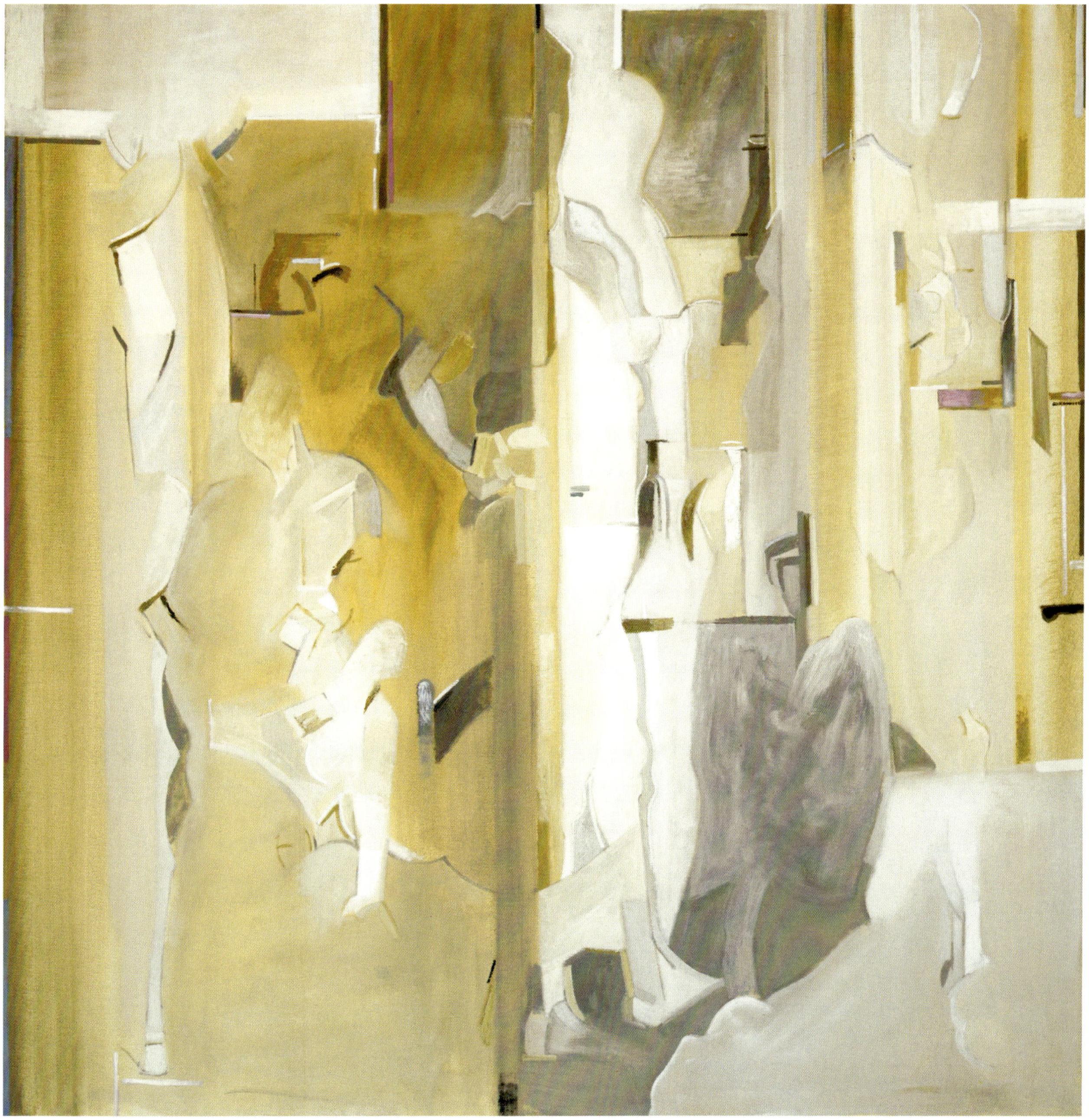

Figures and Objects in a Room 1960

Oil on canvas
152.5 x 152.5 cm

Smith visited Madrid and Toledo in 1954. He went partly to see Velàzquez's *Las Meninas*, a large painting, reproductions of which keep one curiously under-informed. He found himself also deeply impressed by Titian's *Entombment of Christ*. He made drawings; above all he looked and was affected by the starkness of Spain's harsh lights and shadows and by all those black clothes. His 1955 show at the Beaux Arts Gallery included pictures of bull-fights: people and animals caught in motion, silhouetted in the relief-like space formed by the hard light. Alan Clutton-Brock reviewed the show in *The Listener*, commenting first on how hardboard encouraged the production of large paintings: the young artist of today 'declaims as if he had to stop the passer-by in a busy street. This is of course in line with the doctrine of social realism ... [in which] the harsh conviction of the image counts for more than any charm. ... Mr Smith complains of the sink'. He found Smith's paintings of bull-fights violent and emotional 'in too deliberate and artificial a way'. The whole review riled Jack Smith enough to make him write a letter:

> *Sir, – I would like to point out to Mr Clutton-Brock ... that I did not go out of my way to look for violence in the paintings of bull-fights. In fact, that aspect of the subject interested me least. Nor do I complain of the kitchen sink ...*
>
> *The social realists may complain, but I have never met any painter in this country who is a social realist. Who are they? Perhaps Mr Clutton-Brock could enlighten me. I certainly refuse to accept the label.*[13]

He went to Venice in 1955 and found himself interested, like many another painter, in the interaction of light, water and buildings. He could not afford to go there in 1956 for the Biennale, nor could the other three; subsequently the British Council found it useful to arrange for exhibiting artists to be there during the first days of the Biennales. In 1955 their presence might have helped their paintings to meet with better attention, especially in view of their diversity as individuals as well as artists.

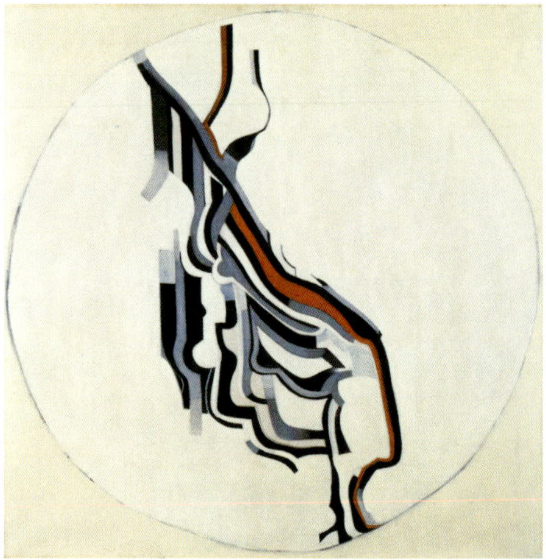

Black, White and Grey Movement No. 2
1962

Oil on canvas
106.5 x 106.5 cm

13. Clutton-Brock's review: *The Listener*, 2 June 1955; Jack Smith's letter: 9 June 1955. In 1959 Clutton-Brock devoted an article to Social Realism, writing mostly of its origins, as he saw it, in Stalin's Russia and of its emergence in post-war French painting, 'consciously and deliberately associated with left wing politics'. He made no mention of Italian realism, but noted the absence of 'political conviction behind the work of Jack Smith, Bratby, Middleditch and others who were influenced by the social realist movement'. They merely painted 'anything that was particularly unpicturesque in their immediate surroundings ... what most of us feel to be among the more tedious necessities of modern life'. He did add: 'their historical position, returning as they did to a visual stimulus after so many painters had avoided any direct observation of reality, may well have given them a sense of sudden liberation.' *Studio*, August/September 1959.

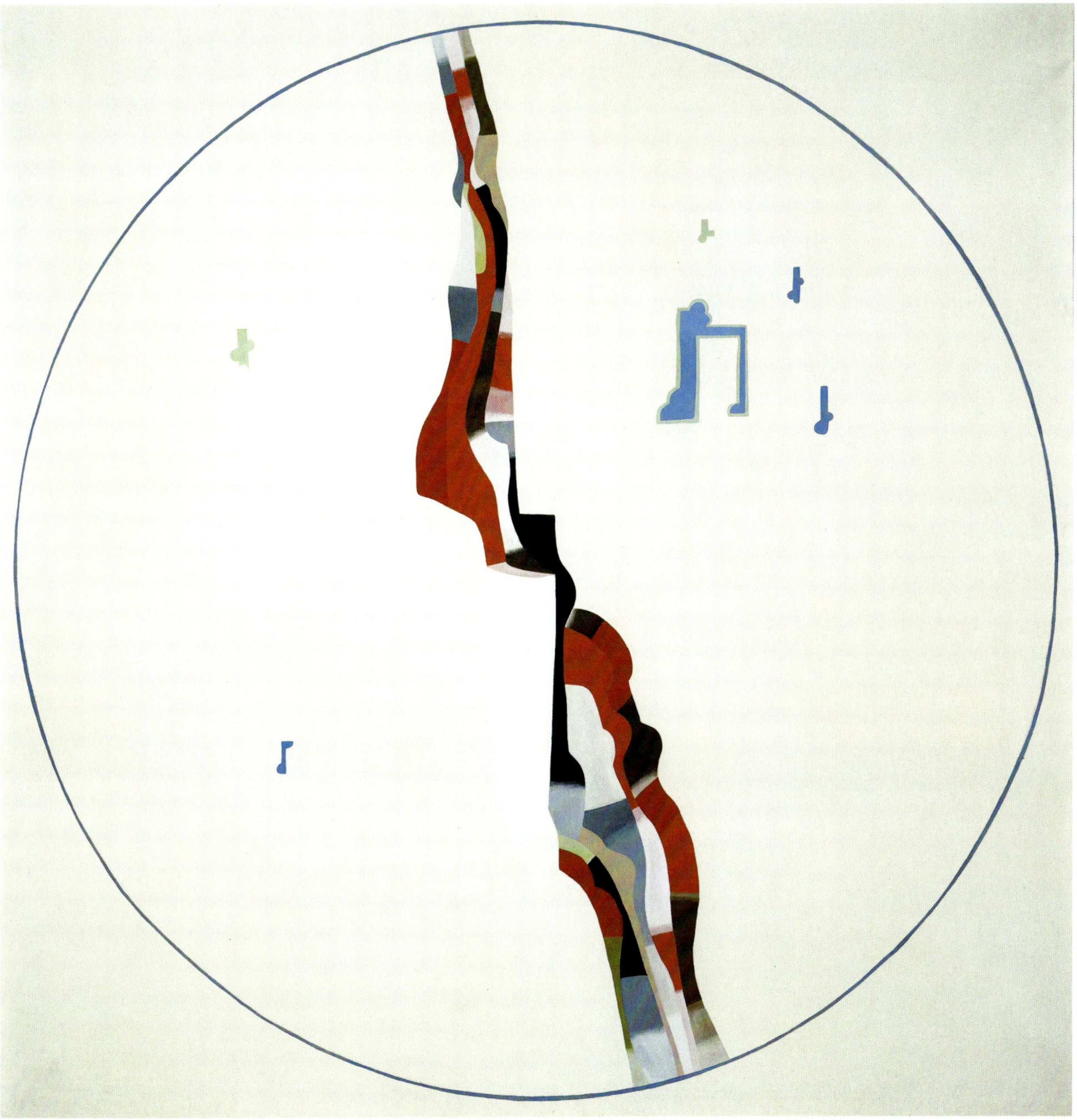

Side to Side No.1 1963

Oil on canvas
152.5 x 152.5 cm

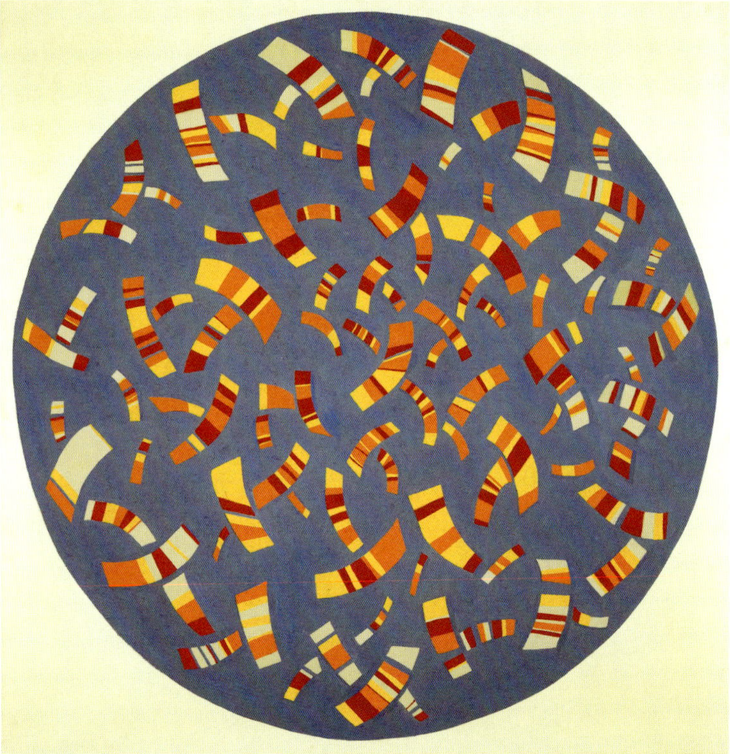

Sea Movement Red Orange & Blue 1962

Oil on canvas
107 x 107 cm

Jack Smith's major exhibition at the Whitechapel Art Gallery in 1959 would be of work done during the preceding decade, opening with a *Sea Painting* done while at St Martin's. The selection, as we shall see, played down the so-called Kitchen Sink aspect of his work, drawing attention to other kinds of subject matter, pursued during the same Beaux Arts years, and then emphasizing the new range of object-based but in effect semi-abstract paintings he had developed since 1957. He was doing what he could to distance himself from the sort of commentary the label had attracted at several levels.

In his article of December 1954, Sylvester had written that 'neither objectivity nor abstraction is the aim of the young painters of the kitchen-sink school'. He itemised what might be seen in the new work: 'every kind of food and drink, every kind of utensil and implement, the usual plain furniture, and even the baby's nappies on the line. Everything but the kitchen sink? The kitchen sink too'. This was lively journalism, and it pointed especially to Jack Smith. In fact, the 'baby's nappies on the line' were towels. The kitchen sink did occasionally feature in Smith's paintings, for example in his 1953 painting *Mother Bathing Child*, bought by the Tate Gallery, ill. p. 11.

Better-off mothers do not wash their babies in a Belfast sink in water

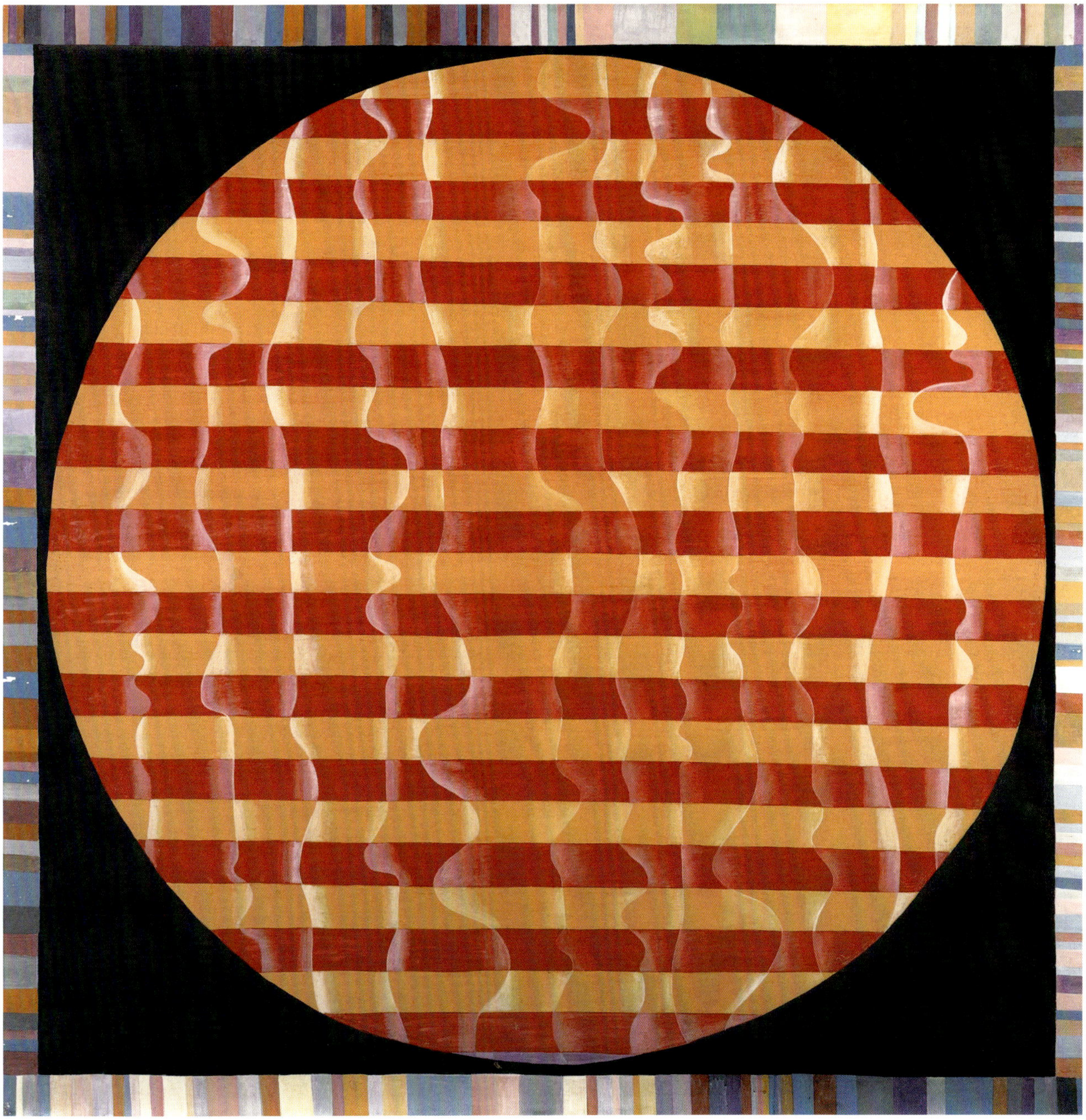

Shimmer, Red and Orange 1962

Oil on canvas

137 x 137 cm

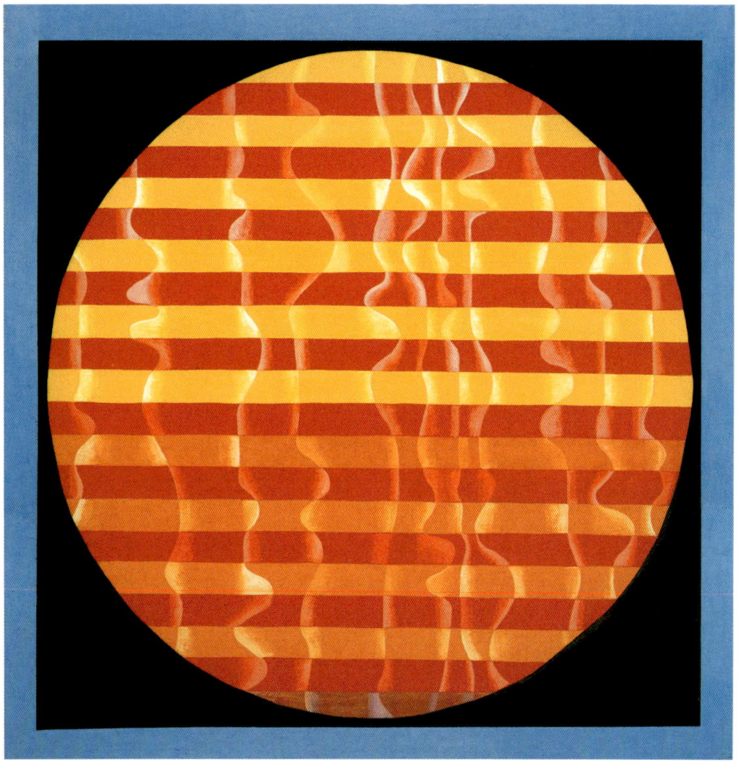

Shimmer 3 1962

Oil on canvas
122 x 122 cm

from a gas-fired geyser. The setting is quite bare – no decoration, no secondary objects. We can read the care and attention lavished by the mother on her child and the child's vulnerability, both caught by the painter in minimal terms. There is no sentimentality on offer. The mother is a strong image, no victim. Her left hand is sponging the child's back. Her left elbow is a powerful moment in the composition, the upper arm lying on the picture plane, the lower arm drastically foreshortened, a *tour de force* of drawing with the brush. We then notice the strong design of her silhouette, with just enough facial detail to give her a living presence, but more like a Poussin head than an Expressionist's. The firmly outlined child is merely a child being washed. It stands on slightly insecure legs, and the little body's angles and axes seem to generate the structure of the whole picture. A peaceful, ordinary action is enshrined by its simple setting. The background is gently angled around the human group. Placing the figures centre-left rather than on the central axis, Smith presses them forward, towards us; reversed, the arrangement would fall apart. No straight lines are perfectly straight, nor are the verticals and horizontals exact, and in this way Smith built a clear but unmechanical structure in which abstract and human elements coexist expressively. Sylvester wrote that Rebeyrolle's interiors would

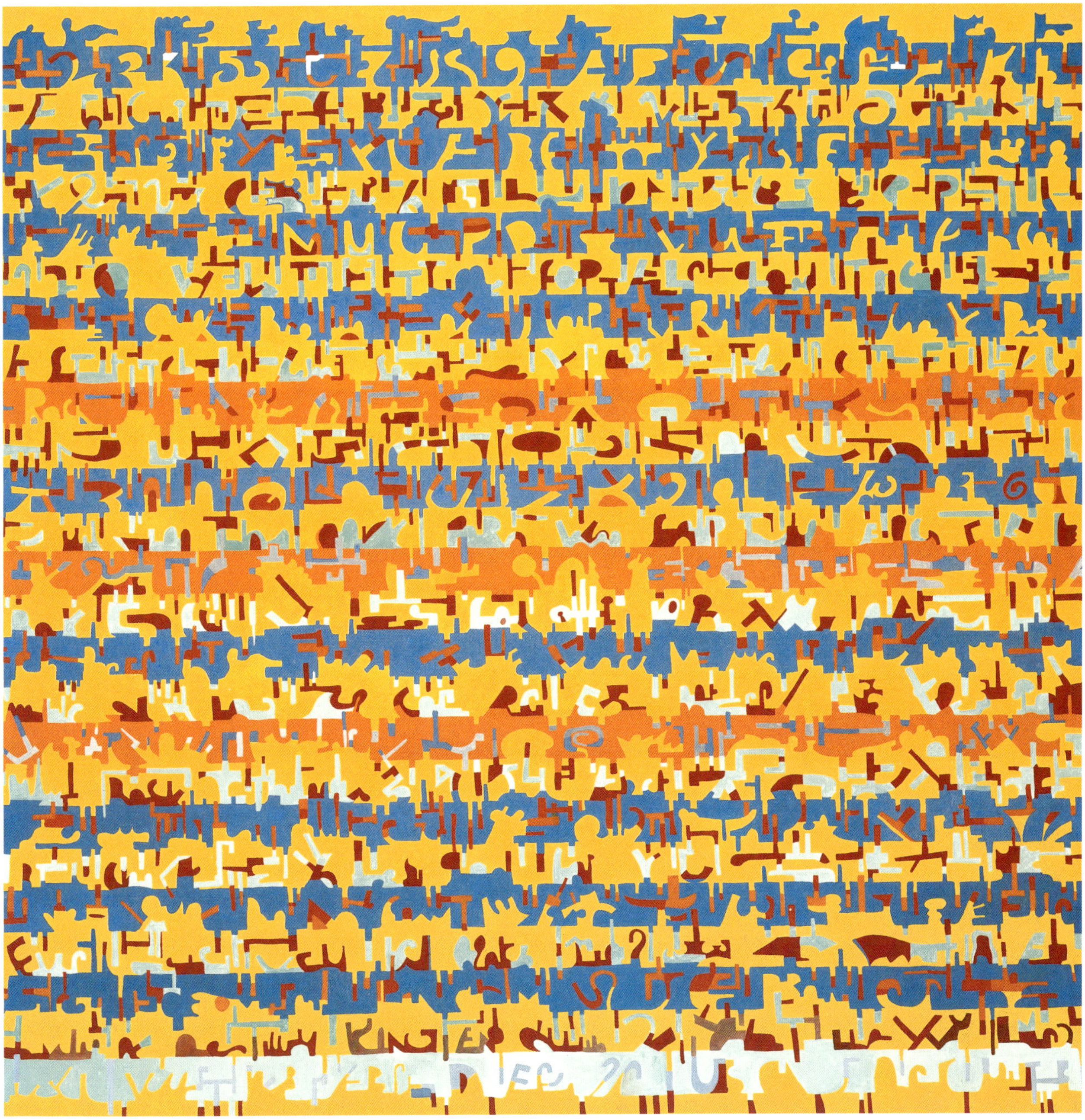

Light Movement 7 1962

Oil on canvas
137 x 137 cm

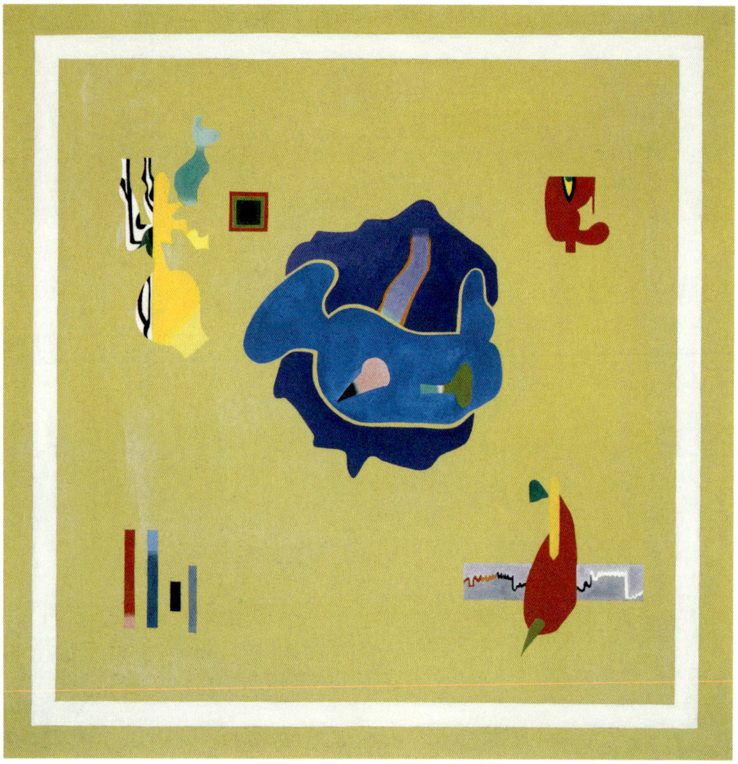

Oceanair 2 1964

Oil on canvas
107 x 107 cm

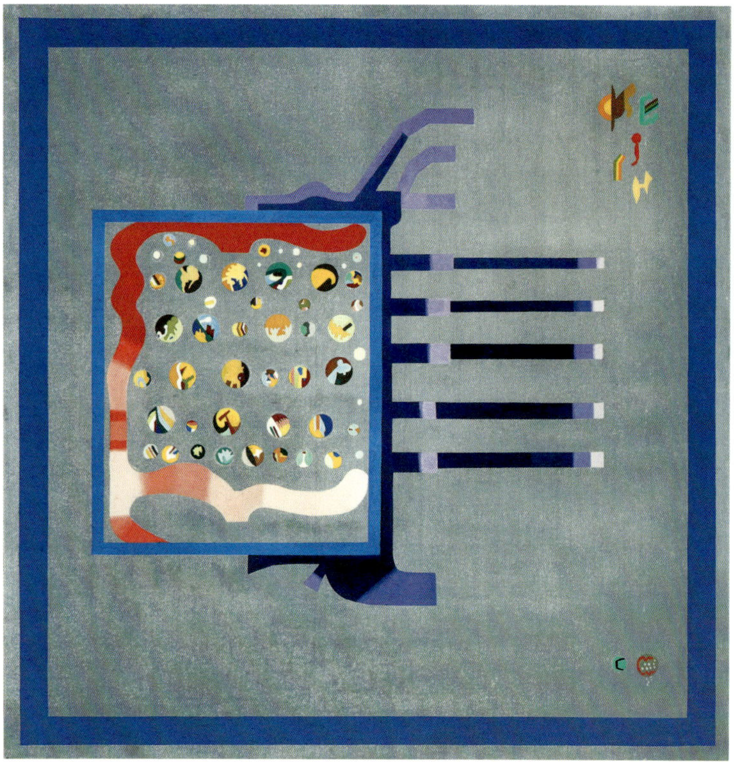

Inside and Outside 1964

Oil on canvas
91.5 x 91.5 cm

'have the air of a peasant's kitchen', whereas Smith's is 'proletarian', suggesting 'a particular social background'. True, though, Sylvester must have known many people of that generation, living in what then seemed modest - today, grim - conditions, sharing kitchens and bathrooms not with friends but with complete strangers while finding their feet on the earnings ladder in a Britain urgently in need of new and better housing.

Sylvester's article was illustrated with a full-page Bratby table-top picture, *Still Life with Chip Fryer*, while Smith's *Children and Dog* (not illustrated) shared a page with Rebeyrolle's *Still Life with Ladder*; the captions give neither dates nor sizes. *Children and Dog* was probably five by four feet and painted in 1953-54; Smith destroyed it later. It was a much busier scene than *Mother Bathing Child*. Centre foreground, a stool; mostly to the right of that and further back, a dining table, fairly cluttered with kitchen things, fruit, vegetables and cooking utensils as well as crockery, glasses etc. Beyond that rising surface we see a chair-back and then a door and a dark opening. The floorboards recede perspectivally, and on the left support two young children and a dog. A little girl kneels with her back to us; we see only her skirt, lower legs and feet, and one arm as she pushes a little wooden cart. Beyond her, in effect making one shape with her, is the other child, perhaps a boy, squatting frontally on the floor. Between her and us is the dog, seated, looking towards us. It could all be lively and charming. Or it could all have that 'effect of austere melancholy' which Sylvester ascribes to Buffet's painting, on which, at the end of his essay, he heaps praise with a generosity he must have regretted since.[14] It is neither, but calm and in its way dignified, without any hint of complaint. *Children and Dog* and *Mother Bathing Child* are strong images, part of the great tradition of realistic genre-painting that burgeoned in the seventeenth century and the nineteenth. While *Mother Bathing Child* recalls painters who honoured ordinary human activities, such as Millet in his small prints as well as in his sometimes too-imposing paintings, *Children and Dog* is closer to the *Intimisme* of Bonnard in which the domestic

---

14. Even Quentin Bell, an artist as well as a writer, wrote about 'some excellent works by Buffet' showing at the Mayor Gallery in November 1954 (*The Listener*, 19 November 1965). In the same article Bell reported on the London Group's annual exhibition, noting 'a tendency which exists among the younger painters of England and France to use a small and sombre palette. ... Mr Uglow's large nude and Jack Smith's enormous, tottering, slum-bound child have rather more colour but show the same healthy reluctance to indulge in pure, brilliant hues. Colour is indeed a thing that a painter may safely be left to discover after long and patient research within a limited field has made it appear at its true value'. A number of critics' reactions, and painters', confirm Buffet's extraordinary appeal in the early 1950s. I always thought his work thoroughly meretricious, and understand his temporary fame as reflecting the period's taste for agreeably pessimistic images and the discomfort felt by many in the face of empire-building abstract painting in Europe and the USA.

interior, its occupants and its still-life contents, are fused pictorially.

Sylvester in 1954 clearly preferred Bratby's noisier paintings for the 'compelling sense of modern life' yielded by their profusion of packaged groceries. He accused Smith of being entirely under van Gogh's influence yet failing to match the Dutchman's 'passionate identification with the object, both its form and its meaning'. For Smith, 'his subject has served as a pretext for making a picture: the glasses and jugs are too beautiful to be true to this stark setting'. It is difficult to see any influence from van Gogh in Smith's work. I recall young painters inclined to some form of realism in the 1950s doffing their caps to 'Vincent' and getting impatient when there was too much talk of Cézanne as *the* 'father of modern art'. Bratby's manner of painting echoes van Gogh's in the use of emphatic lines of paint, but more to dramatize the surface than to convey the structure of objects or to heighten the effect of colours. Smith's way of painting was quite different. The setting of *Children and Dog* is certainly plain, serviceable rather than luxurious: glasses and jugs under light can be beautiful wherever they were bought, and it is odd to see a critic condemning a painter for using his eyes and not limiting his responses to the mean spirit ascribed to him. Sylvester thought much better of Smith's work subsequently.

The Kitchen Sink tag had evidently little to say about Smith's paintings. It came closest to fitting Bratby's which did, for a while, feature table-tops crowded with familiar groceries and utensils. Some of Smith's paintings were of kitchen interiors and some were of other rooms. Neither Greaves nor Middleditch haunted kitchens in their art; they did not paint interiors with any frequency. Yet the association with penury and ugliness conditioned readings of their work, and led to impatience when it didn't comply with expectations. In September 1957 Lawrence Alloway, an increasingly influential London critic, wrote that the terms used for the 1954-55 work of the Beaux Arts painters no longer apply. He implied that the 'kitchen sink' emphasis had always been misleading. What had been seen as 'squalor' was merely 'clutter', and its character was 'often idyllic'. In February 1959 Sylvester would stress that he had never meant his reference to 'kitchen sink' to indicate a preference for squalid subjects: he had been pointing to the painters' interest in what is ordinary and had not meant only English painters.[15]

All other qualities in the work are ignored. Smith's *After the Meal* (1952), ill. p.13, was painted on canvas but is not on that account different in manner from his paintings on board. In the foreground a dining table; everything on it is

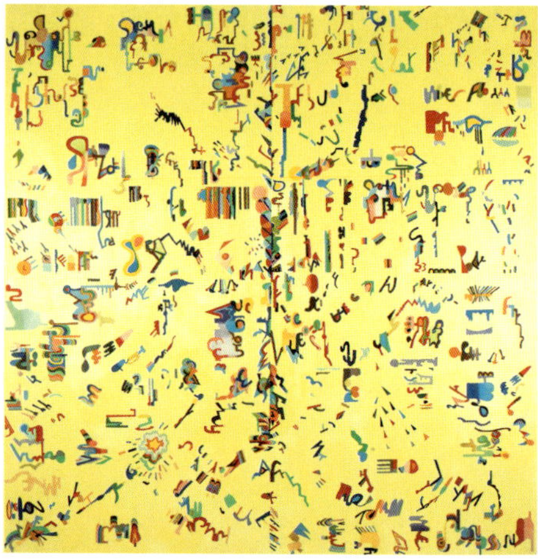

Various Activities Central & Out 1965

Oil on canvas
152 x 152 cm
Royal Pavilion, Libraries and Museums, Brighton & Hove

15. Alloway in *The Listener*, 19 September 1957; Sylvester in ibid., 19 February 1959. In 1961 Alloway went to New York for a visit of some months and remained there.

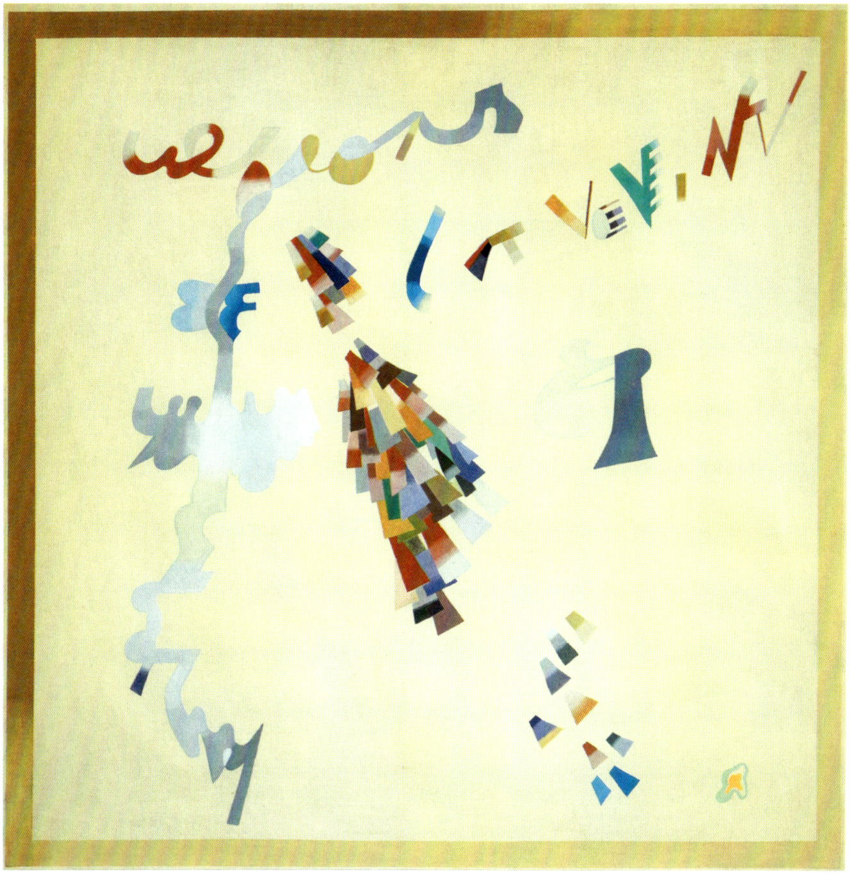

Various Activities (Dance) 1965

Oil on canvas
91.5 x 91.5 cm

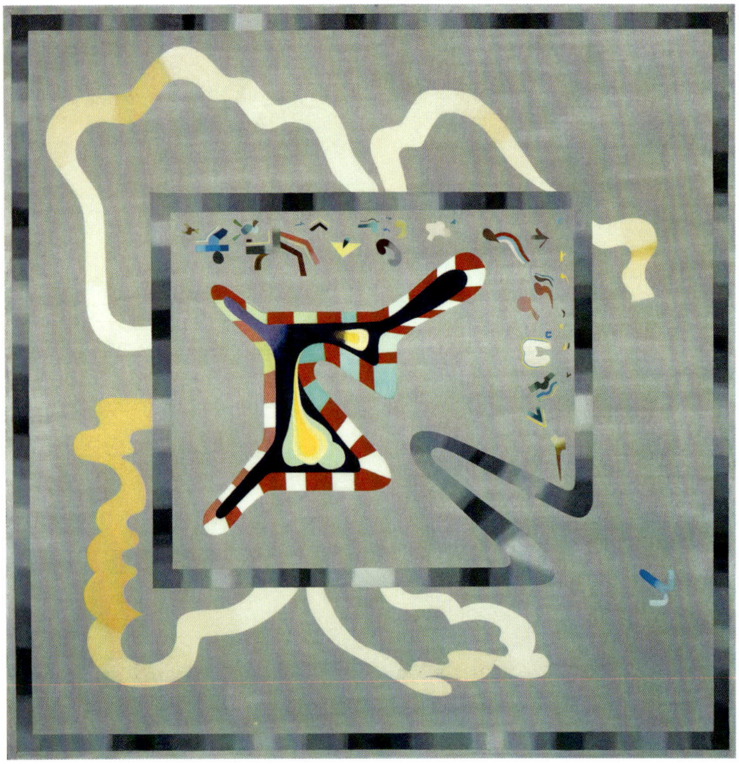

Inner. Outer 1965

Oil on canvas
107 x 107 cm

clean, unused but placed informally. There are two chairs, one on the left, unoccupied, the other central, with its back to us. In this a woman sits holding a baby; we see only her shoulders, her hair and her left cheek, while the baby looks over her shoulder. Another woman stands by an open doorway; here we see the complete figure and she looks towards us. The table and the floorboards together take our eyes into the space of the room, but this directional pull is counteracted by the chairs, by walls and by floorboards making lines across the picture beyond the doorway where we glimpse another room. There is little explicit colour, but the greys and browns are richly modulated, cool and warm, and light tones dominate. I emphasize the spatial structuring of the picture because it is complex and evidently important to the artist. The human element matters too. The woman is rendered in simplified terms, yet her turning, hesitating pose communicates well, as does her face, though this too is rendered without much detail.

Interior with Child (1953), ill. p.9, is more even in tone. Its space is less complicated: a wall parallel to the picture-plane closes it almost entirely. The floorboards lie across the picture too but are painted quite softly. Our entry into the picture is aided by the decorative margin of a carpet rising at about forty degrees to the horizontal from the left foreground to almost halfway up the right edge. Along this margin, a child runs towards us, almost full-face. She is frozen in motion, concentrating on her progress. On the left we see part of a round table set for a meal. Table-cloth, glasses, dishes and cutlery, a few flowers in a decorative jug. A dog ambles in from the left, towards the running girl. Another, shyer dog is under a high-chair in the right top quarter of the picture. This is a substantially different picture from *After the Meal*, displaying interest in other elements and effects. Both compositions make potent use of diagonals, but, here motion commands our attention, not silence. The girl dominates the picture; she is running towards us. She, too, is not represented in great detail, yet we see a particular child, more a portrait than a type. The colours are mostly warm: creams, ochres, browns; there are a few bluish touches.

Child Walking with Check Tablecloth (1953), ill. p.10, is presumably a kitchen scene. A table-top slopes away from us, occupying much of the left half of the painting until it is lost behind a line of washing that goes across and up from the left. Both elements are directional, but whereas the edge of the table takes us into the picture space, the washing blocks the space and behind the washing is a dark wall, slanted towards us, left to right. Wall, washing and table frame a space rather like a niche in which is a little boy, a toddler, walking unsteadily, a small image but wholly alive. The painting contrasts light and dark, with the floor providing middle tones. The 'table-cloth' represents oilcloth printed with a strong pattern of black lines and white, red and black colours. The checks are painted unevenly and give an effect of motion as they seem to swarm into the picture. The toddler in *Child Walking with Wicker Stool* (1954, not illustrated) is running towards us and is much larger in the picture. The only other three-dimensional object in it is the stool, quite large, to the right of the child and further back. The lines constructing the figure are especially important here, including again the drawing of the alert face. The child is placed left of centre and feels very close. No clutter: a quietly monumental image.

Table Still Life with Bowl of Cherries (1954-55, not illustrated) does not include a person but is redolent of human beings. We see a gate-leg table close to the far wall but leaving space for a hint of chair-back and a coat dropped over it. We see the floor, with undefined floorboards lying across our approach. What is defined is the objects on the table. Cups, glassware, cutlery, cruets etc., but also food. Cabbages and a cauliflower; bread on a breadboard with a bread-knife next to it; the cherries of the title in a shallow bowl, but also some other fruit, plums and greengages perhaps; four large peppers. Peppers do not go with penury. There is no mess. Everything feels positive. St Martin's is near the National Gallery, and Jack Smith went there quite frequently and found friends among the Old Masters, notably Chardin and Vermeer. It was Chardin's eloquent economy that struck him most profoundly: achieving so much with a few things carefully placed in a limited space.

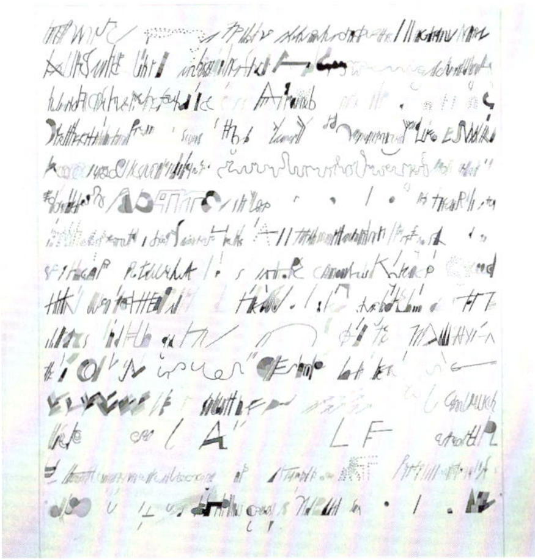

Various Activities No.5 1966

Oil on canvas
152.5 x 152.5 cm
Gothenburg Museum, Sweden

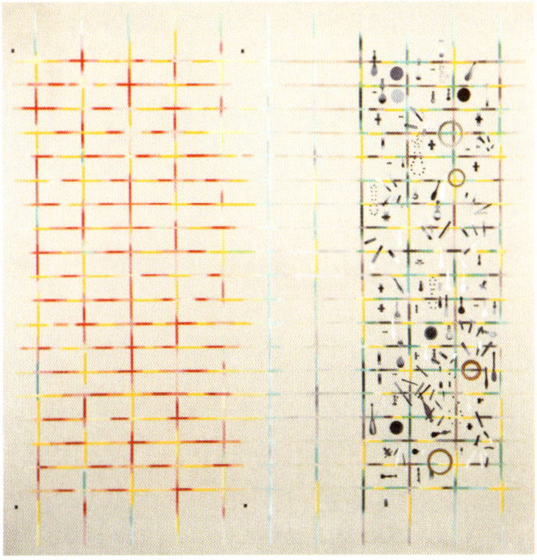

Silences and Sounds No. 3 1968

Oil on canvas
136.5 x 136.5 cm
© Crown copyright: UK Government Art Collection

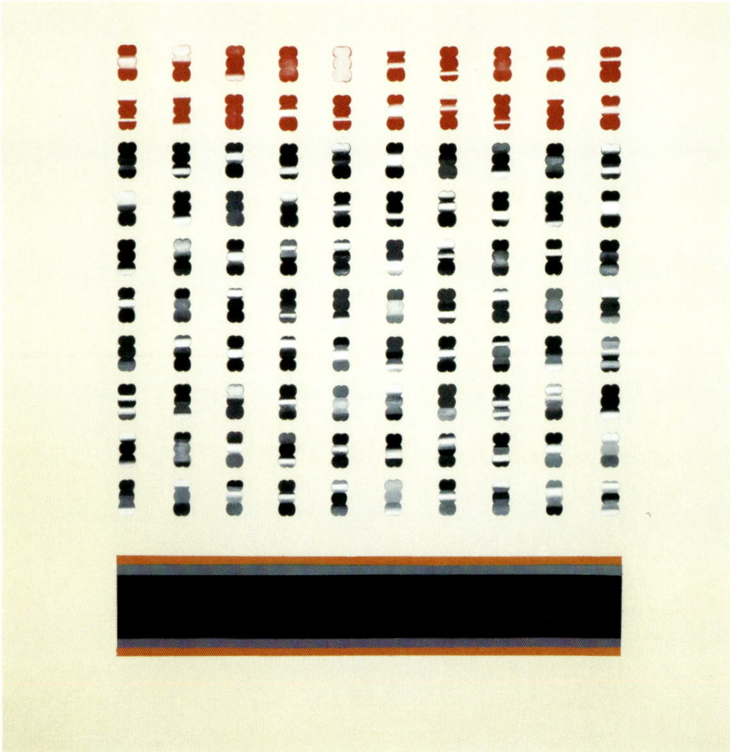

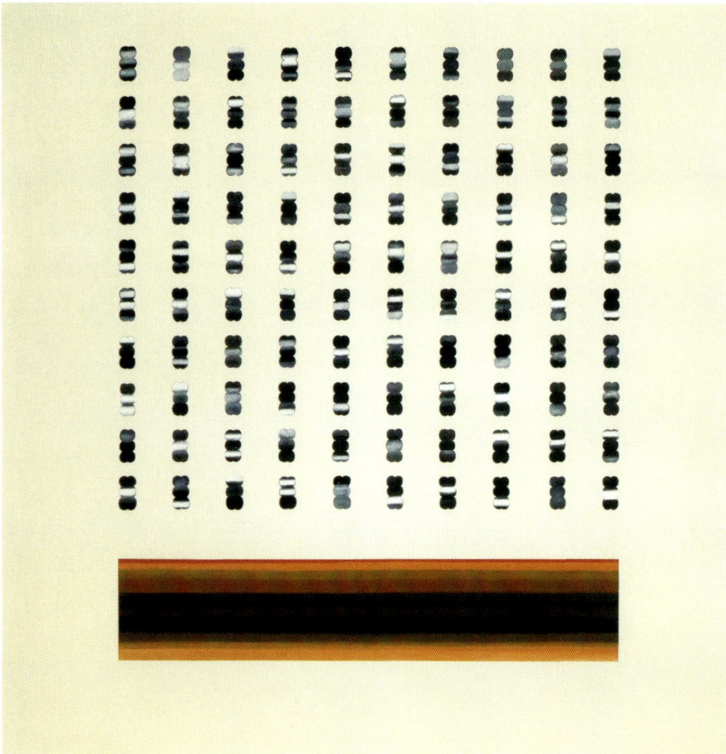

100 Twice (diptych) **1969**

Oil on canvas
107 x 107 cm each

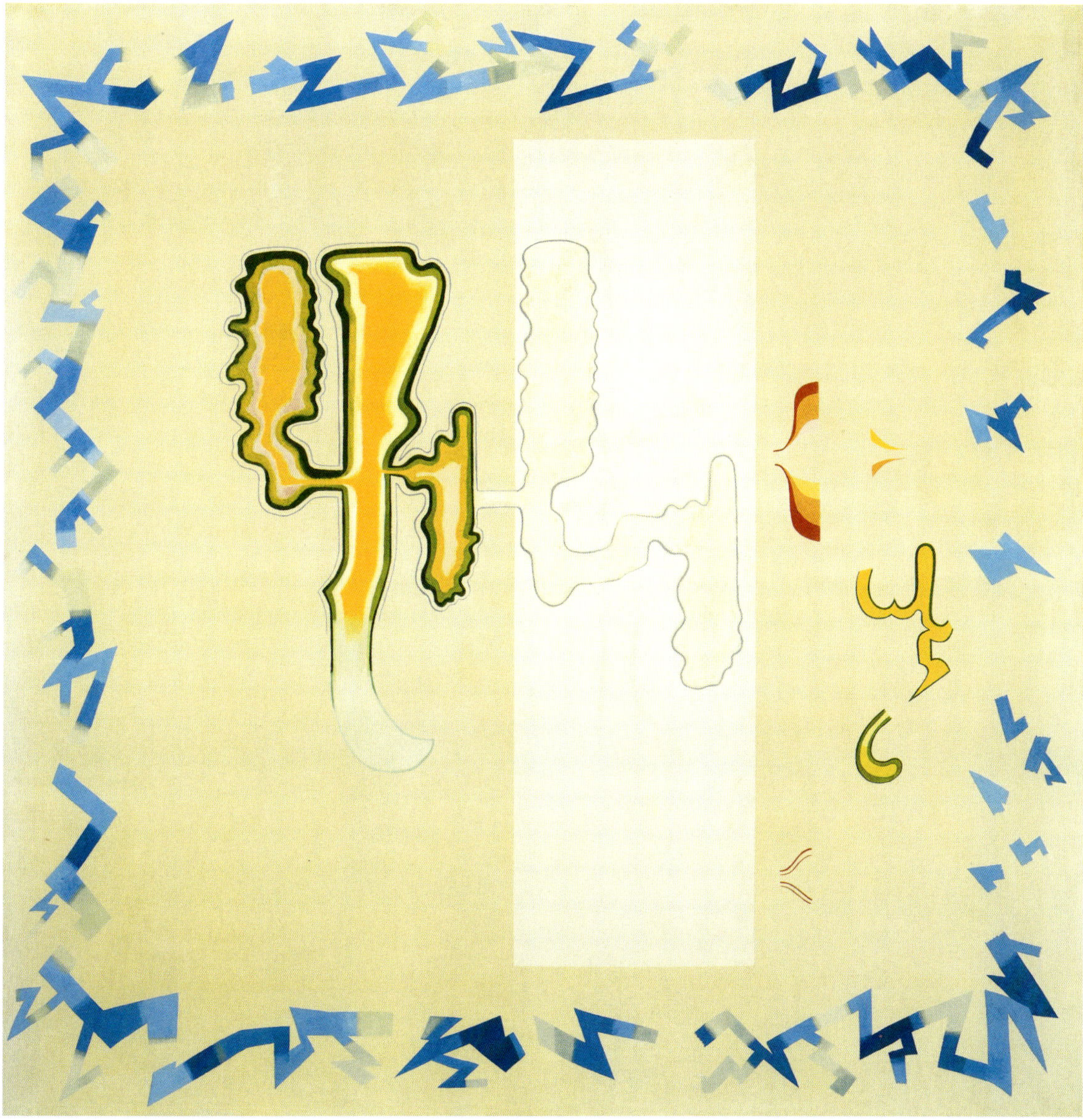

Nature No. 1 1965

Oil on canvas
122 x 122 cm

Smith did not paint only interiors and still lifes in those years. *Snowstorm in a City* (1952-53), ill. p.14, is filled with blowing, swirling forms and with white and near-white brushstrokes; there are few hints in it of the city. In 1952-53 he also painted *Fireworks over Water* (not illustrated). In his catalogue essay of 1959 Mark Roskill would refer to such images as 'compounded from fantastications on visual themes'. *Night Sky with Stars* (1957, not illustrated) is of clustered lights amid darkness, the stars like myriad sparklers in a brown, grey and white sky, a joyous vision of sudden lights not a million miles from that of Whistler's notorious *Nocturne in Black and Gold: The Falling Rocket*. All three paintings, Smith's and Whistler's, pivot on creating equivalents for precious momentary experiences. Smith's 1955 Beaux Arts show included a *Standing Nude*, a *Portrait of the Girl with Red Hair*, sea paintings and still lifes, as well as pictures of bull-fights, all reflecting his visit to Spain the previous year.[16] M.H.Middleton, writing for *The Spectator*, felt Smith had been led to using 'inflationary and stereotyped formulae'; the critic missed the 'human drama which filled his earlier paintings of children'.[17] Certainly *The Wounded Bullfighter* (1955, not illustrated) does not make much of the drama: there is no blood, no excitement even. The visit to Venice produced paintings of an old woman, and also paintings called *Head* in which the heads are firmly abstracted to clustered forms distantly related to early Cubism. Smith says he destroyed many of these paintings, and others throughout his career, more to gain space or in preparation for moving house than by way of rejecting them. In 1955 he painted two pictures of burning chairs: two old chairs he had decided to get rid of, burned in the garden, and found himself attracted by the motif's combination of ordinariness and strangeness, ill. p17. Also, in 1955, a sixty by forty inches painting of a black coat lying close to an electric fire, one of those circular reflectors with a central, candle-like element we used a lot in those days. The coat is not in danger; it was the pairing of the soft black formless heap and the crisp, orange object that needed painting.

The most striking development in Smith's work of 1956 is his interest in light, which now becomes dominant and programmatic. An example is *Shirt in Sunlight*, ill. p17, included in his Whitechapel show of 1959. A shirt hangs from a washing-line in a bare corner, a striking silhouette in the middle of the picture.

16. Peter de Francia reviewed the exhibition with characteristic care, questioning some aspects but finding the whole very impressive, in *Art News and Review*, 14 May 1955, mentioning these titles among others.
17. *The Spectator*, 27 May 1955. Middleton turned from commenting on Smith's paintings to dealing with Elisabeth Frink's first solo exhibition. The new paragraph opens: 'Frenzy and violence are present too at the ...'

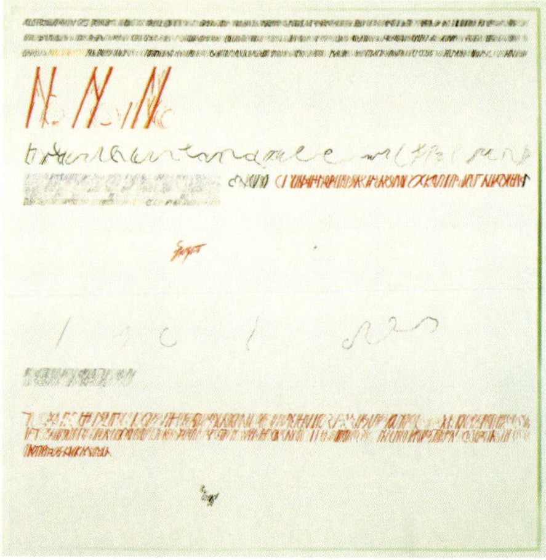

Document 1969

Oil on canvas
107 x 107 cm

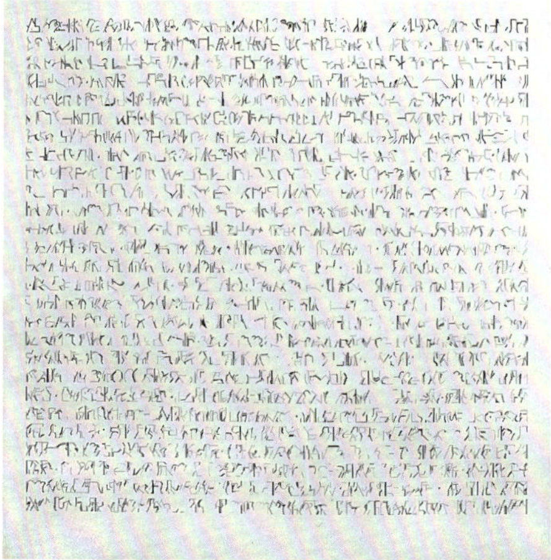

Written Activity No.8 1969

Oil on canvas
167.5 x 167.5 cm
National Museums and Galleries of Wales

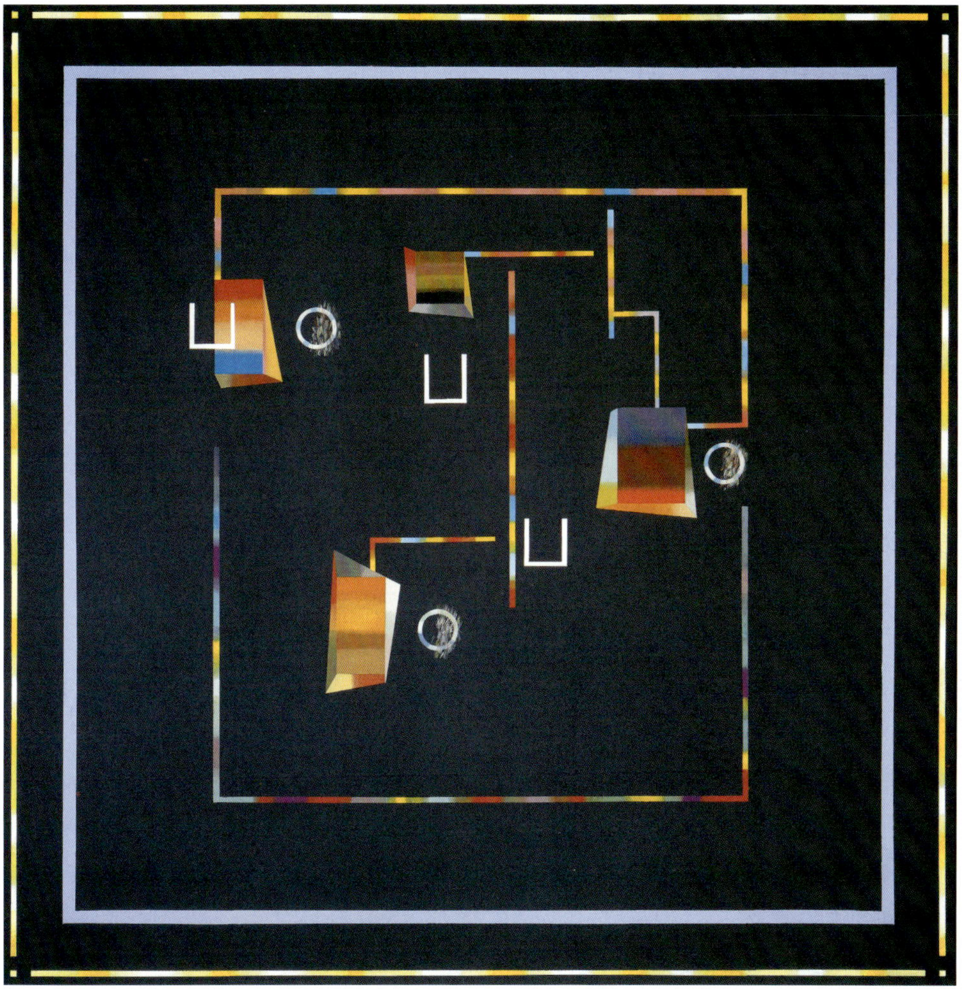

Sounds and Silences on Black 1971

Oil on board
107 x 107 cm

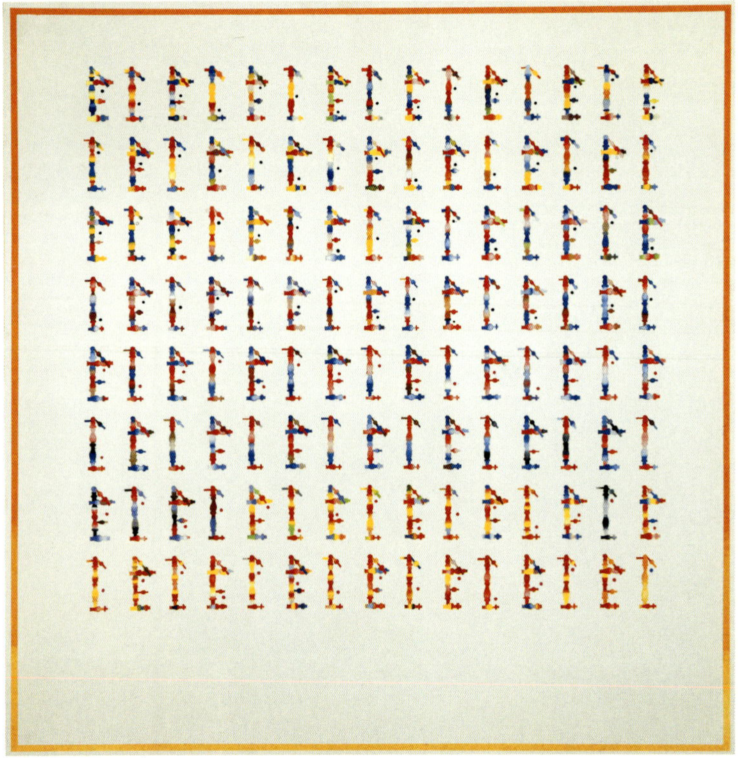

120 Major 105 Minor 1972

Oil on board
107 x 107 cm

Light from a window gives it three-dimensionality by means of tone as well as drawing. The theme is nominally ordinary, but the clear, almost geometrical structure and the almost human presence of the shirt gives it dramatic significance as well as visual force.

This interest, in light and dark but also in the visual force and emotional potency of objects, culminated in *Creation and Crucifixion* (1956), ill. p12. Painted on four four by five foot boards, it offers something like an anthology of what had chiefly concerned Smith since 1954. Clothes on chairs, a washing-line and objects on a table: all of them full of life. Several of the objects seem active, cutlery, glasses and two plaice spilling out from under a cloth: this arrangement, suggested by a chance juxtaposition of things, indicates 'creation'. The 'Crucifixion' theme relates to the shirts. He had earlier painted a shirt left hanging over a chair and called it *Crucifixion*. He wanted to 'make the ordinary miraculous'. Many a modern painter, embarking on a major statement, has drawn on religious formulae. Smith's horizontal composition echoes traditional representations of the three crosses on Calvary, and its mood is sombre though its general effect is lively thanks to contrasts of form and of light and dark, and the positive colours displayed in the hanging shirt, the electric fire and the patterned oilcloth on the right. He painted it in a small studio he rented from George Fullard in Stanley Studios, Fulham, just big enough to take this ten-foot picture. Smith arranged to get it to the first John Moores Liverpool

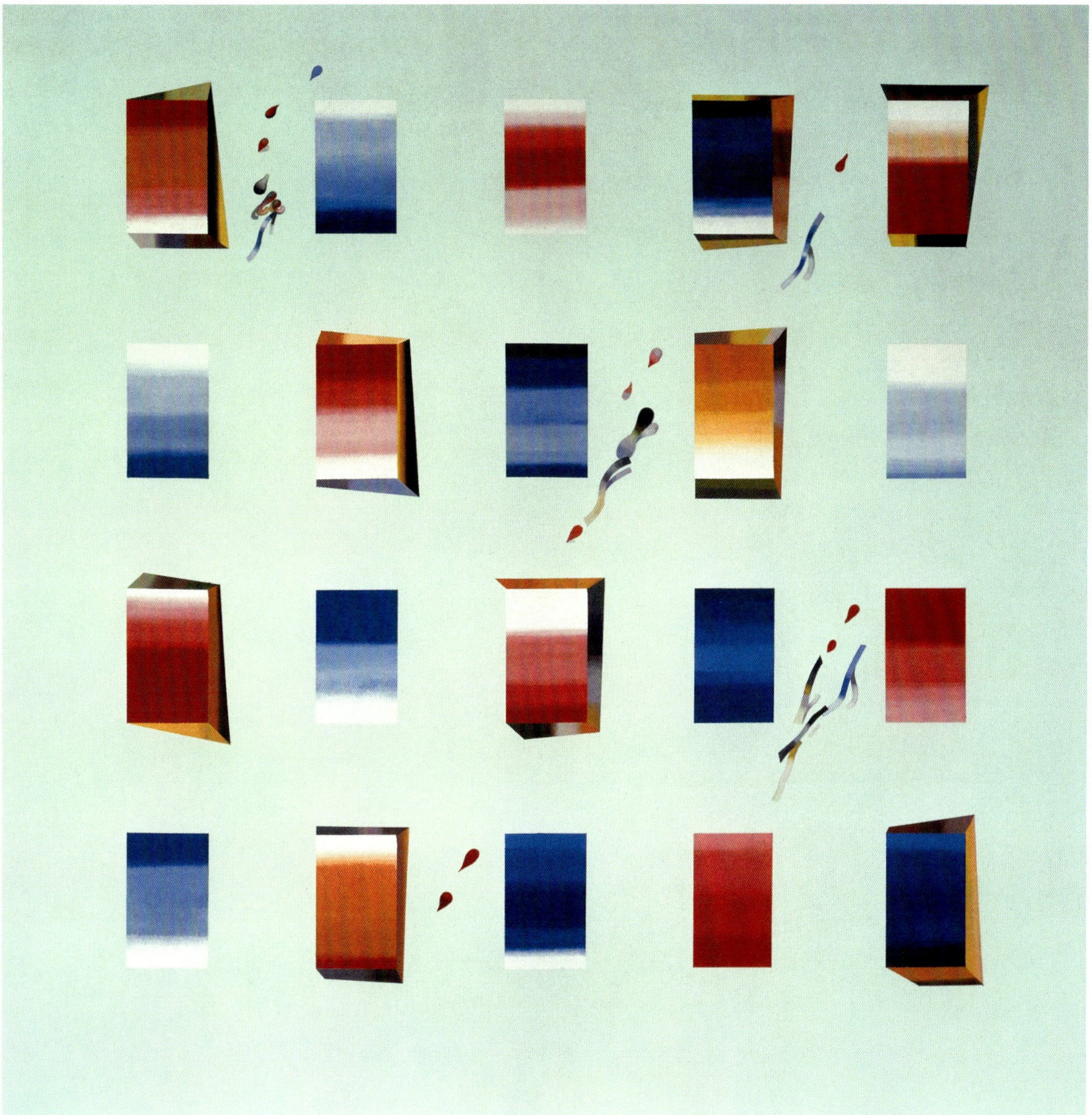

Activities Major and Minor 1972

Oil on wood
122 x 122 cm
© Tate, London 2000

competition the same year. The jury awarded him the first prize of £1000 and the painting was bought for the city collection.

In 1957 Sylvester was impatient at finding Smith's new work different from what he expected, and differently titled. He suggested that titles such as *Patch of Light over Cylinders* were in error, and did not fit what was shown. 'What we have here', he wrote, 'is not a confusion of identity, as in cubism, but a complete loss of identity.' The new paintings seemed to him to stem from Impressionist usage: it doesn't matter what things actually are. 'Smith's new paintings claim to be paintings of light, but I think we should regard light as no more than their point of departure...' Yet before ending his piece Sylvester had interesting second thoughts. After his 'vastly over-rated student-paintings of kitchens', Smith has now achieved work

> *of considerable importance for the future of painting. He has found a way of painting that takes advantage of the freedom painting has won, and yet manages to convey that sense of reality which ... painting has got to have if it is to mean anything to us when we are not actually looking at it. The originality and the power of the works at the Beaux Arts suggest that Smith may become one of that select band of English artists who have some effect upon the course of painting in general.*[18]

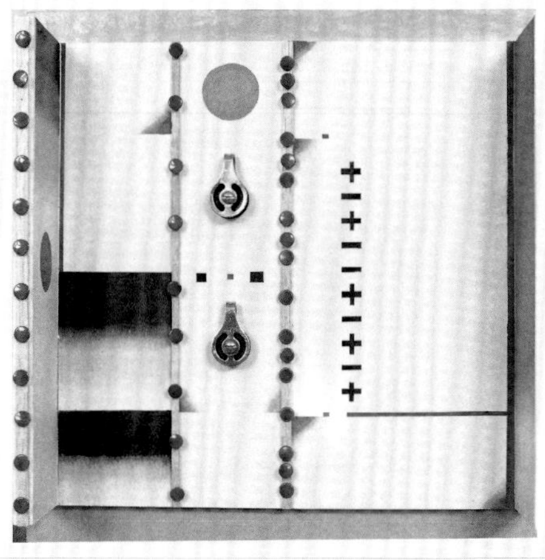

Object I. Metal and Paint 1979

Mixed media
38 x 38 x 13 cm
Private collection

It must have been from some similar feeling that Bryan Robertson offered Jack Smith a retrospective show at the Whitechapel Art Gallery, to be held in May-June 1959. In his brief preface to the catalogue Robertson pointed out that Smith at thirty-one was the youngest artist to be given such a show there. It would be, he argued, of special value to exhibit Smith's work at 'the moment of synthesis when an artist's artistic identity appears to go through a metamorphosis but when in fact his purpose and his technical equipment appear, fully realized, for the first time'. The exhibition, though spanning ten years (the first exhibit was a *Sea Painting* of 1949), featured mostly recent work: *Creation and Crucifixion* was number sixteen in a show of eighty-two paintings, thirty-seven drawings and nine reliefs.

Again, much of the work has been destroyed since, though fourteen exhibits were, and remain, in public and private collections. The catalogue with its sixteen black-and-white plates is therefore a precious document. It has a substantial foreword by a young art historian, the late Mark Roskill. His words are rather elaborate but his general emphasis is wholly apt. The selection, primarily controlled by the painter, included very few pictures of the Kitchen

18. *NS*, 2 November 1957.

Sink phase. Number 5, *Child Walking*, is now known as *Child Walking with Wicker Stool*, discussed above. Though he does not use the phrase 'Kitchen Sink', Roskill too notes 'the pathological character of the child's tense, painful and ungainly attempt to move across a room'. After *Creation and Crucifixion* Smith's work displays 'a change of subject', 'but the formal evolution is quite logical and self-entailing'. Painting a visual experience has to be for Smith 'a *recreation*, a pursuance of the impression in a conjunction of mind and eye parallel to the original vision but not identical with it'. Smith 'is concerned with the character of momentary perception under *multiple* simultaneous aspects...: he is preoccupied with movement as much as with light, and with directions of movement, and with sound where this is a correlate of movement'. Roskill goes on to discuss the ambiguities and contradictions involved in constructing such images in paint. The reliefs, some in white plaster, some painted to suggest bronze, examine how light falling on objects transforms our reading of them, adjusting their apparent nature. In the paintings there had to be a similar concern with how the material would contribute to this, the paint itself being to some degree three-dimensional and the repository of light.

Many of the paintings of 1958-59, still lifes and sea paintings, show him summarizing a mass of impressions both as forms and as colour contrasts, and setting them down as a continuum, not a fixed and final *tableau*. Thus *Light amongst Bottles* (1958) presents almost every aspect of the subject as waves of paint running across the canvas. The subject could almost be the chandelier Smith said he might have painted had he lived with one: the form he gives to light and shadow here belong more to their notation than to bottles or to chandeliers, and everything hovers or presses forward as brushed paint. In *Objects on a Table II* (1959) and other still lifes, there is some differentiation between the objects but we'd be hard pressed to identify them. There is no doubt that these pictures are made of paint, with a brush moving mostly horizontally both to record the action of light and to hold real light and shadow in the ridges and grooves. A series of paintings titled *Sea: Rise and Fall* — all of 1959 and thirty-six inches square; numbers I and III are illustrated in the catalogue – treats the motif diagrammatically. In number I, great arcs of paint swing over each other almost symmetrically in thick and thin paint, with spray coming from them here and there like fronds. There is some sense of forwards and backwards, edge and hollow, but horizontal lines invite a left-to-right reading and thus a sense of time. In number III, where intense blue suggest the sky while black and then brown stand for the water, the horizontal lines are more emphatic, almost breaks in the surface, while the graph-like line of the sea itself, going across the painting as if across a monitor, brings with it thick

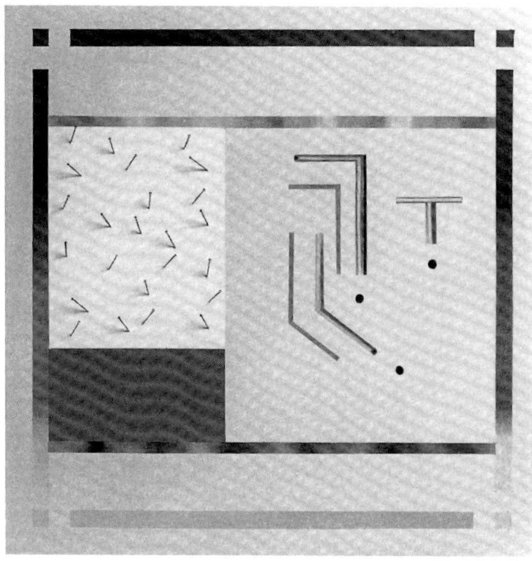

25 Pins White above Blue 1974

Mixed media on canvas
30.5 x 30.5 cm
Private collection

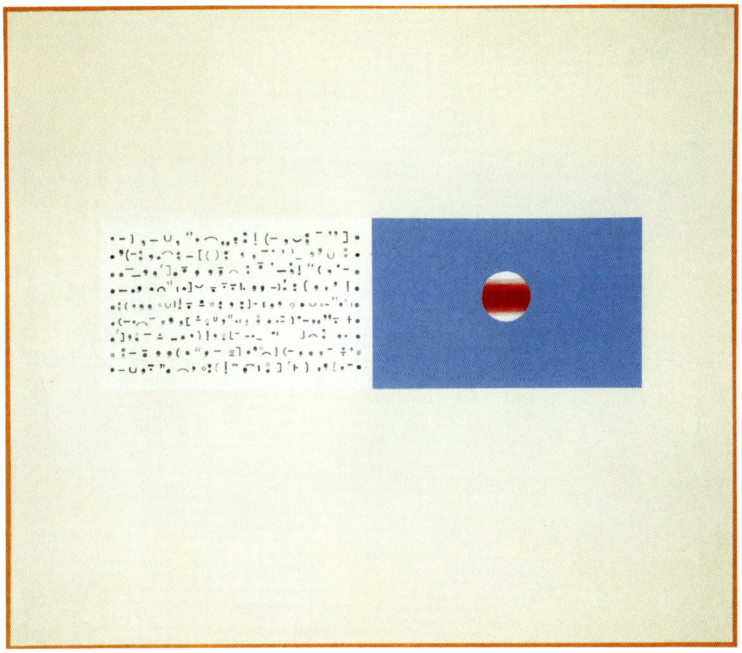

Sound Notation 1974

Oil on board
79 x 91 cm

paint, brushed to form a band following the line. Smith mixed marble dust into his paint, the best permanent way of giving mass to oils. The reliefs are not illustrated in the catalogue and Smith has nothing to represent them now. They were abstract but related to still life, and the paintings suggest that there was something about them of Boccioni's way of stretching forms to indicate motion and energy, here used to speak of light and shadow.

Berger wrote with remarkable clarity about this important exhibition in conjunction with a show of four St Ives painters at the Waddington Galleries. The anonymous critic of *The Times* suggested that the best Smiths 'might be compared in their seriousness with early analytical Cubist works' in their search for a new formal language. This raised in Berger's mind the problem of subjectivity *versus* communication. 'Is it possible that such works are establishing new truths which will in the end become part of our experience of art and therefore finally of life too? ... Or are they indeed as limited and in the strict sense of the word as meaningless as they seem?' He obviously found Smith's paintings, and also Roger Hilton's in their way, very impressive as objects and as evidence of intelligent pursuits. But he concluded that about their work, (as also about any others) the question has to be asked: 'What can art serve here and now?' and gave his answer in terms he used repeatedly before giving up art criticism as his main activity. 'But my conclusion is that their works are useless, because I am unable to see how they help or will help men to know and claim their social rights.'[19]

19. *NS*, 6 June 1959, page 792.

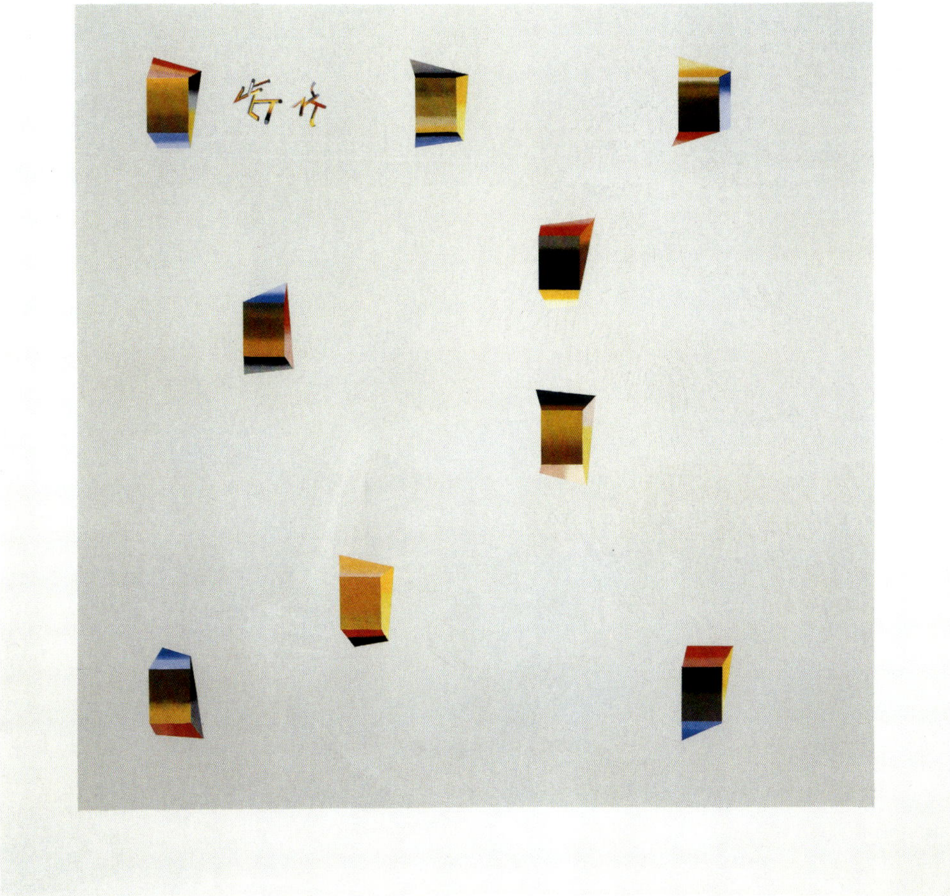

11 Activities, 9 Major 2 Minor 1973

Oil on board
106 x 106 cm

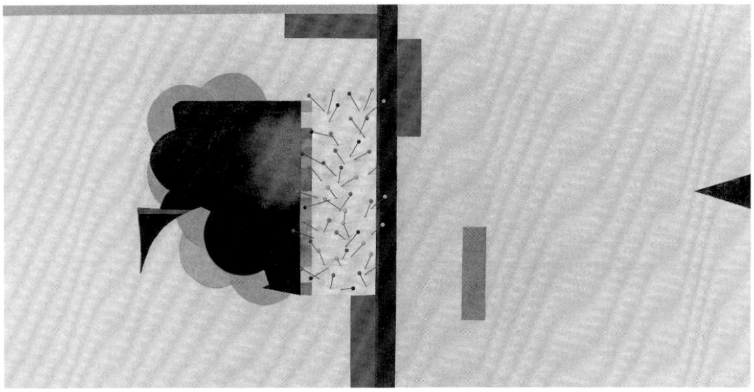

46 Pins and Other Elements 1979/80

Mixed media on board
32 x 62 cm
Private collection

The art critic of *The Spectator* announced himself a convert:

The present writer must admit to having been consistently wrong about Jack Smith's painting for the last seven years. It seemed once that the horrific infants stumping across barren acres of sackcloth, and coloured in turpentine starved of life and pigment, had an air of deadly finality about them. His most recent work has moved away from that work and his paint and plaster reliefs are luxuriant sometimes to ugliness. But the cold realities he tries to capture remain precise, distant and personal. The concern is still with light, light which does not illumine objects, but through which objects and people may be dimly discerned whose character is determined by the light itself. If this does not always work it often achieves great beauty, and a sort of all-of-a-pieceness which, by half blinding one, produces sensations of cold spaces of sea and air which are almost terrifying in their loneliness and their grasp on the imagination.[20]

It is not often that critics admit so openly to a change of heart, but we may wonder at this swing from finding 'horrific infants' to 'sensations ... almost terrifying in their loneliness'. The earlier reading was obviously caused or confirmed by the general need to find an angry young man; the later, though again pessimistic, surprises us with its headlong acceptance of Smith's more analytical, almost abstract, treatment. The backdrop to these responses was the *The New American Painting* exhibition at the Tate Gallery, consisting of substantial groups of work by the Abstract Expressionists. The 1956 show, *Modern American Art* had included one room of samples of their work; the 1959 show, in February-March, made a powerful impression on many British artists but had left most critics hesitating between admiration and disdain. In this situation Smith's latest work was isolated between the New York

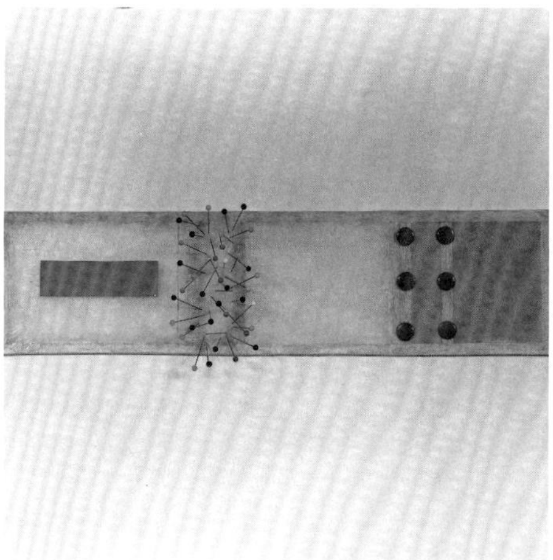

Sounds and Silences. 40 Pins 1978

Mixed media
30.5 x 30.5 cm
Private collection

20. Simon Hodgson, *The Spectator*, 12 June 1959, pages 856-58.

programme of venturing forth guided only by one's heart, and the post-war abstract art of France and Italy, often fine confections formed and repeated in the name of anxiety but including such entertainments as that offered by Georges Mathieu who dashed off, in public, large abstract paintings consisting of linear scrawls that came to look like signatures. With all this spontaneous combustion, real and imagined, on offer from both sides of the Atlantic, while abstract art in the UK was either tied to St Ives's nature lyricism or to London's Constructive art of apparently impersonal geometry, Smith's work must have looked strange indeed, highly individual and quasi-scientific.

Roskill's 1959 text had included a paragraph on 'the personality behind the work':

> *This personality is courageous, self-reliant, assertive. ... Smith has carved out his own field of survey and exploration, on the basis of an attitude that sets the exploration of visual truth above any compromise with forms of art involving an aesthetic tastefulness of picture-making ... The cast of mind here in operation has distinctly visionary features ... With Smith, the interaction of a certain impatience of spirit with rigorous attention to detail seems to contribute in large measure to the staying power of his talent.*

Roskill ended by suggesting that Smith 'has a definite place in the line of British artists who have empowered a basic rationalism with a concomitant visionary intensity'.

In quoting this a year later, Sylvester turned 'British' into 'English', three times in the same sentence, and prefaced the quotation by pointing to 'Smith's Englishness'. This may be what Roskill meant. But by misquoting him, Sylvester was able to aim the theme of 'visionary intensity' in a particular direction. He was writing an introduction to Smith's solo exhibition at the Matthiesen Gallery, shown during October-November 1960. He found that various aspects of Smith's latest paintings, but especially their 'visionary character', reminded him of Paul Nash's best work. Nash's standing was not high at that time. In praising him, Sylvester made him British: 'one of the really authentic and imaginative British painters of our time'. Following Sylvester and placing Smith into 'a line of *English* artists' raises the question whether other key Englishmen may not help us to see his work more clearly. I am thinking of Blake and of Turner: both essential to Nash, one of them a visionary needing to deliver transcendental messages through visual as well as verbal images, the other firmly rooted in this world but becoming visionary as he questioned, with ever-increasing intensity, the complex interactions through which he perceived the flux of experience.

Sylvester's text pivoted on thoughts about silence and light and how we

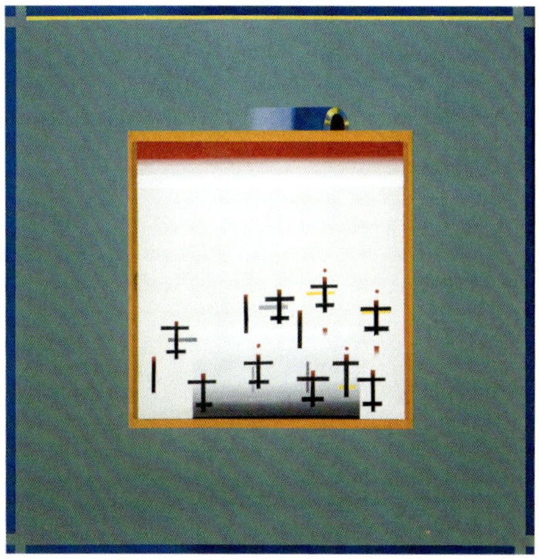

Sound Infiltration 1977

Oil on board with relief
63 x 63 cm

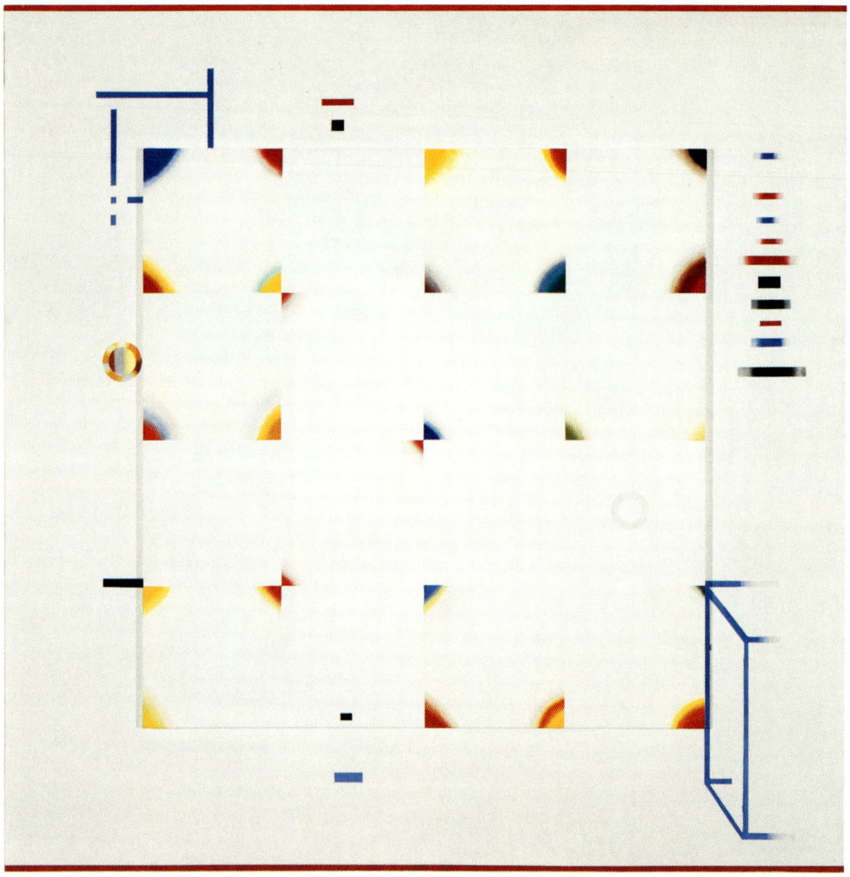

Light Sensation 1979

Oil on board with relief
91.5 x 91.5 cm

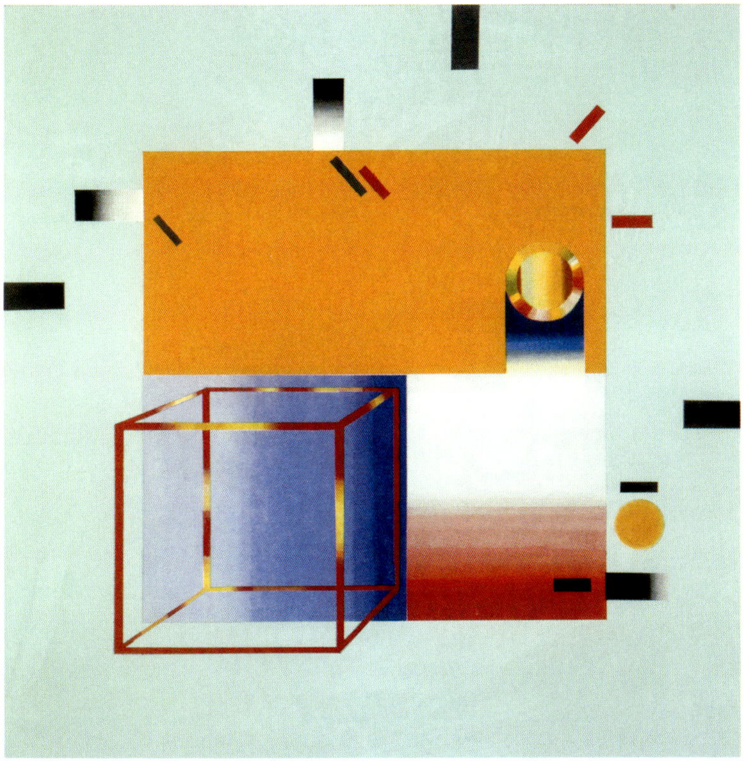

Light and Object Sensation. Sound 1980

Oil and acrylic on board
60 x 60 cm

know the world through them: 'We are never in any doubt that Smith's paintings are of something in the physical world ... they are paintings of specific visual experiences'. But we cannot know the identity of the objects occasioning those experiences, 'with the result that we are able to be aware of certain aspects of their appearance which would tend to elude us once they were named and thereby circumscribed by our preconceptions of them. ... Smith stakes everything on painting things as if their identity could not be fixed'. Those who write seriously about art know that art teaches them anew every day. Sylvester was here completing what we now call a learning curve which began in 1957 when he accused Smith of abandoning the identity of things yet admitted the originality and power of his work. Now, in 1960, probably following a hint from the painter and thinking of silence and light, Sylvester brought in the example of Vermeer. We recall Smith's early recognition of his need to achieve Mondrian's clarity. Vermeer's art, and Mondrian's, speak of passionate intensity without parading the artist, as hero, victim or medium. Both artists stand high in Smith's estimation to this day. Vermeer is the perfect model for an art that goes beyond acute seeing to the act – familiar but still rarely the goal of artists of perceiving without knowing, without getting to the stage of identifying. Sylvester summarized it well: Smith 'is concerned with light because light is a solvent for the names of objects'. The tradition-minded viewer may be perplexed by seeing paintings which, even when they have

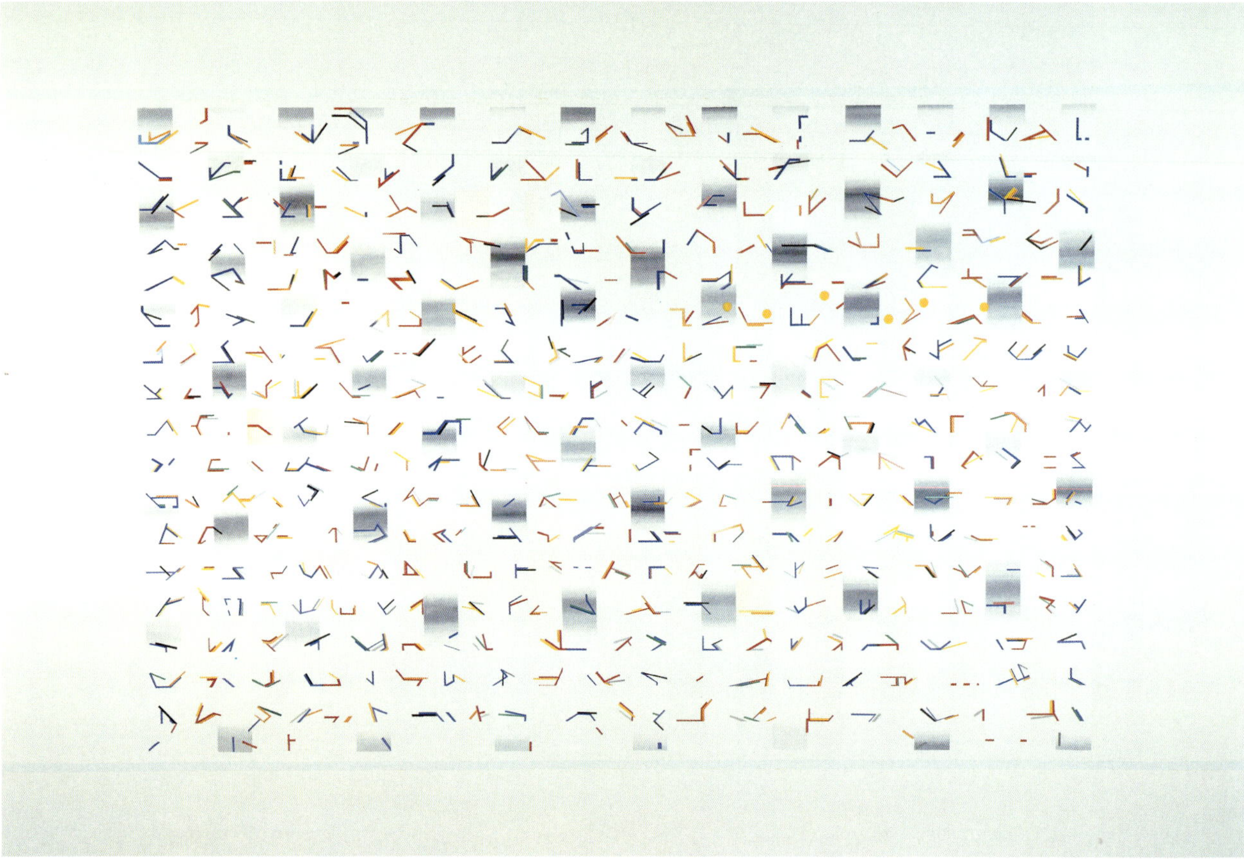

Bridge No. 3 1980

Acrylic on canvas
244 x 366 cm

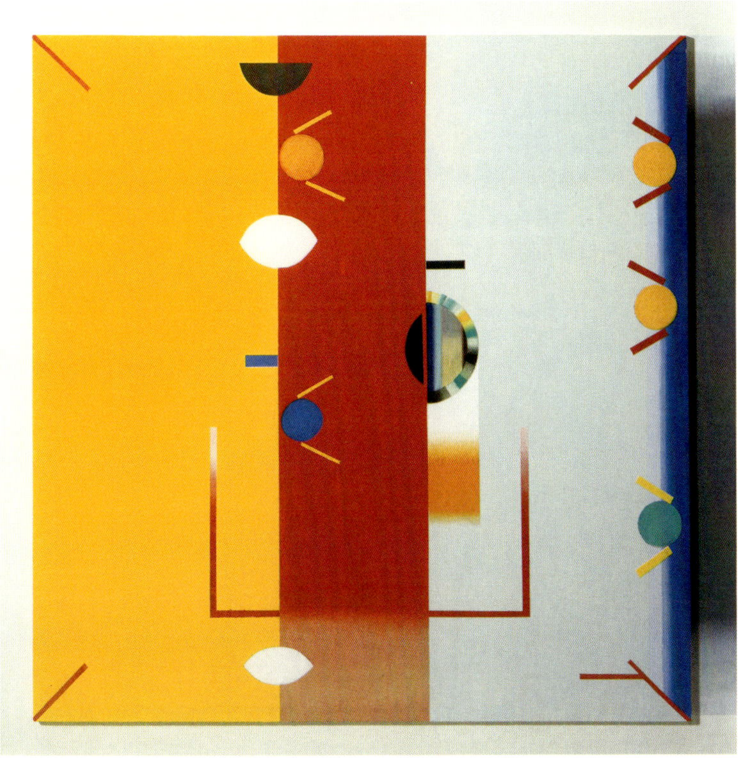

Light and Object Sensation No. 2 1980

Oil on board with relief
71 x 71 cm

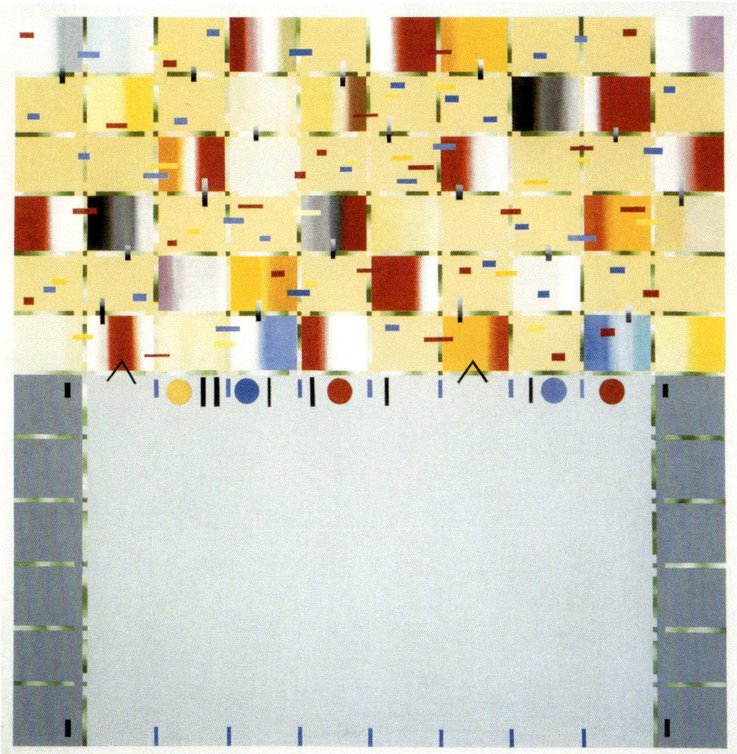

Sounds and Silence 2 1980/81

Oil on board
107 x 107 cm

accurate titles, remain illegible. The problem comes from a change of aim and method that demands from us a new approach: 'Whereas painters in the Renaissance tradition crystallized their experience in a scene, the modern painter invents a construction which is a metaphor for his experience'.

It is more or less impossible today to reconstruct, or imagine, the collective impact of Jack Smith's 1959 show at the Whitechapel and 1960 show at Matthiesen's. Too much of the work has gone and the reproductions are too few and almost all in black and white. Hindsight suggests that both these shows – exceptionally large at the Whitechapel, but very substantial also at the prestigious Matthiesen Gallery — caught Jack Smith in transition. The Whitechapel exhibition cannot have done him any harm, in loosening both the Kitchen Sink label and the group association. Everyone could see that here was an intensely individualistic vision demanding original methods and devoid both of any hint of socio-political commentary. But it did not show the emergence of the fully-formed artist. The Matthiesen show consisted of twenty-seven paintings on canvas, twenty-one pencil drawings, and three 1959 sculptures of modest dimensions in white plaster: one called *Bas-Relief*, the others *Construction for Painting* but presumably low reliefs too. It displayed a first step in his rapid progress towards the art that he now wishes to be identified with, not so much for reasons of pictorial character or beauty or strength as for the fact that it lives on an infinite plane of invention and expression-within-discipline. This will need demonstrating, as also its links back to the work of around 1958-60. What then looked like a terminus was a transit station. Nothing in Smith's progress is wasted.

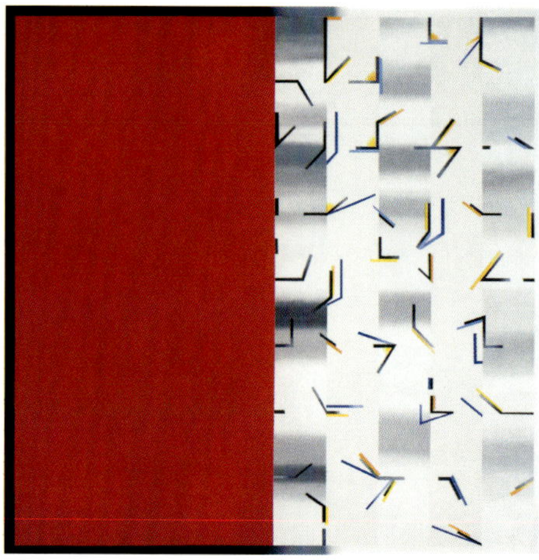

Activities to the Right of Red 1980

Oil on board
107 x 107 cm

The Matthiesen show confirmed Smith's singular vision while demonstrating its capacity for change and development. It restated light as Smith's primary subject, now almost exclusively in relation to figures and still-life objects. (Only one title refers to the sea.) The list of paintings ends with three five foot square paintings called *Figures and Objects in a Room*, ill. p.25 and all but three of the drawings were of figures. These figures are far removed indeed from those of his Kensington interiors. Those are concise but affecting emblems. Two black and white illustrations in the Matthiesen catalogue are of paintings relatively early in what was on show there: number four, *Figure with Easels*, and number seven, *Figure in Light and Objects*. The figure in number four is just legible as a figure, seated in the centre, with head and hints of limbs. It suggests an assembly of painted forms curving this way and that, altogether relief-like on the canvas but floating weightlessly in a shallow space. This space is articulated by small geometrical forms suggesting easels and small paintings on them, all held in a

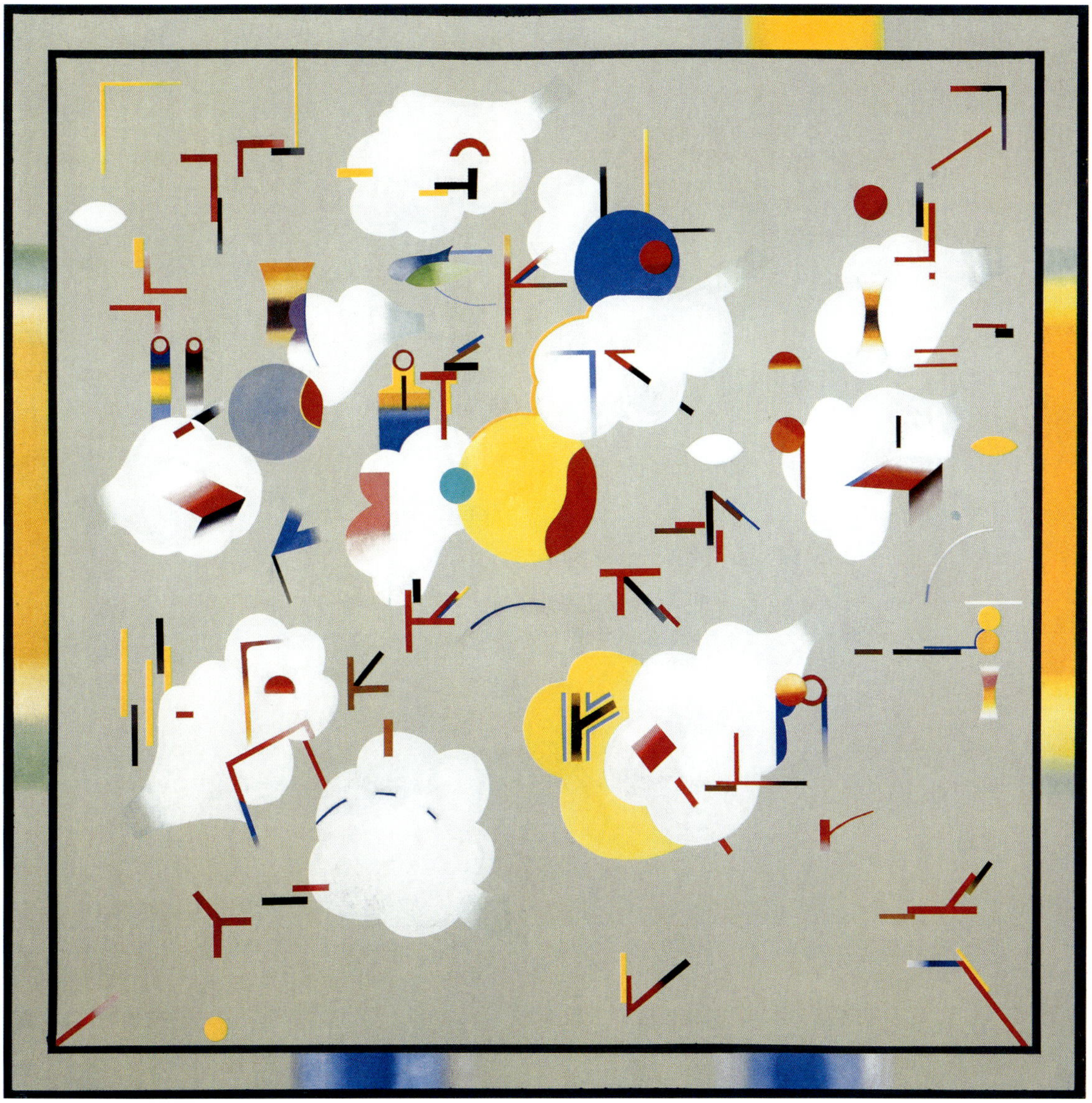

Diagram. Sound and Light 1982

Oil on board
119.5 x 122 cm

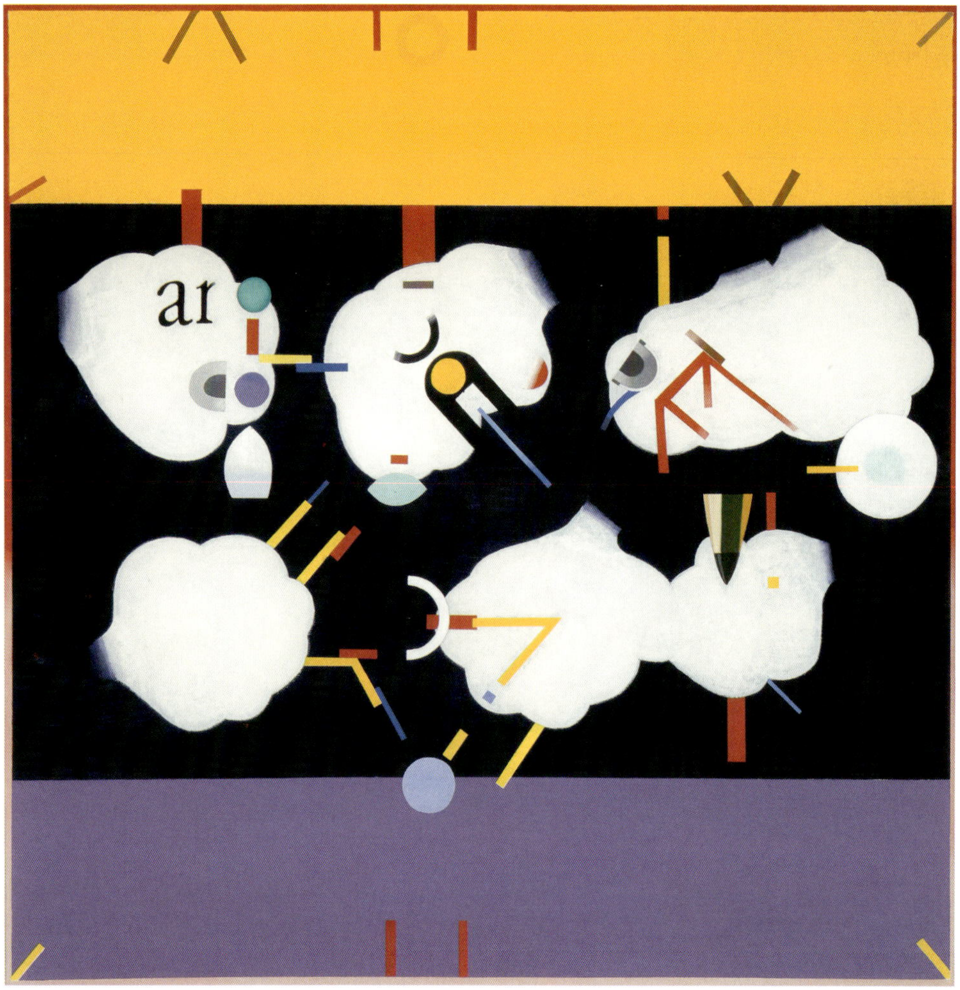

Inside. Outside Sensation 1981

Oil on board
107 x 107 cm

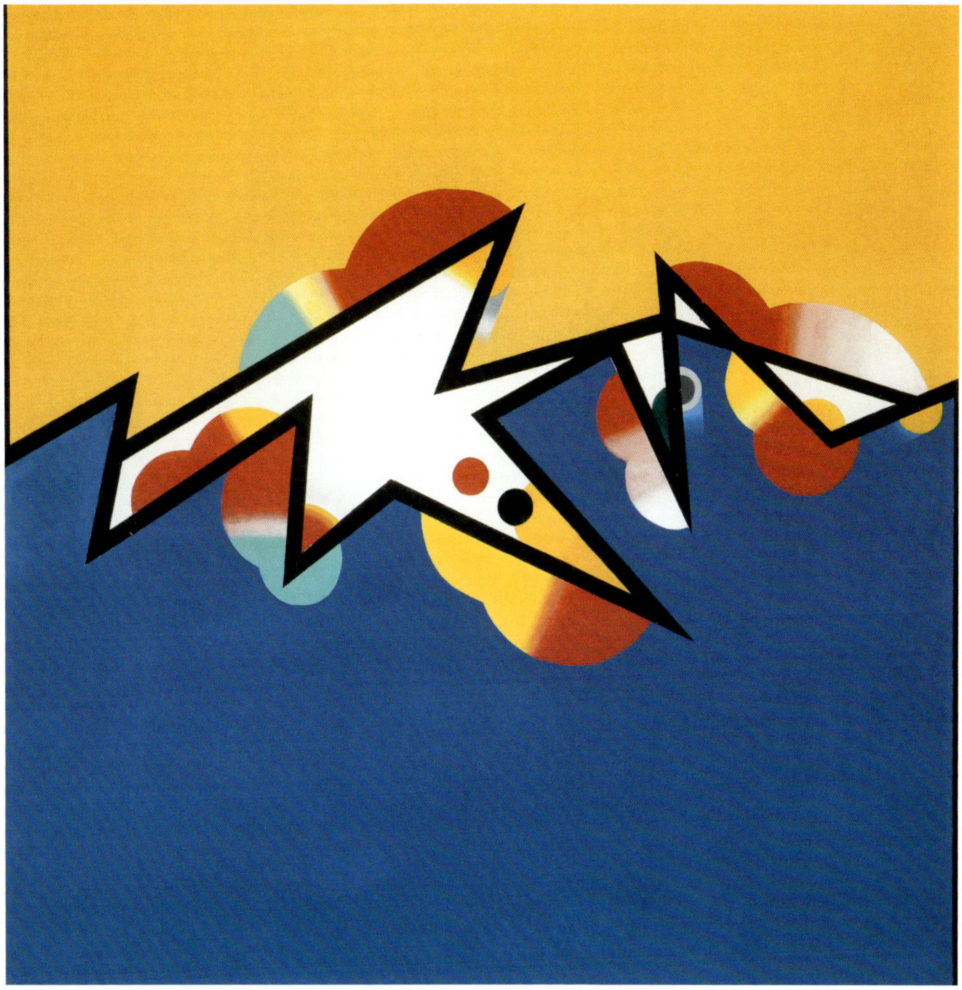

Zig Zag 6 1982

Oil on board
105 x 105 cm

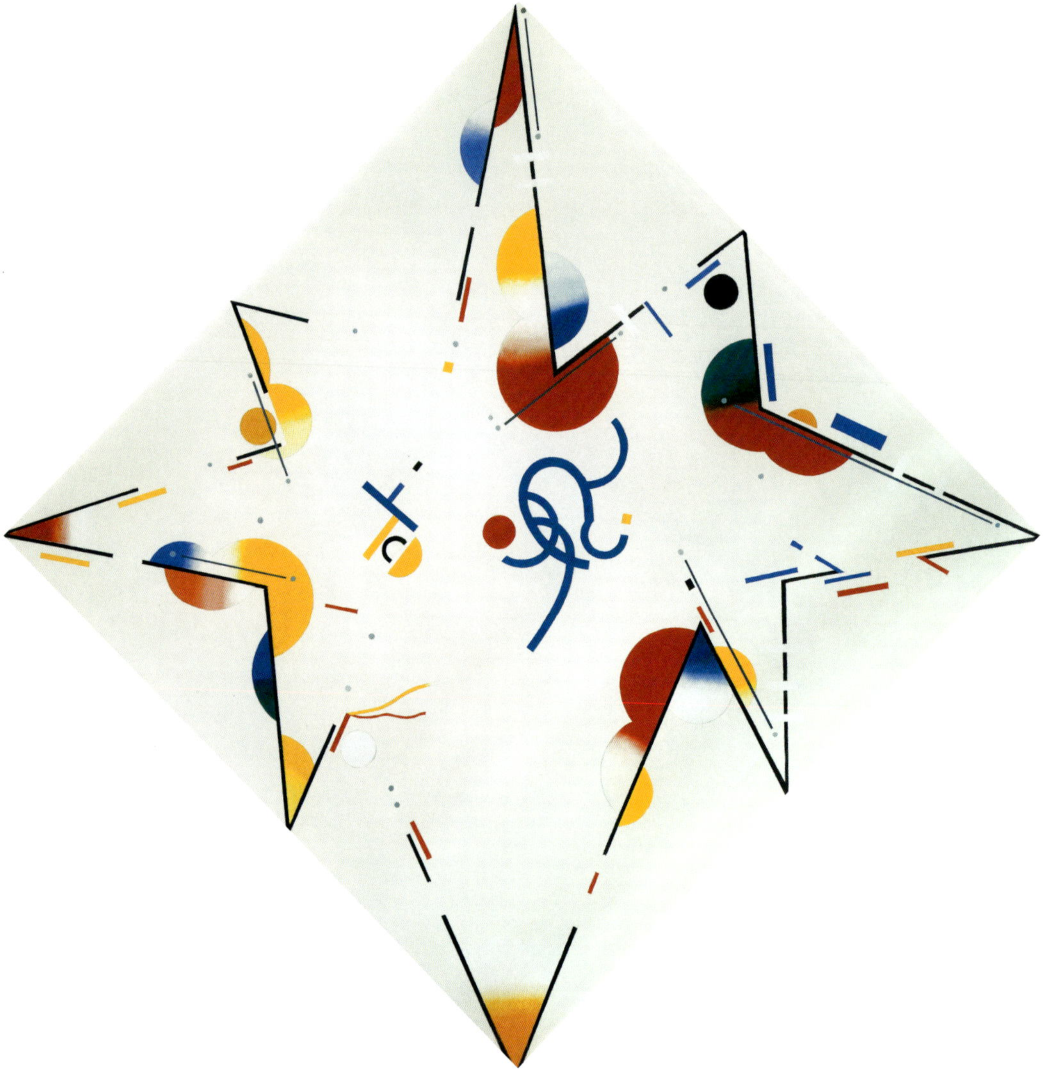

Sounds. (Fractured) 3 1982

Oil on board
90 x 90 cm

mysterious light and, again, weightless. The idiom of the figure is distantly Cubist, but more like a Cubist sculpture than a Cubist painting, and again recalling the forms used by Boccioni. The figure in number seven is quite different. It is seen in a relatively dark setting that hints at an interior by means of passages of textured paint in horizontal and vertical patches. Compared with that, the figure is unsculptural and immaterial, a multiform assemblage of curved and angular portions, all flat or quite shallow, and all in light tones that make it, or her, a ghostly presence, a phenomenon of light.

Four paintings from the exhibition survive. *Still Life in Shadow* (1959), ill. p.20, shows a few objects, mostly squat bottles, with space between them on a tilted table-top. They are more drawn than painted and exist as visible elements primarily because of light falling on them or shadows adhering to them. A few abstract signs here and there indicate other objects and the edge of the table, but the arrangement presents no difficulty though each object has lost its independence and some of its identity. *Jug and Other Objects* (1959-60), ill. p.24, is wholly different. The 'other objects' are arranged and delineated to make a horizontal silhouette, almost a roof-scape, either side of the main and central feature, a Synthetic Cubist cluster of polyphonic profiles that have something of Ben Nicholson's 1950s large still lifes about them. These overlapping shapes are in red, brown, pink and white; they suggest a jug and vases or pots pushed together, almost merging. The objects left and right are almost unpainted, and melt downward into the unpainted canvas that is the lower half of the picture. The upper half is partly unpainted on the left, painted a luminous mid-grey on the right, and a resonant blue behind the jug etc., as well as continuing some way to the left. Bands of grey and white rise from that central group to the top of the picture and leave one in doubt whether there is any picture space between them and the grey 'background'. It is an exhilarating image because of its insubstantiality and, though leaving us unsure of what is what and exactly where it is, its clarity and, yes, silence.

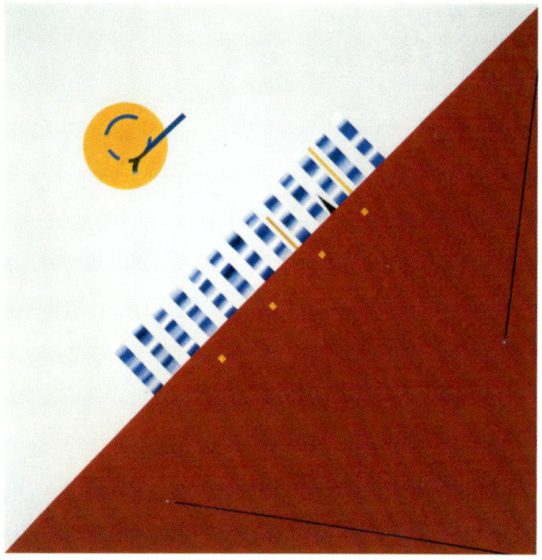

Sound and Light out of Red 1982

Oil on board
107 x 107 cm

Two of the three listed *Figures and Objects in a Room* (all 1960) survive. One of them is numbered '2', ill. p.19; the other has no number, ill. p.25. They are similar in their high tonality: creams, off-whites, pale ochre, here and there dark linear accents and a sudden flash of brighter colour, pink or blue or violet. The forms indicated in them are mostly vertical and will, if we look patiently, reveal figures among easels. This verticality on a square canvas makes for calm, and this is enhanced by the pale tones and the sense of the seen space being remembered as light coming into the room and towards us. Silence? Stillness certainly, nothing happening but the light partly revealing, partly diverting us from our desire to know everything. These are not bland pictures but as full of local incident as they are bathed in general serenity. There is plenty to look at and move between. And though there is plenty of mobility for us in navigating around these compositions, we are not asked to observe motion. They have none of Boccioni's physical assertiveness, but rather something like the opposite: reticence and a tentative approach to things half seen, half remembered.

The cover of the Matthiesen catalogue is in colour. It records a painting that even with its title remains abstract: *Light and Dark Machine with Objects* (1960, not illustrated). We do not see a machine but glimpse something that may be one, perhaps accompanied by 'objects'. Almost all the surface is structured by intermitting horizontal bands, like a screen of figured glass. The subject here is the light/dark interference and what suggestion it yields of something existing behind it. Historically one is again reminded of the Italian Futurists, in this case of Balla who around 1912-14 worked on patterns of colour that would produce sensations of light, and also on patterns of line and tonal contrast that would signal machines in motion. Smith finished a similar painting a little later in 1960, *Objects, Strips of Light + Shadow*, exploring the relief-effect created by contrasting bands of light and dark tones. In another 1960 painting he deployed vertical bands in a similar manner and to similar effect. Both the horizontal and the vertical banding were to bear fruit in his work of the next years.

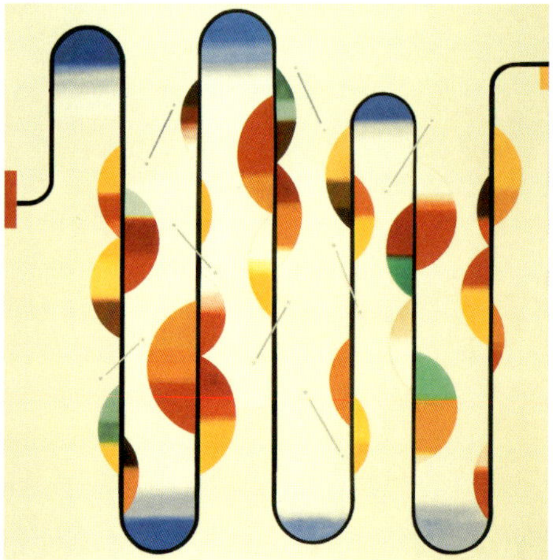

Rise and Fall. Light and Sound 1984

Oil on canvas
91.5 x 91.5 cm

The end of the 1950s was a time when 'going abstract' was an issue attracting praise and competition (did Kandinsky go abstract before Malevich? at which point can we call Mondrian's work abstract?) as well as blame. In Britain, while critics hesitated to make up their minds about it, many artists responded positively to the American exhibitions and the new horizons they indicated. Some British painters became more conscious of their European roots and were content with them; many others, especially among the young, worked ingeniously in what today looks like a mid-Atlantic idiom. But the 1950s had also seen the emergence of a tradition belonging to both sides of the Atlantic and in many respects hostile to the idea of art as a measure of civilization. Robert Motherwell's anthology of Dada texts and productions was published in 1951 into a world that had largely forgotten the movement and its messages. 'Anti-art' suddenly became a subject for debate, better informed as the years passed and further books were published. In Britain the BBC contributed at a high level with a series of radio talks on the *Third Programme*, initiated by Basil Taylor's 'Art – Anti-Art' broadcast in November 1959, and published in the widely-read weekly, *The Listener*.[21] With the sudden onset of Pop art in Britain and America in 1961 the whole situation seemed to be even worse than that described by Doris Lessing in 1957, not merely 'a confusion of standards and the uncertainty of values'. Among serious participants and bystanders, admiration for any section of artistic production had to go with opposition to others, often threaded through with doubts about the absolute virtue of any of it. Meanwhile the media, with colour supplements adding words and colour images to television's offerings, began to present the contemporary art world as something between a fairground and a sports arena. Pop art was fun, but was condemned by many for dragging art down to the level of advertising and mass

21. *The Listener*, 12 November 1959, pages 819-22.

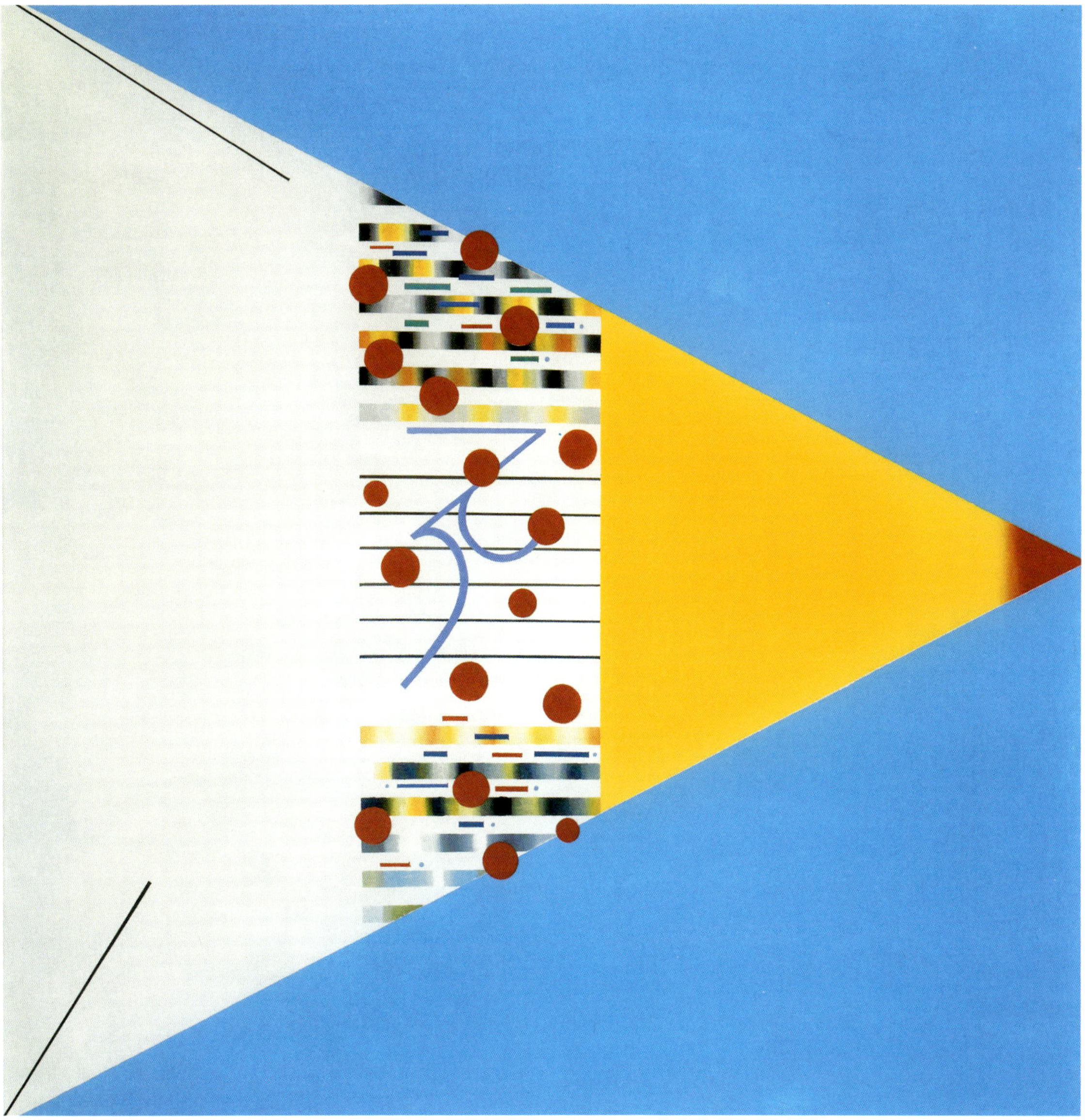

Light and Sound 1982

Oil on board
122 x 122 cm

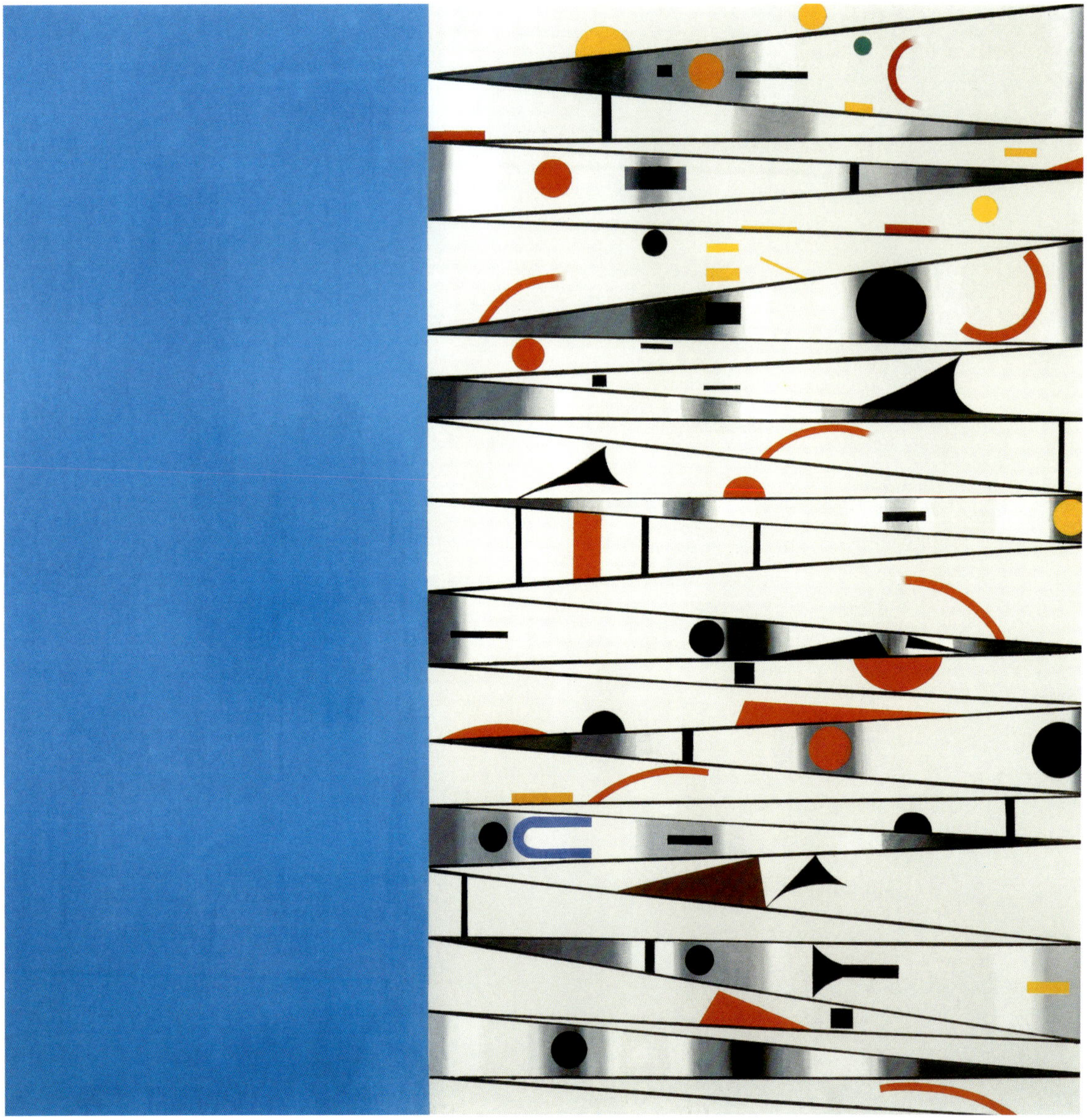

The Blue Song Painting 1984

Oil on canvas
122 x 122 cm

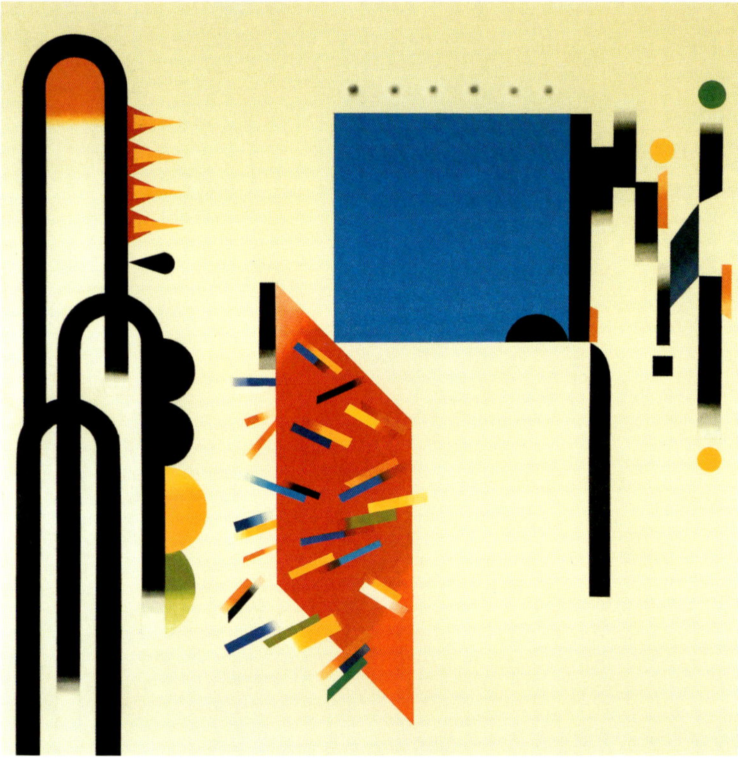

Portrait of a Composer I 1987

Oil on canvas

91.5 x 91.5 cm

Collection: Matthew and Huei Flowers

entertainments, just when painting had achieved unprecedented sublimities, notably the new American painting. Abstract art could accommodate Pop flavours but was not suddenly going to reach out to the masses.

Jack Smith's persistent working out of visual experience left him on the figurative side of the abstract/figurative confrontation, more marked in England perhaps than elsewhere and still noticeable today. He had been deeply impressed by the large Pollock exhibition at the Whitechapel Art Gallery in 1958.[22] He was aware of competing tendencies in current British art, which around 1960 included St Ives abstraction, emboldened by American example but not detached from its attachment to nature; the Constructive abstract art promoted by Pasmore and his friends, rigorous in theory but often inflected by English lyricism; and by the younger Constructive artists who became public during the 1960s as 'Systems' but had for some time been working in a spirit of objective research. Their public success was always less than they deserved in a country suspicious of art theory, but their influence was marked in the art schools where they taught, at a time when specialist art history and general studies courses, as well as libraries, were developing. The promotion in London

22. Generally, this focused display got a warmer reception from the London critics than the broader American show. Pollock's art could not answer Berger's demands, yet Berger found it excellent in itself, so good that 'through it one can see the disintegration of our culture'. *NS*, 22 November 1958, pages 722-23.

of large, wholly abstract painting, and then also sculpture, in the 'Situation' exhibitions of 1960-61 asserted an un-English professionalism in the attitudes and productions of relatively young British artists, as well as their aversion to the English habit of self-deprecating lyricism. That their bid for public attention was trumped by Pop art's emergence was abetted by the English reluctance to be interested in more than one kind of art, preferably one artist, at a time. But for that, we might have been helped to attend to the vitality to be found in the work of all these movements. It was, perhaps inevitably, figurative art that got media attention and, especially with the rise to fame of Francis Bacon (whose 1962 retrospective show at the Tate Gallery fixed him in public awareness), respect from the critics. In spite of its rapid development and many fine exhibitions during the 60s, abstract painting and sculpture continued to be thought of as aberrant.

From 1957 on, Jack Smith was teaching part-time in London art schools, at Chelsea School of Art and then at Hornsey and Wimbledon and in the Royal College's sculpture department. Chelsea was growing into an exceptionally energetic and broadly-based art school, large enough to provide a wide range of partisan teaching, ranging from convinced naturalistic representation to free abstract art and Constructive art. Many young and purposeful artists taught there part-time. We forget today how much England's major art schools then functioned as meeting places for the new artists of the 1960s, fully active on the national art scene and increasingly articulate in their discussions, among themselves and in their role as tutors. Jack Smith's old friend George Fullard was head of sculpture at Chelsea. Jack Smith himself would return there in 1972 as head of painting. Meanwhile, he exhibited frequently in respected London galleries – a second time at Matthiesen in 1963, at the Grosvenor Gallery in 1965, at Marlborough Fine Art in 1968, as well as in solo and group exhibitions abroad, in New York, Gothenburg, Brisbane etc. But his work never benefited from the persisting critical support that might have penetrated public doubt. He was 'going abstract' in the early 60s, abandoning even the references to the sea and other favourite motifs that survive into his titling for a few years. This left commentators little to discuss unless they were prepared to enter his new world of abstract signs, choreographed pictorially to deliver sensations and experiences stimulated by many external sources but often coming most directly from his own current work. All mature creative artists, in any medium, find their work driven by its internal momentum even when they are responding also to material encountered in the world around them.

He is not given, unlike some artists, to explaining himself. As a teacher

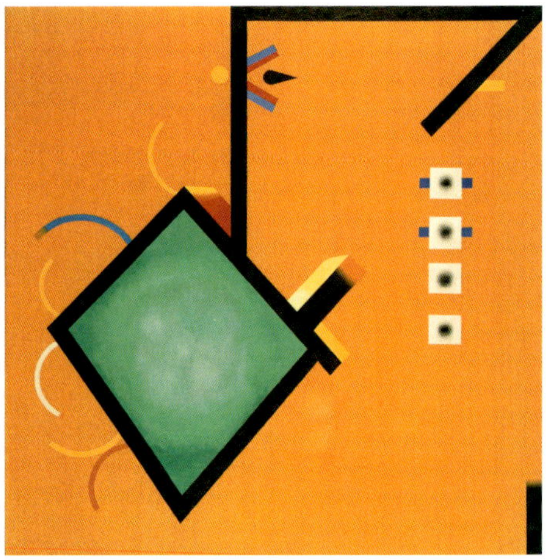

Portrait of a C. M. Composer 1987

Oil on canvas
91.5 x 91.5 cm
Private collection

over many years, he is practised in finding words for artistic values. Speaking about his own work he tends to be brief and specific, drawing attention to this or that aspect of a painting rather than offering metaphysical justifications for what he does. None the less, in 1965 he agreed to publish a statement of his ideas and principles in the pages of *London Magazine*, where short articles on contemporary art, and occasional illustrations of it, mingled with new poetry and prose and with literary criticism. It came out just before his show at the Grosvenor Gallery opened, and is reprinted here on page 5.[23] He also agreed to be interviewed by the art critic Charles S.Spencer. The article resulting from this appeared during the exhibition. It is valuable principally for Smith's words, some of them from his published statement but also others going beyond it, and for the excellent illustrations. Spencer's introductory paragraphs sketch the painter's history and reiterate some of Sylvester's 1960 points. If this is slightly disappointing, the presentation of this combination of words and images in Britain's major art journal had to be an important moment for the artist. From 1965 on, and into the 1970s, he was repeatedly included in export exhibitions of contemporary British art, and was certainly more firmly part of the developing London art scene than he had been since he distanced himself from his Beaux Arts associations.[24]

> *Explanations are like having to make rational whatever magic one has. I doubt whether art ought to be written about at all. We live in an age of explanation.*

Quoted by Charles Spencer, who added that he 'sympathised and agreed', those words give me pause too. But am I offering explanations? Artists speaking to each other and discussing work in art schools do not explain what is being

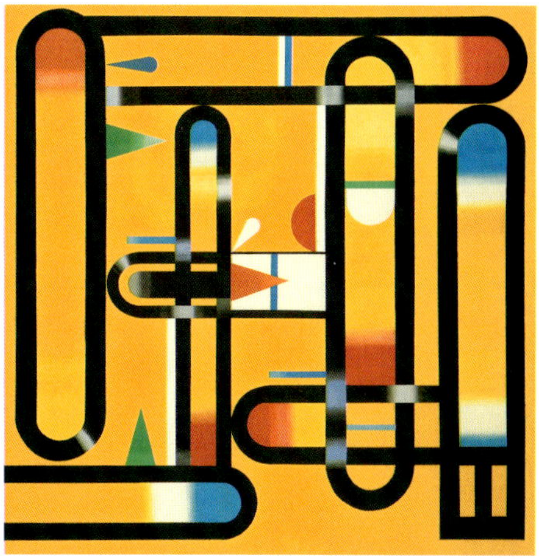

Sound and Light 1987

Oil on canvas

91.5 x 91.5 cm

23. As printed in *London Magazine*, March 1965, 'Notes on Painting' omits his last three sentences, perhaps to fit the page.
24. Charles S.Spencer, 'Jack Smith – Movement and sound in new paintings', *Studio International*, April 1965. Spencer made some odd mistakes in his contribution, for instance when he refers to, and echoes, Sylvester's comparison of Smith's paintings to the visionary art of Paul Nash but calls him 'John Nash', confusing those brothers and attributing visionary qualities to the art of the one who did not allow himself any. The issue as a whole gives a revealing impression of what G.S.Whittet, the editor welcomed at that time. The main article is by Herbert Read, hitherto the most generous of champions of modern art, now seventy-two. He complained of 'the disintegration of form in modern art' and found it primarily in Pop art. I think that, like other critics of mature years, he was really recording his fear that the new art was increasingly infected with what he referred to privately as 'beatnikery' (see Benedict Read and David Thistlewood (eds.), *Herbert Read – a British Vision of World Art*, Leeds City Art Galleries 1993, page 165). Read's view was that 'Whether as an extension of perceptual experience or as a realisation of inner feeling, the main purpose of the modern artist has been to establish being. He has redeemed vision from its merely reproductive task ... and has dared to be creative, that is to say, to transcend the accepted level of existence'. Much Pop art prided itself on not transcending the everyday world. Read's words could be a statement in support of Jack Smith's development as outlined a few pages further on.

done, but draw attention to aspects of it, important in themselves and perhaps indicative of a general intention. Good art explains itself if we give it our attention and if we are willing to receive its multifarious signals. My task is to draw attention to Jack Smith's work and, with luck, to hold it here long enough for some contact to be made. Its context, inside his studio and as provided by the world outside, help us all to make some sense of his intuitive purpose: painting primarily for himself, he is also addressing himself to a public, even when it seems reluctant to listen.

Perhaps the most useful part of Spencer's article is the paragraph in which he reports on Smith's second Matthiesen show, in 1963. This 'included titles like *Light Movement*, *Sea Movement* and reliefs described as *First and Second Movement* or *Four Movements*. The latter are of great significance since the painted reliefs and free-standing sculpture were efforts to free himself from the desire to paint three-dimensionally or create space. The reference to 'movements' was a conscious search for the purity and diversity of music.'
Spencer reported that Smith's latest paintings have 'quite definite origins – Music, Fairgrounds and Roundabouts, Sea and Aeroplanes, objects or activities which involve sound and movement', adding that Smith's very first exhibition (in 1962) included a picture of *Roundabout Horses*. The new paintings (six are illustrated in the Matthiesen catalogue, all 1963 and '64 and square or nearly square in format) present non-referential compositions containing many or a few hieroglyphic forms, in themselves flat but often implying layers and sequence by the way they lie over others. Smith agreed that his newest work could be called 'diagrams of experience', adding, 'I like the straight face of a diagram. I don't think this disqualifies emotion; you can paint dispassionately. A painting can be diagrammatic rather than descriptive'. *Painted Relief* (1963, not illustrated) consisted of five boards mounted centrally on top of each other, becoming more oblong from the largest at the back to the smallest. Each has a different language of coloured forms: free geometrical patterning; bands of contrasting tones and colours painted as though radiating from the hidden centre and thus in themselves three-dimensional in effect; large, curling, swirling forms apparently moving like oil in water; a free geometrical pattern similar to that of the first panel; a pattern of black and white stripes of irregular widths but systematically placed in vertical and horizontal groups; an area of rising and falling curved forms, smaller than those of the third level; and finally a blue area largely filled by a central ovoid divided into four colour areas in some of which hover smaller, clear and firm shapes. The visual richness of this presentation is astounding. The original must have been as noisy as ... a fairground, perhaps, with its conflicting sounds, sights and motions all around one.

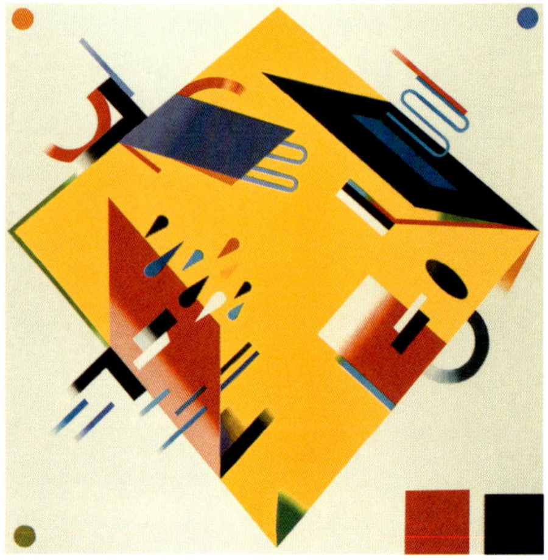

Musical Painting 1987

Oil on canvas
91.5 x 91.5 cm
Private collection

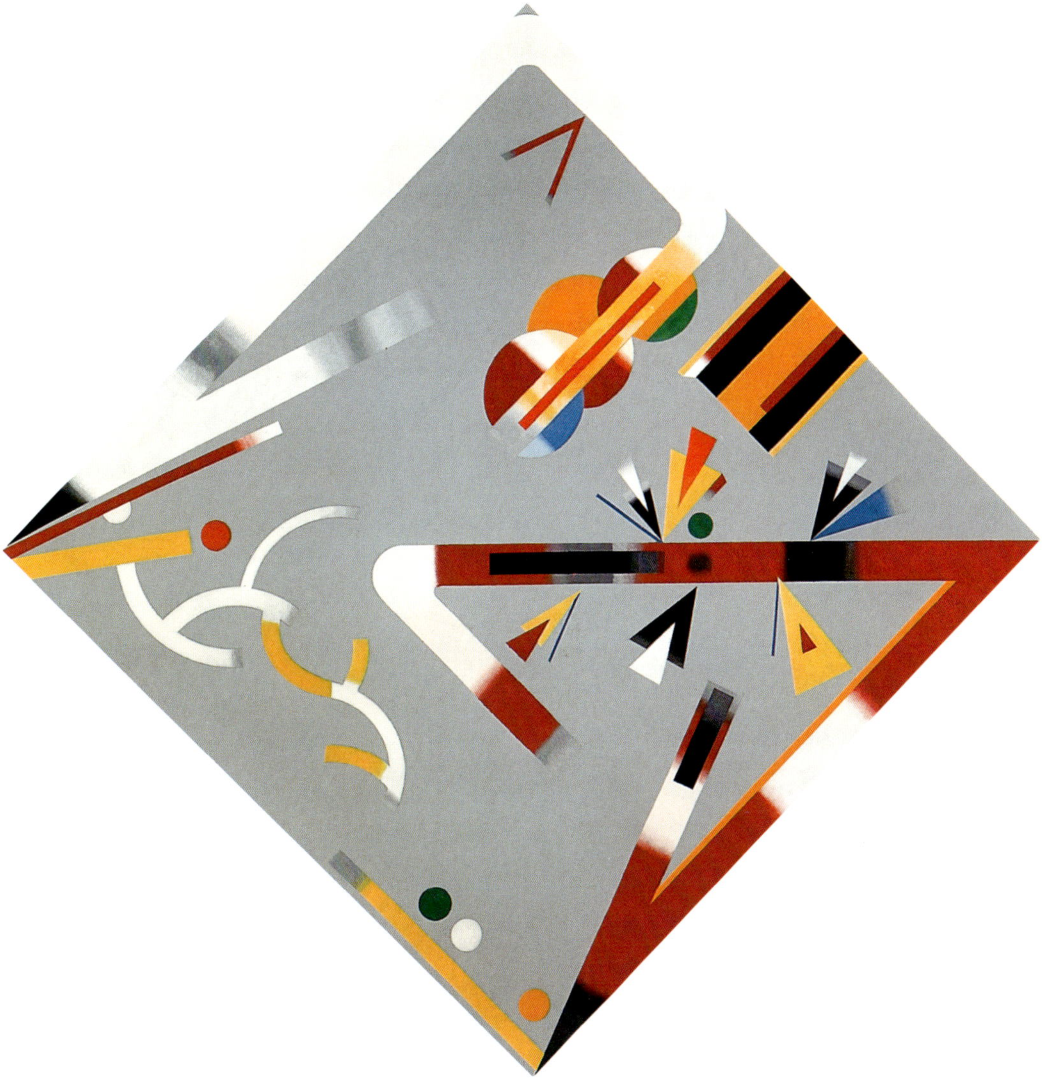

Another illustration shows a sculpture. An earlier photograph of his studio, taken in 1957, includes a number of canvases but is especially valuable for what it shows of two recent reliefs. One is painted a dark colour to suggest bronze and, though seen whole, is difficult to make out. Its forms seem to be soft and irregular. Closer to us but only partly visible, is a relief, framed in battens like a painting and similar to Smith's last still-life pictures, such as *Jug and Other Objects*, discussed above. The forms are crisply defined but in low relief, white on white, and one can well imagine how such a composition and light falling on it could propose a wealth of painted variations. The sculpture illustrated in *Studio* is of another sort. It is free-standing and consists of pre-cast forms joined to the outer and inner sides of a hollow block, all in white plaster. The title is one that Smith was adapting for paintings: *Inside and Outside No.1*

Areas of Energy 1986

Oil on canvas
76.5 x 76.5 cm
Private collection

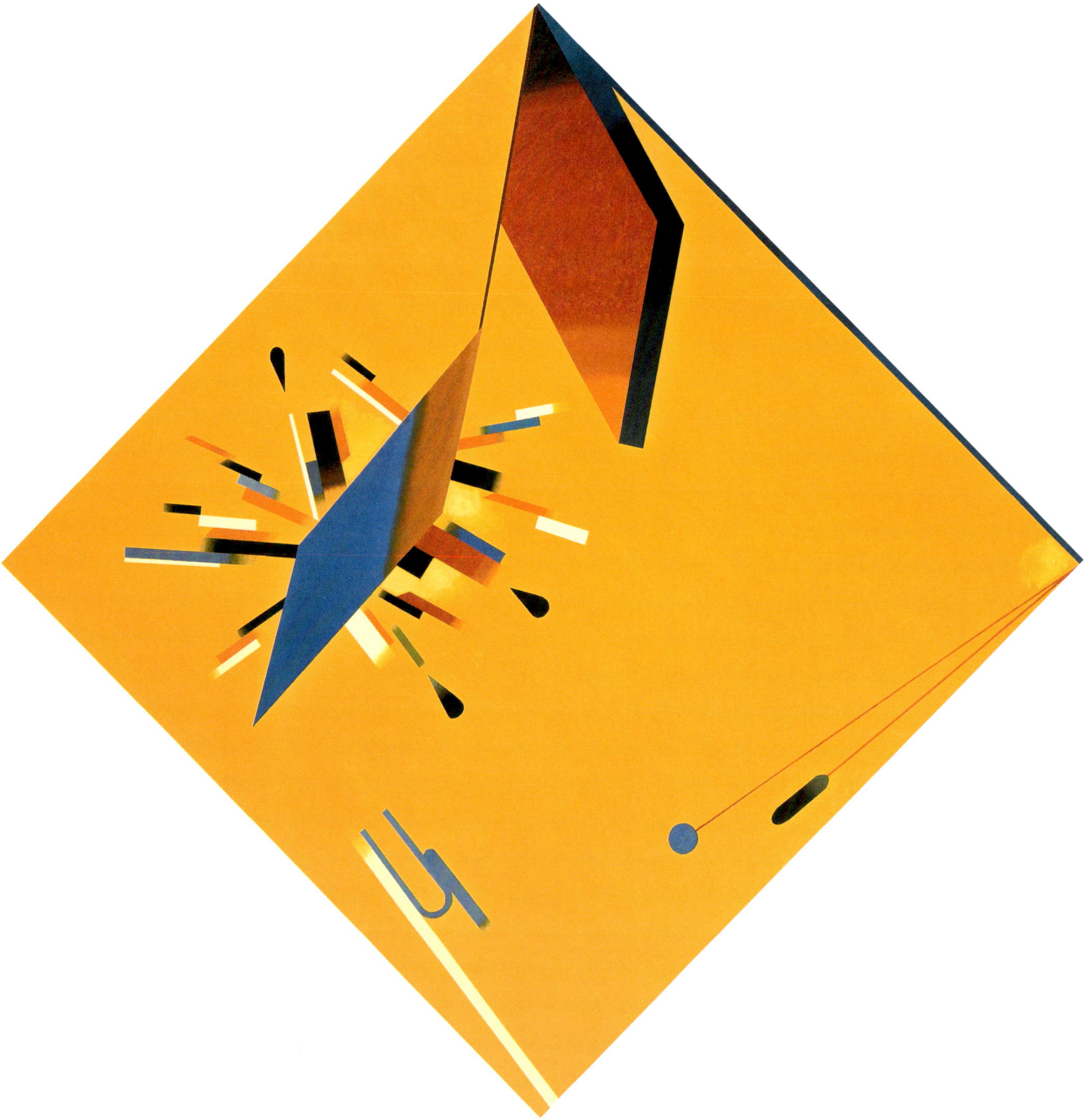

Sounds and Silences 1987

Oil on canvas
270 x 270 cm
Private collection

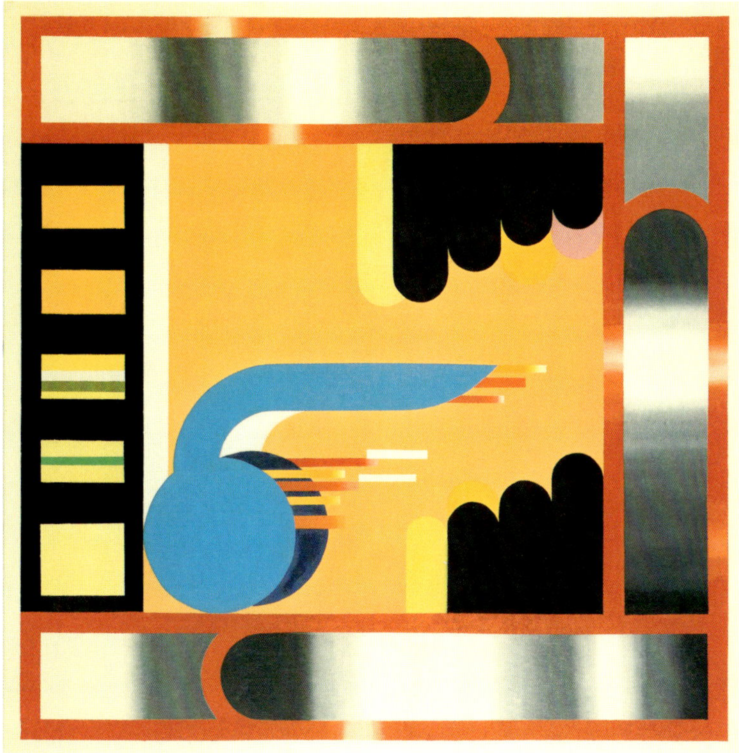

Musical Painting, Sound and Light 1988/89

Oil on canvas
91.5 x 91.5 cm

(1964, not illustrated). There are many objects in and on this block, some relatively large, many quite small. Though abstract, most of them play with things in the real world, or parts of things – the handles of tools, fruits, heels of shoes, partially inflated balloons perhaps, spirals suggesting drills, etc. Their association here, particularly their inhabiting the interior, has a partly Surrealist flavour. In its all-out originality as sculpture, it connects distantly with the new sculpture being pursued in London at the time, by William Tucker, Phillip King and a number of other sculptors, mostly in their late twenties. Their work was shown in 1965 at the Whitechapel Art Gallery as the second *New Generation* exhibition. In his preface to the catalogue, Bryan Robertson pointed out the echoes to be found in this sculpture of the new painting, a selection of which he had shown the previous year. In both kinds of work new forms and new qualities of light and colour were being explored with a freedom which came from ignoring the abstract/figurative division and as well as that between painting and sculpture, and disregarding all questions of sublimity of expression. These issues were suddenly quite unimportant. What was important was finding new things for painting and sculpture to do, separately and in fusion. What counted now, as Paul Huxley wrote in the 1964 *New Generation* catalogue, was 'making reconnaissance trips rather than supplying answers'. A few years older than these artists, Jack Smith was working in a similar spirit (and had been since he was very much of their age, in 1957-58), intent on the task of finding pictorial equivalents for events and experiences that were of other kinds and had rarely been attempted before. His 1964 sculpture, for all its distant links to Surrealism, can be related very directly to his *Painted Relief* of 1963 - both illustrated in *Studio International* on opposing pages which is not Surrealist at all.

Certainly the new work of 1964-65 has Smith attending to sound where previously he had sought silence. For a painting to indicate sound it has to be of a silent nature first. He told Spencer that 'I want a painting to contain thousands of experiences and images. So much contemporary art is concerned with one statement – it bores me to tears'. This applies evidently to *Inside and Outside: Roundabout No.2* (1964). Two-dimensional, it is subdivided by coloured bands that can be read as advancing rectangles with somewhat different forms and scales operating within each of them. Among the most recent paintings in the Grosvenor show were several Sea and Aeroplane paintings, and the article illustrates one of these. *Oceanair* (1964, not illustrated) has one painted border within which float about fifteen separate formal clusters or units, some simple and geometrical in silhouette, however complex within it, others more like open, stretched organic forms, all painted quite flatly and thus without any added lights or shadows. Spencer states that these paintings 'are based on swimmers and floating objects and the visual play of space, moving backwards and forward over the whole area'. The distribution of these abstract forms is neat without being systematic, so that each appears to have its share of the surface and to speak from it with equal clarity; they invoke ancient hieroglyphs more readily than the Cubism to which Spencer links them.

One of the paintings illustrated in *Studio* is available to us now: *Inside and Outside* (1964), ill. p.32. It still looks intensely original. Left of centre, a blue border functions a little like the plaster block in the 1964 sculpture. It contains a crowd of small circular emblems, accompanied top, left and bottom by snaking bands of reds and pinks. Darker forms start from the outside of this container and extend towards the right. Top and bottom right are some small units that may have escaped from the container, being similar to the emblems in it; they are in bright colours in this otherwise relatively colourless section. All this is surrounded by a luminous blue border close to the four sides of the canvas, but the background colour, a quiet, light grey-blue, continues beyond it, asserting its role as a limitless firmament, and thus an additional outside/inside decision. No form, no colour, is wholly devoid of implications, but there is no reference here to anything outside the painting, no implied narrative. Whatever significance we find belongs to the painting, the parts and the whole, and is the

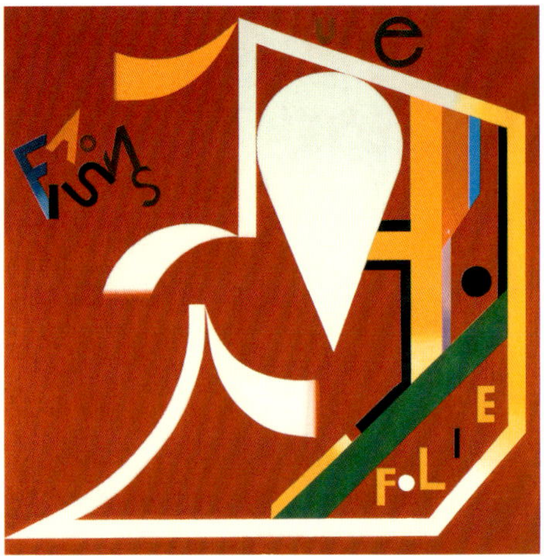

Faisons une Folie 2 1988

Oil on canvas
76 x 76 cm
Private collection

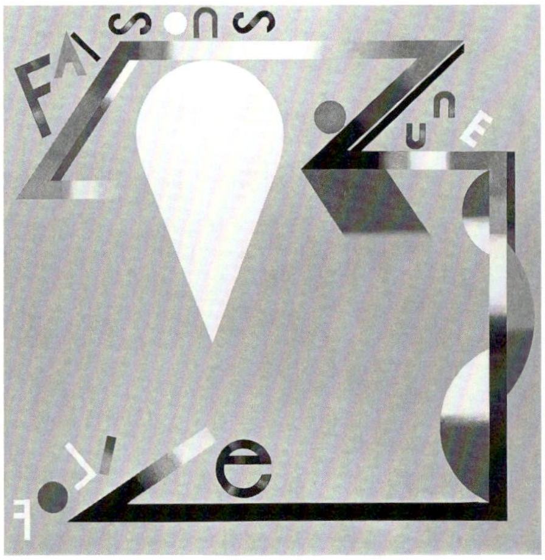

Faisons une Folie 1 1988

Oil on canvas
76 x 76 cm
Private collection

invention of the artist. Is such work, then, nonsense, as academics are still wont to insist? Only if, say, Bach's 'inventions' are nonsense too. Smith's relationship to music will be more fully considered below, as well as the relationship of his abstract pictorial languages to modern enquiries into linguistics. From now on he will work in the spirit of a pioneer, alert to new areas as yet unexplored, but always eager to explore them energetically, almost systematically. Hence his habit of working in series.

Echoing and repeated titles signal a particular pictorial stratagem, to be deployed in varying ways until its potential has been proven and perhaps used up. New titles signal a new venture, but some titles seem designed to be unspecific, or perhaps to signal catholicity and openness. One such is *Various Activities*; there were three paintings with that title in the Grosvenor Gallery show. Already in 1963 Smith had used it for a painting whose genesis he described in 1976:

> *At that time I had a sudden revulsion against making what I considered to be compositional pictures, and I decided well, why shouldn't a painting be like a list or an inventory. I remember standing in front of this canvas and trying to make an equivalent form for every object in my studio.*

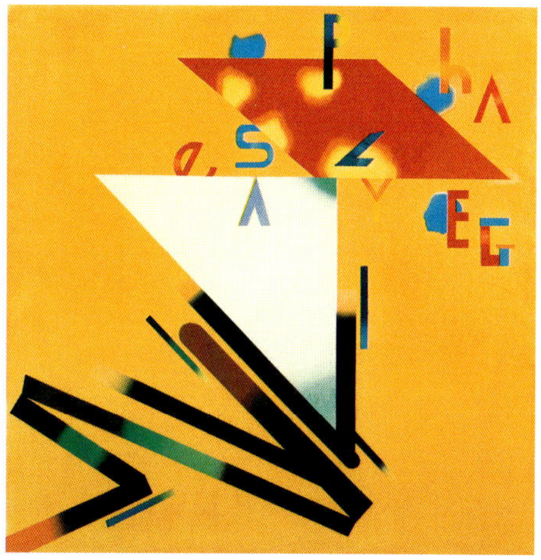

Portrait of A.P. Choreographer 1988

Oil on canvas
76 x 76 cm

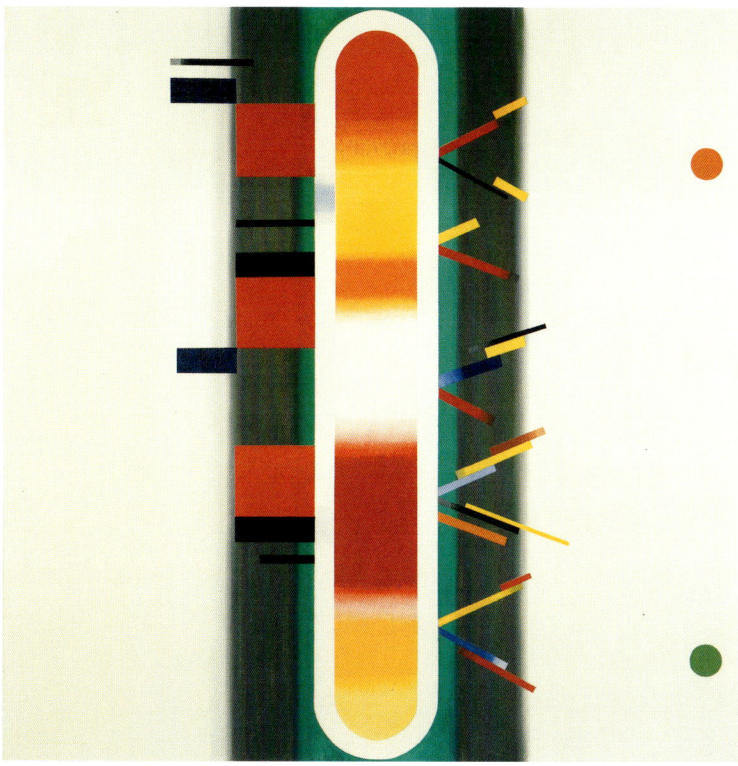

Sound and Light. Central and Out 1988

Oil on canvas
91.5 x 91.5 cm
Private collection

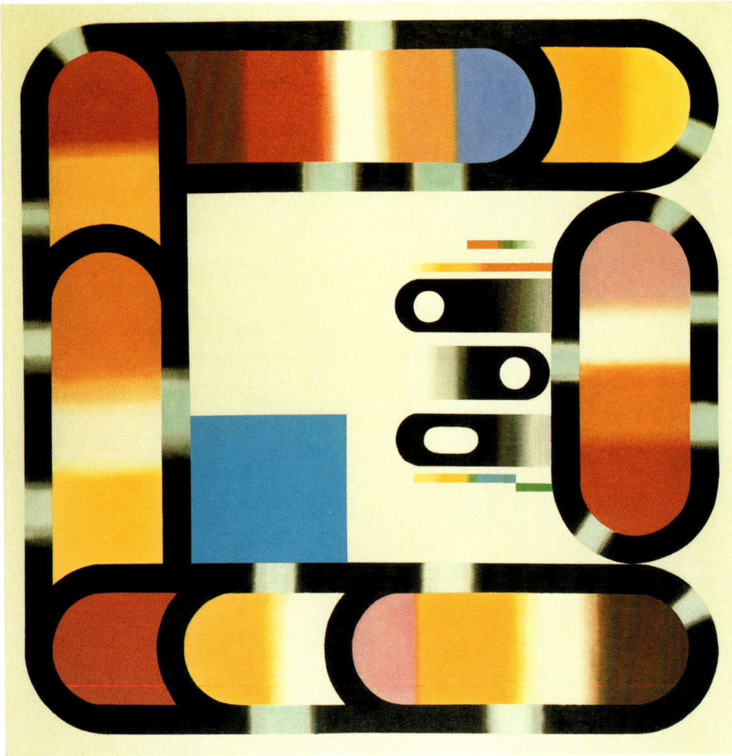

Sound of Light (Early One Morning) I 1988

Oil on canvas
91.5 x 91.5 cm
Private collection

> *One invented the forms, just as I invented the forms equivalent to sounds in other pictures. It was that kind of invention, and yet it's still based on a visual reality.*[25]

It is a fifty four inch square canvas covered quite evenly with more than three hundred little abstract motifs, some of them solid little shapes, some more like writing or printing and almost making words. They are more or less in rows though some extend through two rows. The general effect is all neat and shipshape and there is lots of colour involved in the motifs, so that this is a busy but organized picture, positive and without a weak spot. A particularly intense example of this sort is *Various Activities Central & Out* (1965), ill. p.34. Here, over a reticent yellow ground that keeps them hovering a little, Smith has painted a multitude of small, neat, multicoloured abstract forms, some detached, some connecting, here and there a cluster or a vacant space. Some of them form chains and imply direction; others want to stay where they are. Some suggest legible script. No backward or forward space is implied, but as we look a general structure emerges, a concentration of forms on the vertical central axis, so that the whole array appears to have been generated by the picture's spine. The all-over impression is one of lightness and gaiety; a closer look

25. See note 31.

reveals little local dramas, and effects of dispersion and ease as well as of agitation and compression. This is self-evidently a painting to be taken in gradually and read like a document, not glanced at for its general effect only. Jack Smith told me that he had painted all the little forms on a white ground, before deciding that pale yellow would enhance their colour and laboriously repainting the entire field around the forms. He did this with such care that there is no sign anywhere in this well-preserved work that the background was painted last. A very different painting with the same series title is *Various Activities (Dance)* (1965), ill. p.35. The subtitle inclines us to see movement; in any case, almost everything in it surges or drifts, most obviously the multicoloured snippets crossing the centre of the canvas like a school of fish and the looser and smaller group following on behind them. Cursive forms meander up the left side of the picture towards others, close to handwriting, floating at the top. Only the grey keyhole shape, in the right half, feels stationary. These forms – perhaps they should be called 'events' — occupy a ground that is almost no colour at all, and are surrounded by a border of, in effect, sepia, a brown that becomes lighter and darker along the four edges of the picture.

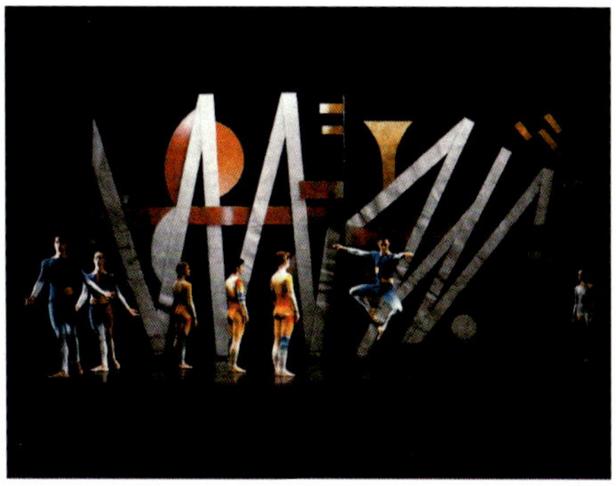

Designs for Carmen Arcadiae Mechanicae Perpetuum,
Rambert Dance Company
Photograph: Catherine Ashmore

Malevich composed abstract forms in and after 1915 to invent Suprematism. Under his influence Kandinsky clarified his pictorial language after 1918, and became a leader in the movement Van Doesburg and Max Bill proposed to call Concrete art, signifying its abstention from references to the external world. Malevich's paintings are representational, picturing his vision of a cosmic world. Kandinsky, even at his most apparently abstract, would sometimes introduce existing visual material, from nature and from art. Bill liked to source his often majestic displays of abstract form and colour in mathematical ideas. Kenneth Martin, whom Smith admires, invented systems for himself in which chance activates a predetermined painting procedure. Jack Smith has not worked with systems of any kind, nor from any starting point other than that provided by his own painting, developing ideas further or stimulated by alternative ideas arising in the process of working.

These are not nit-picking distinctions. They are the first steps towards understanding abstract art as something more than an arbitrary style. The enmity of abstract and figurative art was insisted on by critics and art historians dealing with early Modernism and has been re-imposed whenever major tendencies showed up either side of the barricades – as when the *New American Painting* exhibition landed in London, and also when, in 1981, a group of critics and curators announced 'A New Spirit in Painting', meaning figurative painting after decades of abstract and Conceptual art. A lot of weakly academic painting has been promoted since as part of Postmodernism, and welcomed by those who had always feared innovation. A number of artists went on making abstract art, and when they felt they might be thought out of date tagged 'neo' onto the existing term for the work they were doing. Jack Smith has avoided membership of any tendency and adherence to anything with a label. The best modern artists have ignored the figurative/abstract division, working in an area they consider belongs to both categories, or moving across it as they wished. Smith, having demonstrated his responsiveness to visual material belonging to the world around him with a long series of figurative paintings, shifted his attention to what we might call higher common factors: light and shadow, movement and stillness, now attracting his attention as self-sufficient themes. The sea, figures in an interior, fairgrounds etc., became opportunities for exploring immaterial but still real-world phenomena, until he found these too limiting. For him the world of picture-making is ever fruitful. At the same time, he lives in the real world and finds in it an infinity of impulses as well as nature's environment of light, air and space, of growth and metamorphosis.

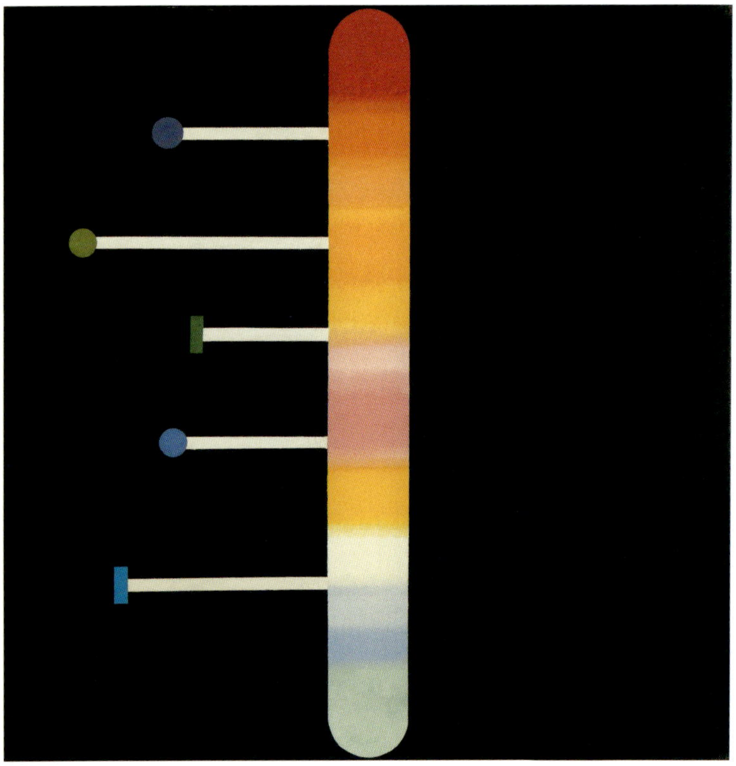

To The Left of Silence 1989

Oil on canvas
91.5 x 91.5 cm
Private collection

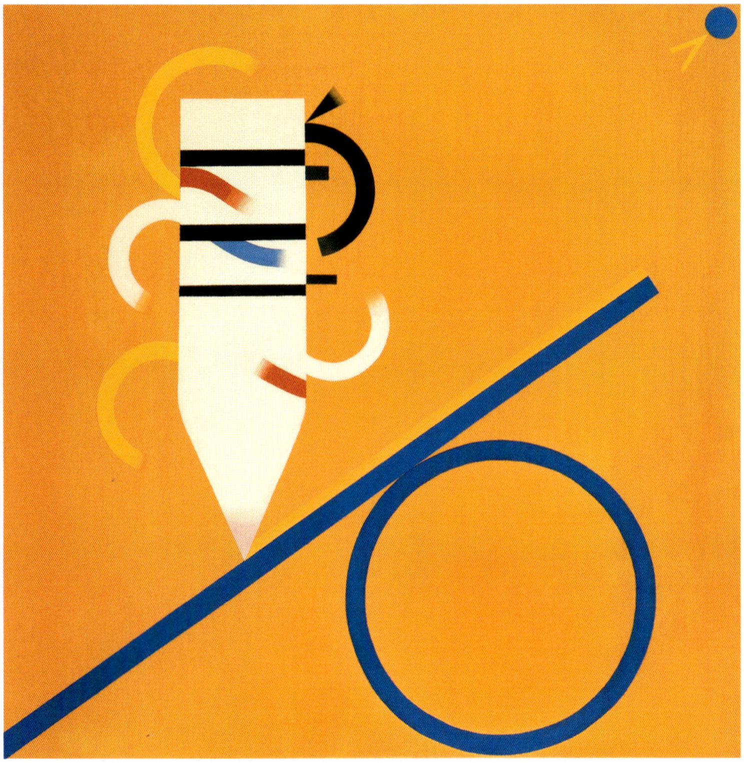

Celebration 1989

Oil on canvas
91.5 x 91.5 cm
BZW, London

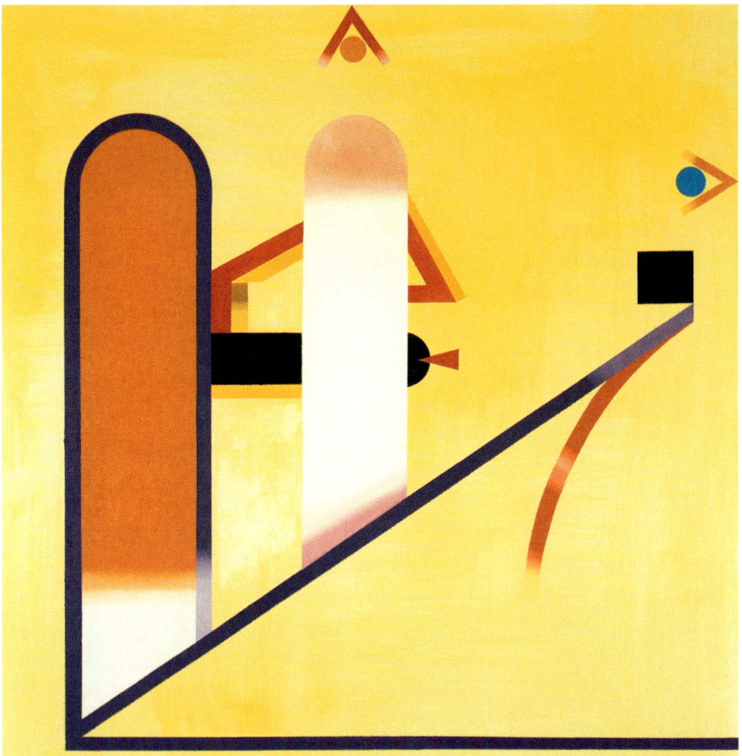

Celebration. Light and Sound 2 1989

Oil on canvas
91.5 x 91.5 cm

The differences between Jack Smith's work since the mid-1960s and that of the early and mid-1950s tempt one to see him as a convert or a renegade according to one's prejudices. There was a gradual shift from representations such as *Child Walking with Wicker Stool* to his abstract inventions such as *Various Activities (Dance)*, via paintings in which non-material aspects of the world were his primary concern. Gradually he distanced himself from scenes of daily-life to enter an apparently infinite world of forms and colours and their interactions. Has he remained the same artist? Did he achieve a 'breakthrough' – a word implying liberation? The only certain, measurable liberation is that of shrugging off the 'Kitchen Sink' label and its implications. Today it is shameful to find key figures in the art world still seeing him as *that* painter, thinking only of *that* work when his name comes up.[26] The mis-named Kitchen Sink phase represents at most five years of Smith's long career. The misreading of that phase lingers, as well as the reluctance to admit that even then Smith was tackling other subjects to which the term 'social realism' could not possibly be attached. When David Sylvester, having inadvertently landed Smith with that label, welcomed his subsequent, different work in 1957 and 1960, the world took little notice, being reluctant to let go of that first handle.

In 1968 Mark Glazebrook wrote about Smith's art in *London Magazine* in connection with his exhibition at Marlborough Fine Art that January.[27] This consisted of thirty-one paintings done during 1965-67 as well as two sculptures and a few drawings and etchings. The titles tell us some of their themes: there were paintings that simulate writing, but also paintings 'about silence', 'about emptiness'; the sculptures were *Contemplation Table* (a six foot long work with forms up to a foot high on it, the whole thing in white) and *Contemplation Object*. Glazebrook gave a general description of the paintings: square canvases, from three feet to six and a half feet square occupied by small forms, often within a square border. 'There is a certain fascination in following the series of logical steps by which Smith's language has reached this point'. As interested in continuities as in disruptions, I too look for what is permanent in

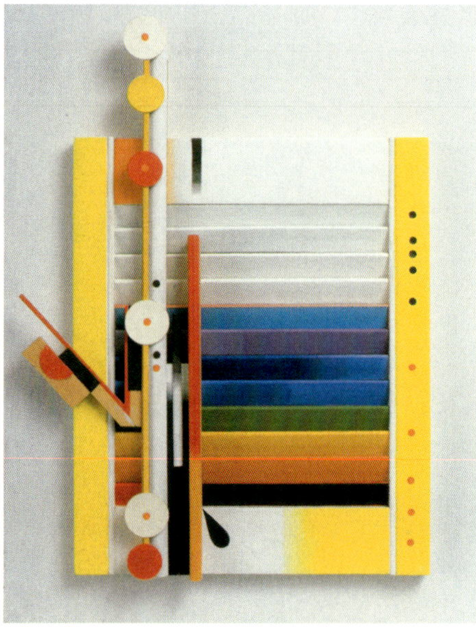

Harmony Structure 1989/90

Painted objects
68.5 x 53.5 cm
Private collection

26. The Tate Gallery, now Tate Britain, has been rehung: *Mother Bathing Child* is the only Jack Smith on show. Neither does Tate Modern exhibit any of his abstract work though the collection includes several examples of it.
27. *London Magazine*, June 1968, pages 86-91. Three Smith paintings are illustrated in black and white: *Written Activity 3*, *Sounds and Silences 1* and *Sounds and Silences 2*. The first is a developed example of Smith's script-like paintings; the other two are paintings in two halves, the right half full of forms that could be hieroglyphs (in *1*) or musical notation (in 2); the left half relatively clear but showing forms and marks of other kinds. No dates or dimensions are given, and since the illustrations are not square what they show is presumably only part of each canvas. It says something about the educated English attitude to abstract art that these illustrations should have been cropped and that no mention of the fact was thought necessary.

artists' work and attitudes to art, not least to defend them against the charge of arbitrary and headlong innovation for innovation's sake, yet hesitate to call the connections I find 'logical'. Perhaps I attach too much meaning to the word. Jack Smith himself uses it in his 1965 *Notes on Painting*: his development from a 1952 painting of a snowscape to his paintings of 1962-63 strikes him as 'absolutely logical', light being his subject in 1952 and ten years later, though in 1952 this light related to 'an outside source' whereas ten years later it was 'a quality within the painting'. That is a link, not a logical progression, and in between, light was less evidently his concern though it was always a positive element in his work. At every stage an artist is confronted by a great number of possibilities, and though each decision may have its own local logic the outcome is not likely to deliver a logical progression. Moreover, one of art's many ambiguities relates to the fact that artists who seem to work logically proceed intuitively. Smith wanted to link his new work back to his old, and light was one connecting element. Others, as Glazebrook points out, are movement and sound; these, together with light, Smith 'has consistently attempted to convey in painted form'. Not quite true: see his *The Wounded Bullfighter*. It is a poor artist who never steps outside his programme, even one found for him retrospectively.

Mondrian's example is relevant. From 1921 until 1940 he worked almost exclusively in one way, exploring the area he had mapped out for himself and finding a wealth of opportunities in it. Kandinsky's work in many respects is closer to Smith's in character, especially if we think of Kandinsky's paintings of the 1920s, when he was at the Bauhaus and influenced by alternative techniques as well as formal methods, and finally in Paris. Kandinsky's range was much larger, so much so that it can be thought centreless. I have wondered at Smith's reluctance to admit to any connection with it. The clue may be given in his 1995 statement (reproduced on page 6), where he says, 'In much contemporary painting there is too much Wagner and not enough Stravinsky'. We can guess what he means: too much everything, not enough economy; too much self-importance, not enough attention to the reality of the elements of music; too much rhetorical grandeur, not enough satisfaction with smaller, more specifically functional creative acts; too many pretentious messages, not enough lightness and space. One of the achievements of early Modernism was to jettison the habit of gravity. Not only the gravity that goes with solemn themes (though this too is relatively rare in modern art), but the sense of physical gravity that goes with representations of things, real or imagined. Notice the frequency with which artists, from the Renaissance on, built the main elements of their multi-figure compositions as pyramids within the picture space, broad

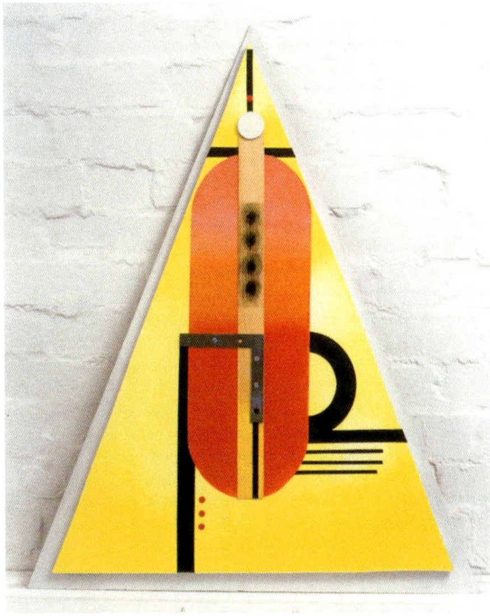

Towards the Light 1990/91

Painted objects
101 x 75.5 cm

and solid at the bottom and tapering upwards. The circular structure of the classical symphony yields a similar quality, leaving a base and then returning, after various activities, to its security. The beginning, middle and end system on which the well-made play and novel were constructed provided them, too, with a teleological line. This applied also to opera, the *Singspiel* as Wagner liked to call it: the sung drama. With Wagner it is continuous, not a sequence of units that leave us breathing spaces (arias, recitatives, choruses, etc.) but an unbroken chain or words and music, and, in the *Ring*, continuity from evening to evening. This, plus the dark auditorium he insisted on and the trick of hiding the orchestra, enabled Wagner to give his operas quasi-hypnotic power. Kandinsky was deeply attached to Wagner's music and historical role, and charged his paintings with complexities they could scarcely bear, especially the great compositions of 1913-14. His manner lightened in the 1920s, influenced by both Schoenberg and Klee, but even then he tended to offer too much, as though nothing could be left unsaid, and some of his major abstract compositions recall those of traditional history painting. Nevertheless, Kandinsky, too, sought and recommended an art of painting without gravity as part of his campaign against materialism. The arrangement of forms and their dimensions enable the painter to achieve an ideal, as opposed to a material, surface. 'Similar possibilities are offered by the correct use of colour, which can recede or advance ... and turn the picture into a being hovering in mid-air.'[28]

Jack Smith's essential move was to break away from the gravity of his realistic paintings, necessarily related to the world's materiality. His interiors, still lifes, bull-fight scenes etc., had to be earth-bound, but in seascapes, snow scenes and paintings of stars and fireworks he explored an apparently weightless world and could modify, and then abandon, his earthy colour schemes. By 1958 when he painted light passing over still life – making light itself the pictorial event – he had almost eliminated gravity. He then used built-up paint to give physical presence to the immaterial motifs he was pursuing, but in the process moved also to all-over structures. His pictorial reliefs may well have guided him here. By 1962 he was painting weightless pictures, using his surfaces as tablets on which to inscribe forms that could resemble runes or light on water, as in *Sea Movement, Red Orange & Blue*, ill. p.28. A series of 1962 paintings uses the title *Shimmer*, as in *Shimmer 3*, ill. p.30, and in *Shimmer, Red and Orange*, ill. p.29. In both cases the subject is presented in a circular form, luminous against a black ground framed by a coloured border. The disk format counteracts any

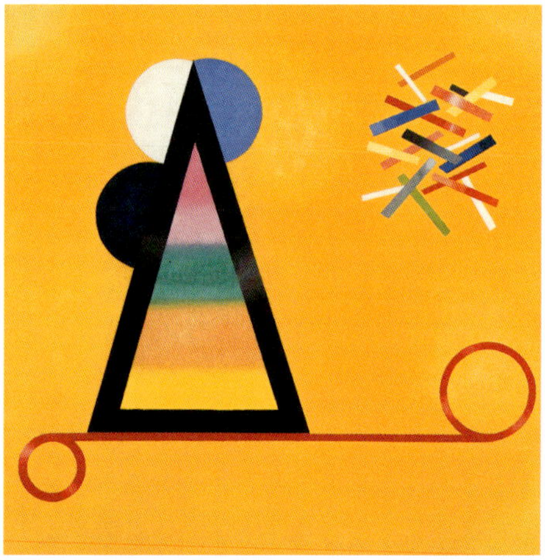

Light and Sound 1990/91

Oil and acrylic on canvas
89 x 89.5 cm

28. In his *On the Spiritual in Art*, 1912. See Kenneth C.Lindsay and Peter Vergo (eds.), *Kandinsky – Complete Writings on Art*, London 1982, vol.1, page 195.

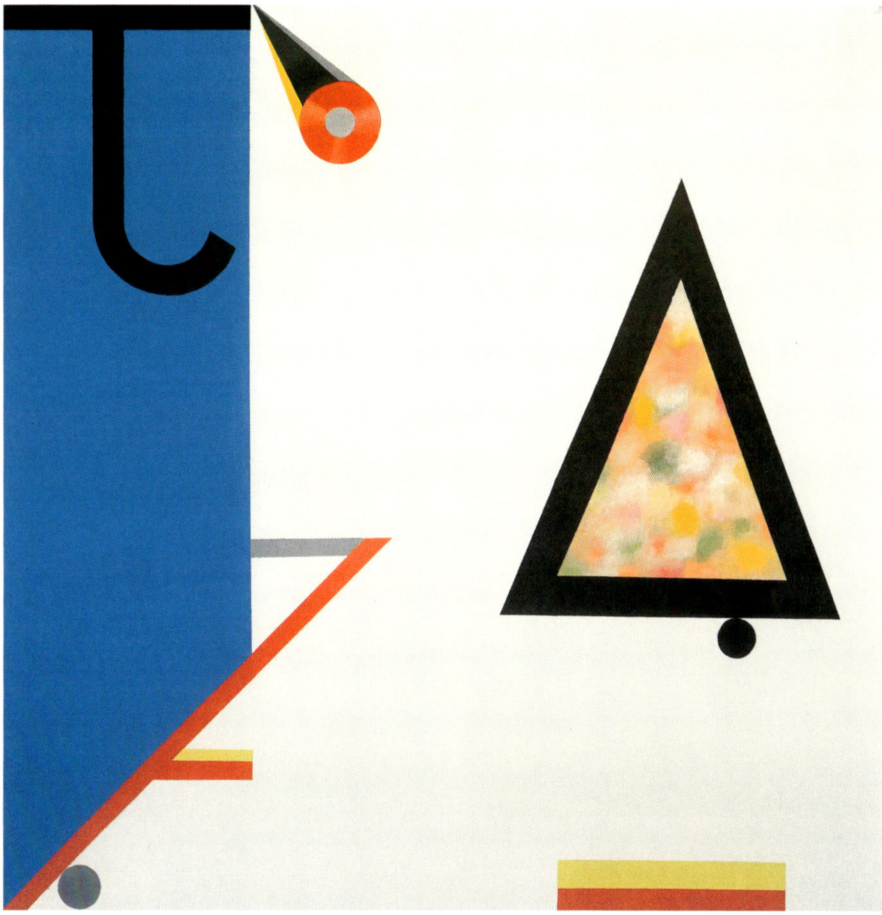

The Triumph of the Triangle 1990

Oil and acrylic on canvas
96 x 96.5 cm

sense of top and bottom and suggests a partial, port-hole or telescopic, view, just as Delaunay's use of it, fifty years earlier, enabled him to invoke the cosmos. Mondrian's use of the diamond format similarly detached his compositions from the earth. The circular format in combination with a watery subject also suggests the water passing through the painting. But this becomes especially compelling when the subject is something we cannot identify as mobile, as in *Side to Side No.1* (1963), ill. p.27. Here a large circle is inscribed on a white canvas. Inside it are a few signs, some of them close to musical notation, while the main motif, clearly stated but in no way referential, is a variegated form that passes through the centre of the circle, fading slightly as it reaches the circumference; it passes neither up nor down, but through. *Side to Side No.2* (1963, not illustrated), confirms his interest in strange formulations of this kind, as does the more elaborate *Black, White and Grey Movement 2*, ill. p.26. Thus, in the same months, Smith was painting elaborately packed, all-over compositions of the *Various Activities* kind and also leaving most of his canvas blank to despatch a formal device through it. With the *Written Activity* series that began in 1965 and continued for some years, and another series of *Diagram* paintings, mostly of 1967, he demonstrated his freedom from the old painterly functions of description and personal expression. Painting, he insists, should have an impersonal presence, though it originates in the artist's particular interests and excitements; it should be light, not heavy, and light also and not dark, except for special effects; it should be clean and craftsmanlike, never unkempt.

Two works of 1969 show how sure Smith by then was of his new domain. *Document*, ill. p.40, came out of the *Written Activity* series. It has neat lines and patches of abstract writing, as well as large areas of unmarked canvas, and here and there scrawls and scratchings that suggest abandoned attempts. All the marks are in black or red on white. Near the top are repetitions of the capital N, leaning more and more to the right and losing its coherence. *100 Twice*, ill. p.38, is a seven-foot diptych, each canvas presenting ten columns of ten clusters of rounded shapes, above broad dark bands of colour. One could interpret this as scientific information, about genes perhaps; one could equally interpret it as sounds, crisp, light chords heard above the deep resonance of an organ. The problem of whether such work is abstract or not falls away: we are confronted by an art independent of art's assumed routines and duties. Both these paintings were in Smith's second Whitechapel exhibition, in January-February 1971, which consisted of seventy-seven paintings, twenty-three drawings, most of them with watercolour, and three etchings, some of these with watercolour too. Words such as 'sounds', 'silence' and 'disturbance' are prominent in the

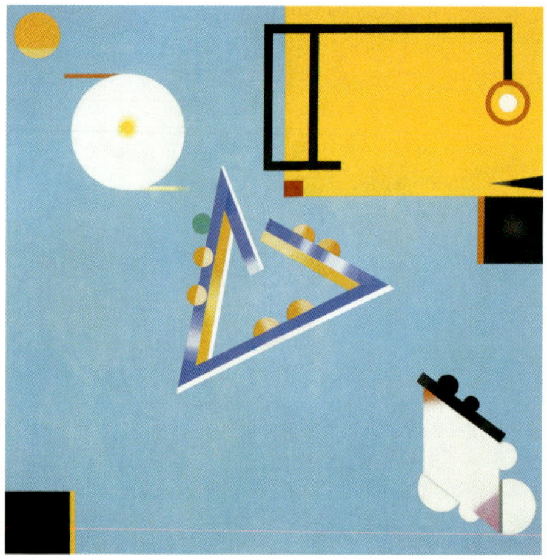

Floating World 1992

Oil on canvas
152.5 x 152.5 cm

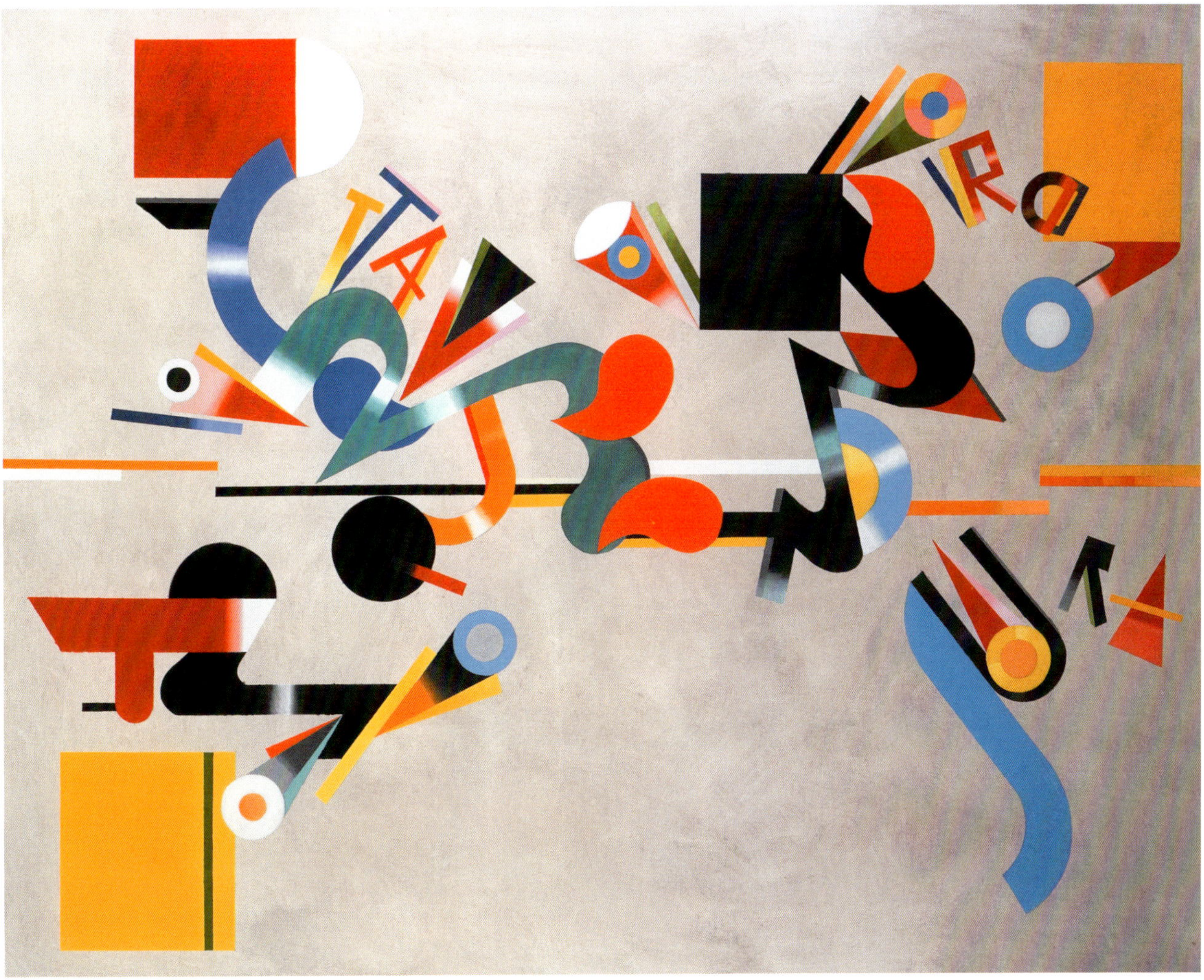

Ta Ra Ra 1991

Oil and acrylic on canvas

127 × 157.5 cm

Virgin Communications Corporate Art Collection

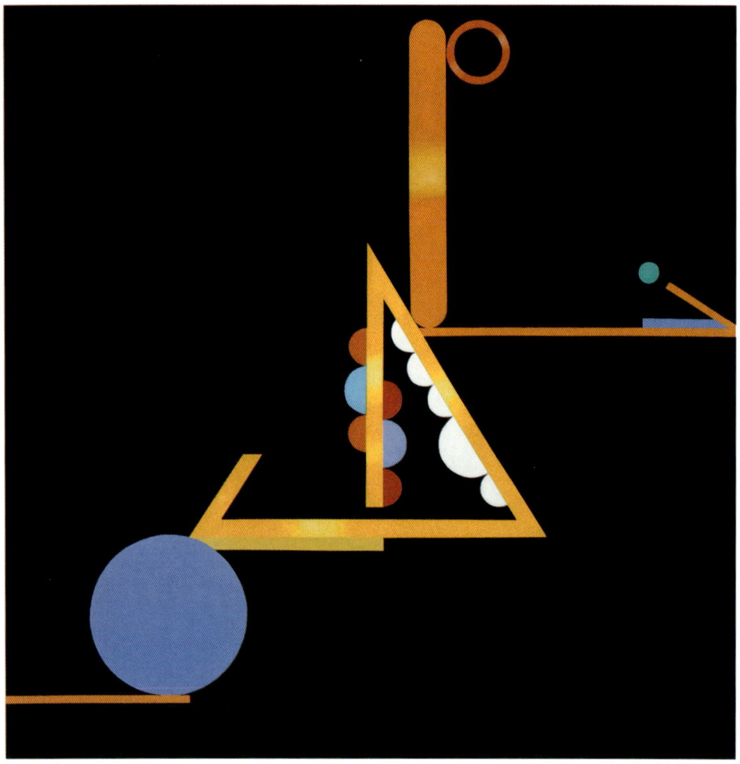

Touching on Black 1992

Oil on canvas
152.5 x 152.5 cm

titles, but others enumerate what they contain or do, as in *19 Horizontals, 2 Verticals and 19 Notes* (1968), or *43 Elements* (1968, on two canvases), or *5 Thoughts* (1970). *Painting for Two Instruments* (1968-9) and one or two other titles hint at music. The first of some new 'notes on the paintings' Smith wrote on this occasion states, 'Some pictures have musical connotations'. He explained that drawings he titled with the word 'hazard' combined a collage area and his development or countering of it by graphic means. They therefore embraced 'two different worlds – the real and the unreal', with the collage section acting as 'a kind of reality'. The display of, in effect, three years' production, 1968-70, was of remarkable power but not to the art world's taste. The only professional critic to notice it was Marina Vaizey, writing for the *Financial Times*. It was a supportive review but not one, Smith says, that could persuade doubters. Smith's notes ended by listing four qualities he considered essential: 'the work must be dynamic', it must have 'austerity and precision', and it must have 'detachment'. Without these, art 'becomes an essay in self indulgence'. Above all, 'Each work should be a celebration'.[29]

---

29. The exhibition is recalled in its 'poster-catalogue', a folded sheet providing basic data about the artist, his notes, part of his 1969 article in *The Journal of Typographical Research* from which I quote later.

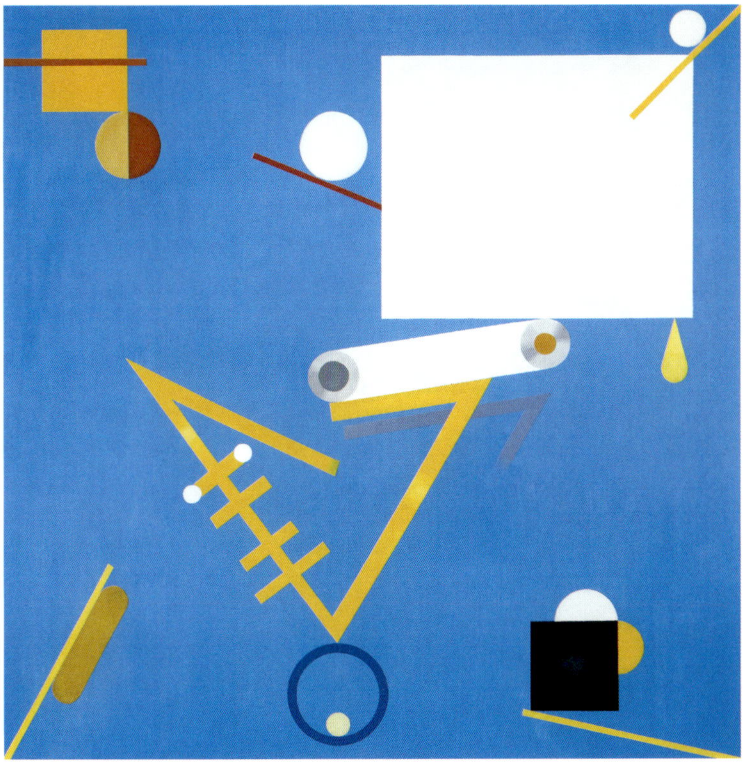

Balancing 1992

Oil on canvas
151 x 151 cm

The conjunction of discipline and celebration is particularly significant. The whole endeavour is serious and dedicated – I don't believe there is a more full-time painter than Jack Smith — but there is almost always an element of play, of inviting chance, in his working. As he had explained to Alan Bowness, he intends his paintings to be beautiful. He works intuitively and wants people to receive his art similarly, without inhibiting prejudices. 'A picture will be beautiful if the parts are correctly put together.' Above all, 'I'd like to produce something which stands outside the hysteria of one's own time'. To paint hysteria would at best be self-indulgent, at worst attention-grabbing. To deliver emotions and sensations, including those of delight, while preserving 'detachment' lest the painter should stand between the work and the viewer, calls for an expressive language which is discrete and in many senses extrinsic, not a personal, self-referential thing, neither heart-on-sleeve nor covered with fingerprints. He had never been a complaining artist; he became an artist in pursuit of marvels.

Jack Smith has a special admiration for the music of Anton Webern, one of the small group to whom Schoenberg in 1923 announced his system of atonal serial composition – 'composition with twelve notes related only to each other'. This released music from the anchorages of key and harmonic structure on which classicism depended. Given a set of twelve equal notes, the composer faces an infinite range of possibilities: the self-imposed limitation brings unimagined freedom. Webern committed himself to it in 1924 and

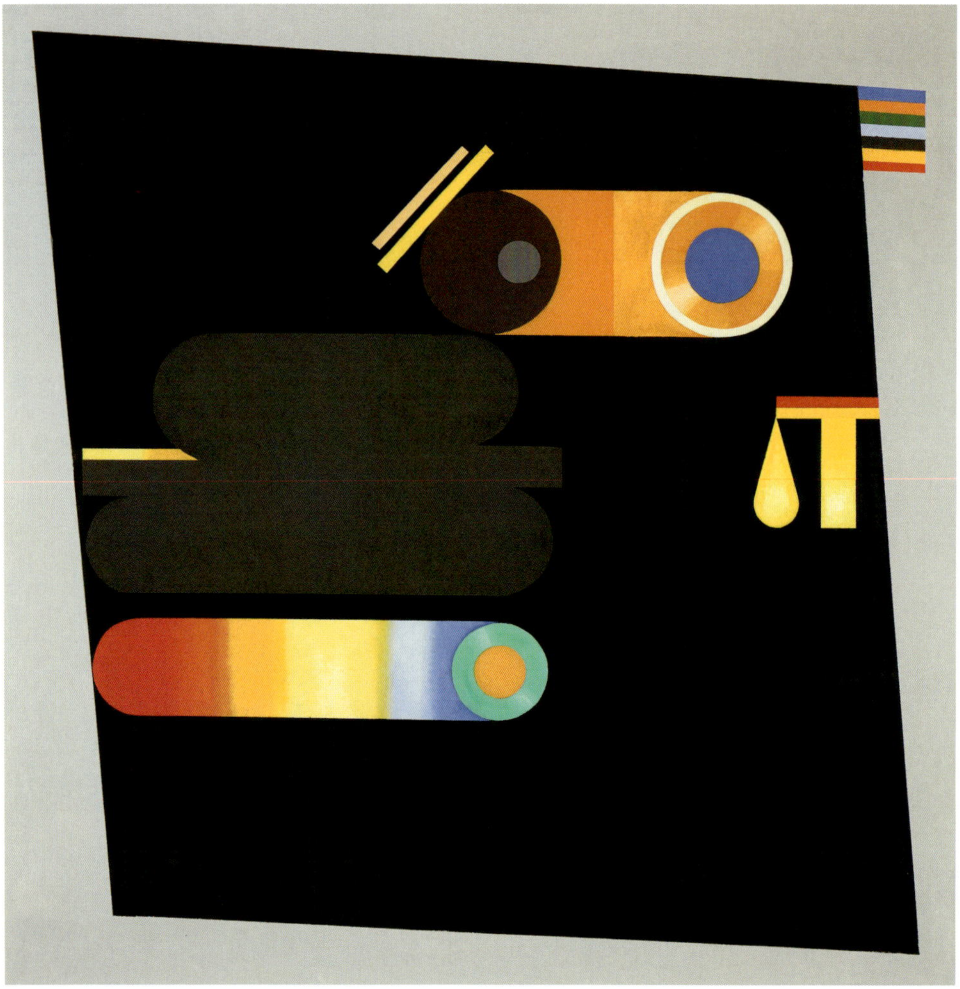

Floating and Touching 1993

Oil on canvas
106 x 106 cm

worked in it with joy and passion until his unnecessary death in 1945 when he was sixty-two. His music's main characteristics are clarity, lightness, brevity. Many of his pieces last less than a minute. It is music free of gravitational pull, music of interrelated sounds, each of which is complete in itself and exists in space and silence. Webern's music is not inimical to the past: coherence was the essential condition, for his music as for the great music of the past. 'At the root of [my music] is the aim of expressing myself as comprehensively as possible'. Like Klee, he stressed that art is a product of human nature and thus of nature itself. 'We take possession of what nature has given us'; nature, not artistic conventions, must be the guide. The composer works out of the need to work (Kandinsky's and Goethe's 'inner necessity'), and thus does not act arbitrarily. He does not need to repeat himself: every piece must be new. Polyphony and metamorphosis are methods essential to the new composer as to the old. Webern summarized the structure of a piece as follows: 'A number of metamorphoses of the first figure gives the theme. This, a new unit, goes itself through various metamorphoses. These, then, joined together as a new unit, provide the over-all form'.

Such words, and the mind-set they reveal, fit also Jack Smith and his art. The other composer he mentions as of special interest to him is Eric Satie. Satie is eminent among those Parisian composers who overcame the dominance of German Romanticism. Satie's method was often humour and mockery, and the musical languages he used for this tended to be archaic as well as ultra-modern. His music for the Cocteau+Picasso+Massine ballet *Parade* is his riposte to *Parsifal*. It is a suite of small, pert pieces which included the noise of sirens, typewriters and aeroplanes. Like other early Modernist works but to unequalled public effect, *Parade* invoked the circus and the fairground, and the chaos of modern life, in its mockery of the routine profundities of traditional high art. Satie's most philosophical work, *Socrates*, a 'symphonic drama' in which he set Plato's words to a sort of plainchant accompanied by a minimal orchestra, has a quality of bareness and stark economy that removes it far from the academic grandeur which was the musical culture of his generation. Both Satie's economy and his readiness to make jokes fit Jack Smith's case.

Smith's mature painting, of the mid-1960s and after, has affinities also with the music of his exact contemporary Stockhausen, in spite of Stockhausen's subsequent aspiration to quasi-Wagnerian grandeur. Moreover, many of Smith's paintings can be seen as equivalent to the graphic scores of such composers as the Englishman Cornelius Cardew, a former student and collaborator of Stockhausen's. Cardew's chief graphic-notation works are *Treatise* (1963-67)

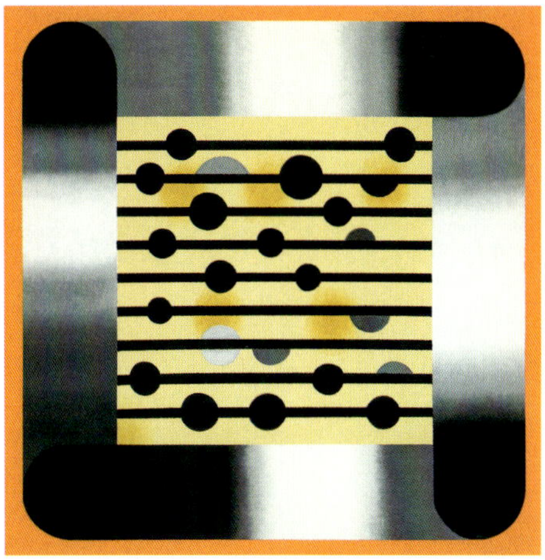

Winter Song 2 1995

Oil on canvas
61 x 61 cm
Private collection

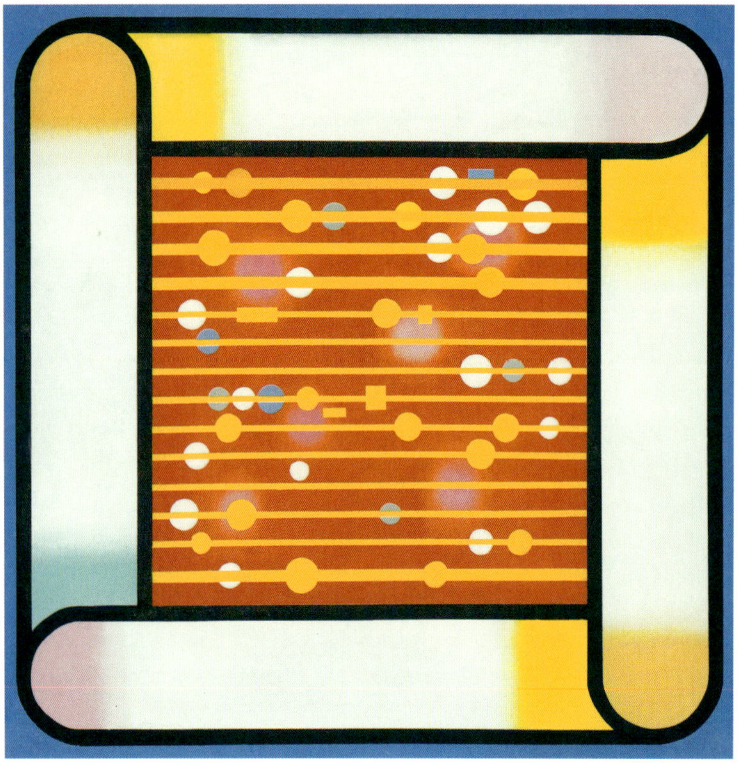

Summer Song 2 1995

Oil on canvas
91.5 x 91.5 cm

and *The Great Learning* (1968-70). He was one of a small group of composers/performers of improvised music who worked in London during the later 1960s and was known as AMM. The idea that 'visual and musical processes are somehow analogous, and that, in realisation, some essence of the original can be captured in the sounding performance' was the theme of an article by Hugo Cole in *The Guardian* of 24 April 1970. I am not here making overt connections between Jack Smith and ideas and practices in modern music but, encouraged by his awareness and sympathy for it, sketching the musical environment in which he attained what he considers his artistic maturity. In *On the Spiritual in Art*, Kandinsky wrote that

> *An artist who sees that the imitation of natural appearances ... is not for him – the kind of creative artist who wants to, and has to, express his own inner world – sees with envy how naturally and easily such goals can be attained in music, the least material of the arts today. Understandably, he may turn toward it and try to find the same means in his own art.*[30]

I am not aware of any direct use of musical forms or methods in Smith's work; what seems clear is the shared interest in attaining a plateau that allows free action and endless exploration. His statement of 1965 had already referred to

30. *On the Spiritual in Art*, page 154; see note 28.

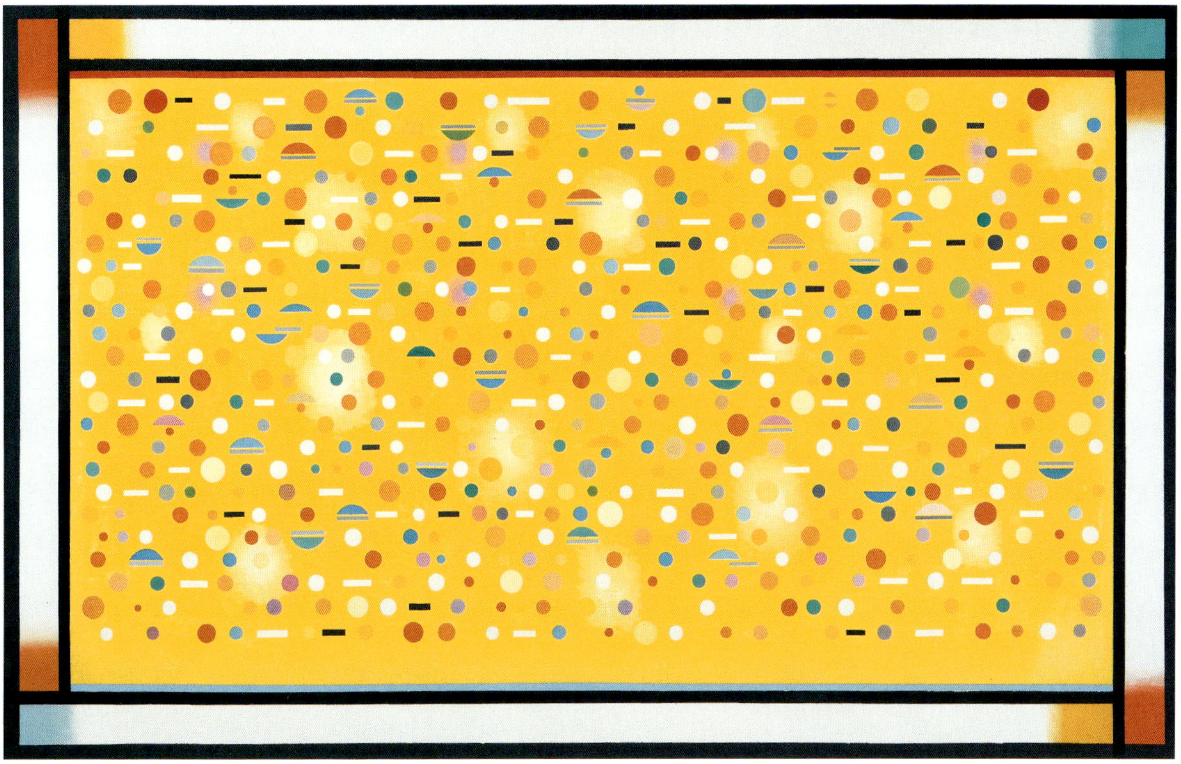

Summer Sensation 1995

Oil on canvas
153 x 244 cm

music and explicitly to 'groups of single notes', suggesting an affinity to Webern's way of disposing sounds. But he is not imitating music. Experience and intuition are of the essence at this level of creative work, and vision sets each day's goal. These are personal resources and powers, but knowledge of what the means available to each art form can carry imposes an objective dimension on the creative process.

In beginning his 'written' paintings of 1965 and after, Smith was, he said, painting the 'sound of words'. He would take a printed sentence as a sequence of sounds and seek a form for each sound. One set of sound forms, inscribed on the canvas, would lead on to the next, but he would also take further material from the printed source in order to continue. It was 'very taxing work. It took me all morning to produce one line', and he could not pursue this continuously, needing to intermit by working on other paintings. So, very different canvases would be in production at the same time. Colour decisions usually preceded starting a written painting. There being no exact formal equivalent for the sounds, much depended on his spirit when doing them, and he welcomed the differences resulting from that.[31] To some extent the variations reveal the artist to himself.

The degree to which Smith's written paintings invite reading like other texts set down from left to right varies. Some pictures are more linear and sequential in their organization; others are less directional. He himself analysed

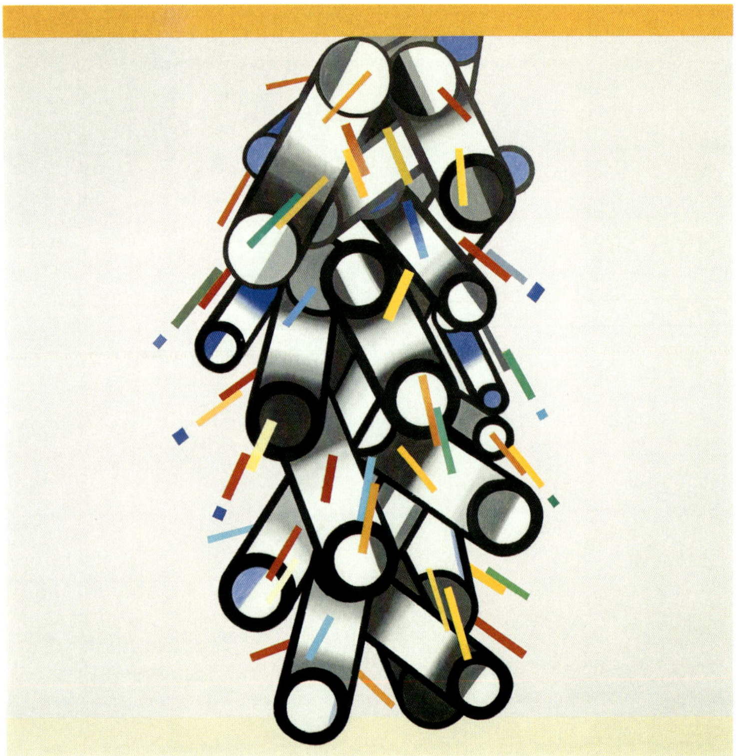

Cascade No. 2 1996

Oil on canvas
91 x 91 cm

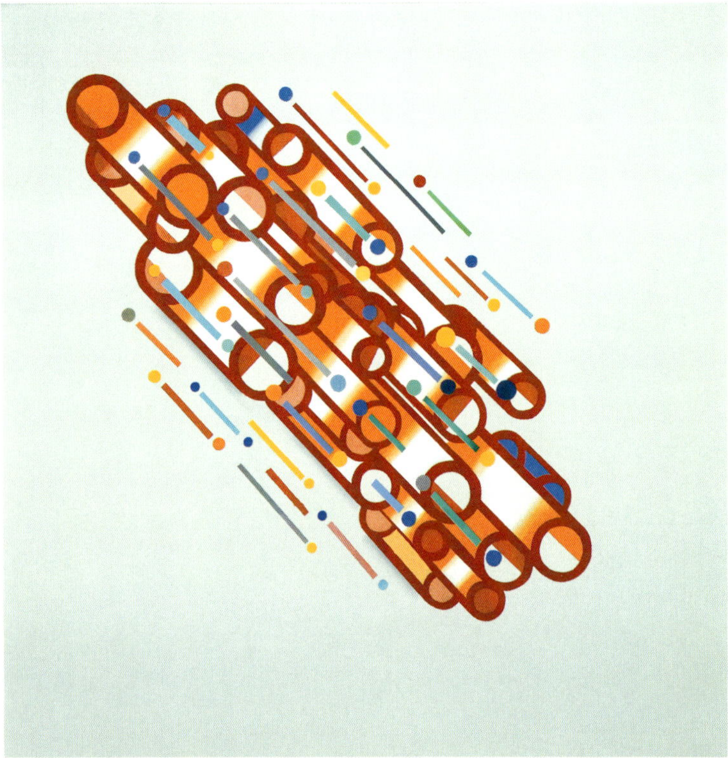

Cascade on Grey 1996

Oil on canvas
91 x 91 cm

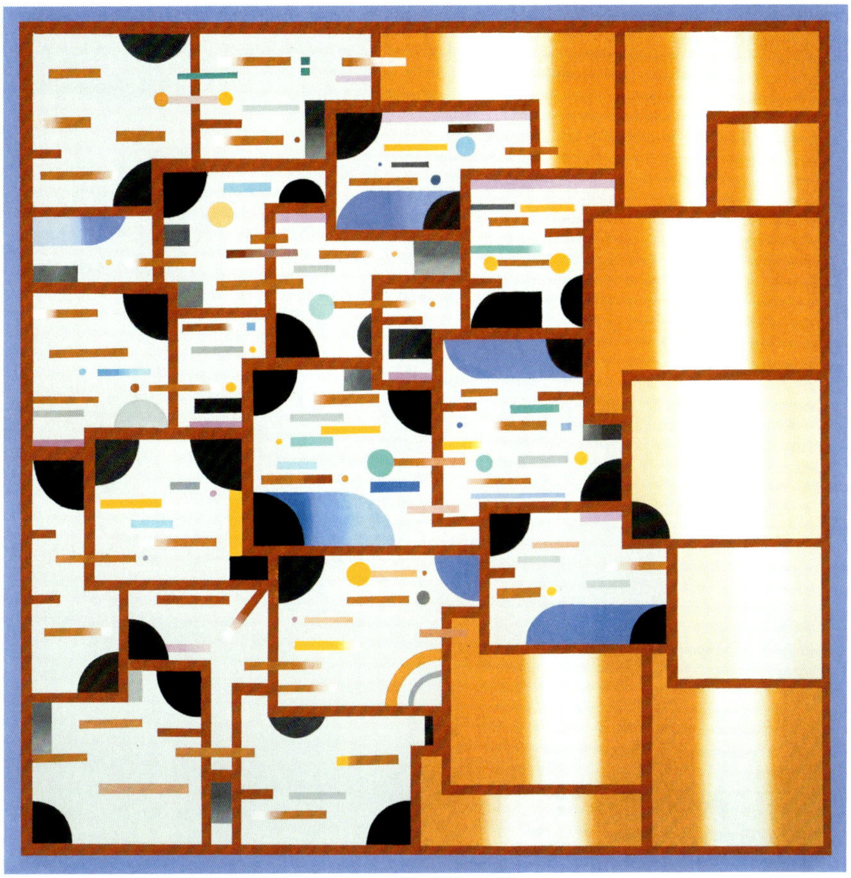

Visual Invention (complex) 1996

Oil on canvas

91 x 91 cm

two examples of 1966 for a typographical journal, mostly in factual terms but also commenting on how such art should be received. The artist's changing emotions and sensations are crucial but are embodied in the work, not to be elucidated by reading. Altogether, 'it is a mistake to try and read any passage as [the paintings] only work visually ... They can be thought of as visual poetry, but they are not to be confused with concrete poetry ... I seem now to be able to build up a visual written language that can deal with any experience or sensation'.[32]

Unlike most Concrete poetry, Smith's written paintings do not contain legible words, nor hint at them, nor affect to represent their subjects by visual arrangements, but deliver in a variety of styles an abstract language whose sense communicates through sensation, not through knowledge and understanding. Helder Macedo's essay, Jack Smith's *Word-Objects and the Language of Signs*, argues that his paintings contradict an assumption underlying semantic theory:

> *The idea of a symbol without referencer seems a logical impossibility. But if, as in the case of Jack Smith's pictorial signs, the referent is the sign itself, the logical impossibility becomes the basis for a transposition of the sign to a plane of meaning in which it acquires all the weight of symbolic significance, becoming both the signifier and the signified.*

He concluded by commenting on Smith's deployment of the spaces left between the signs:

> *In Jack Smith's paintings the spaces acquire a designative value as precise as that of the word-objects. Here again the musical analogy is relevant. There are no sounds without silence ... In this sense, Jack Smith's paintings*

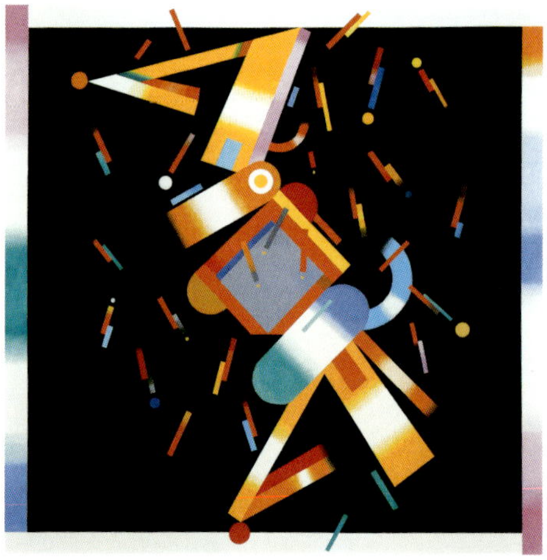

Cascade on Black. Balancing and Touching 1996

Oil on canvas
106 x 106 cm

31. I have slightly abbreviated what Jack Smith said to Alan Bowness in their conversation printed in the book *Jack Smith – Paintings and Drawings 1949-1976*, published by the Ceolfrith Press, Sunderland, in 1977, on pages 7 to 19. This is an unusually interesting question-and-answer dialogue, in which Alan Bowness engaged carefully with Smith's work out of his wide knowledge of modern British art. The book was published in conjunction with an exhibition of the same title at the Sunderland Arts Centre, but did not serve as a catalogue for the exhibition.
32. *The Journal of Typographic Research*, July 1969. Smith's commentary was written for an issue focusing on letterforms in the arts. During the 1960s Concrete poetry was widely produced, exhibited and printed, and discussed in art circles. A Concrete poetry movement had developed in Brazil in the 1950s. In Europe the Swiss writer Eugen Gomringer provided major instances and impulses in his work of the 60s. He had been Max Bill's secretary when Bill was promoting the concept of Concrete art in paintings and sculpture. Gomringer became well known in London for the poems he called 'constellations', using several languages and published from 1953 on. The Institute of Contemporary Arts in London in 1965 presented a major exhibition of international Concrete poetry under the title 'Between Poetry and Painting', curated by a team led by Jasia Reichardt who also wrote an introduction to the illustrated and informative book published by the ICA in place of a catalogue.

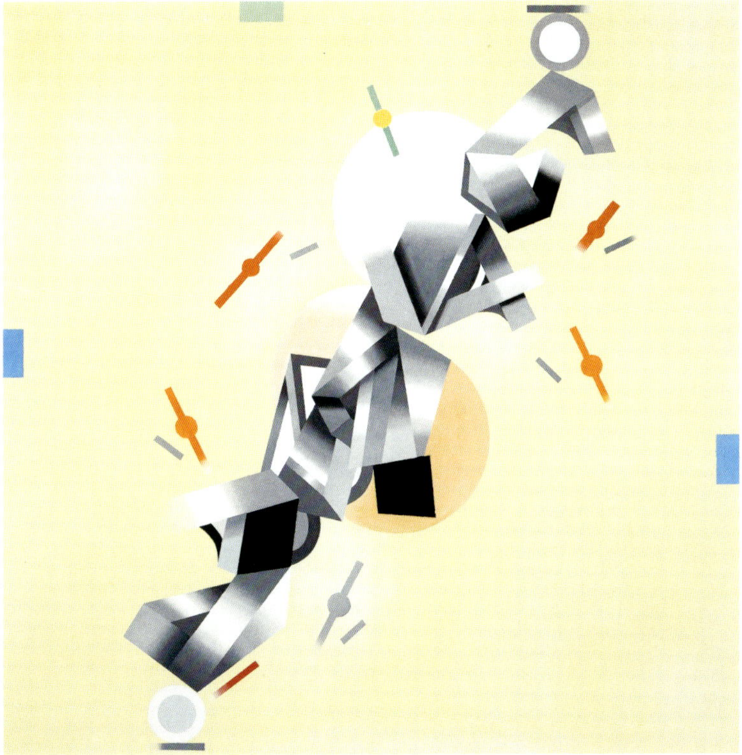

Cascade (Metallic) 1997

Oil on canvas
106 x 106 cm

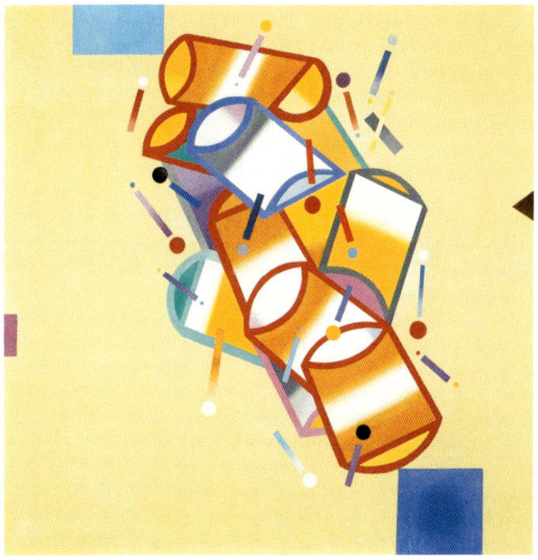

Cascade on Yellow 1997

Oil on canvas
91 x 91 cm

> *give form to sounds and define silence: the absolute language of a mysticism without God, the transformation of the void into the word, of space into meaning.*[33]

The Sunderland Arts Centre exhibition of 1976 was Smith's second retrospective and consisted of about fifty paintings; it toured subsequently to five other centres not large enough to display more than a small selection of the original show. The accompanying book was edited and designed by the director of the Arts Centre, Christopher Carrell. It illustrates many paintings, six of them in colour, and has brief captions giving the essential data. It puts its emphasis work of the 1960s and 70s, proving the energy but also the open-mindedness with which the painter was working in those years. Almost every illustration calls for some degree of readjustment; we turn the page and are amazed to find that having done *this* he could also go on to do *that*, opening up another, unexpected section of the vast field he had discovered. Even within series, his paintings are astonishingly diverse. The differences between series are

33. See note 31. Macedo's text is on pages 49-52 of the Ceolfrith Press's book. A poet and critic, Macedo was living in London in the 1960s. He became Portugal's Director-General for Cultural Affairs after the anti-totalitarian revolution of 1974. Subsequently he returned to London and lectured in Portuguese and Brazilian Studies at King's College, University of London.

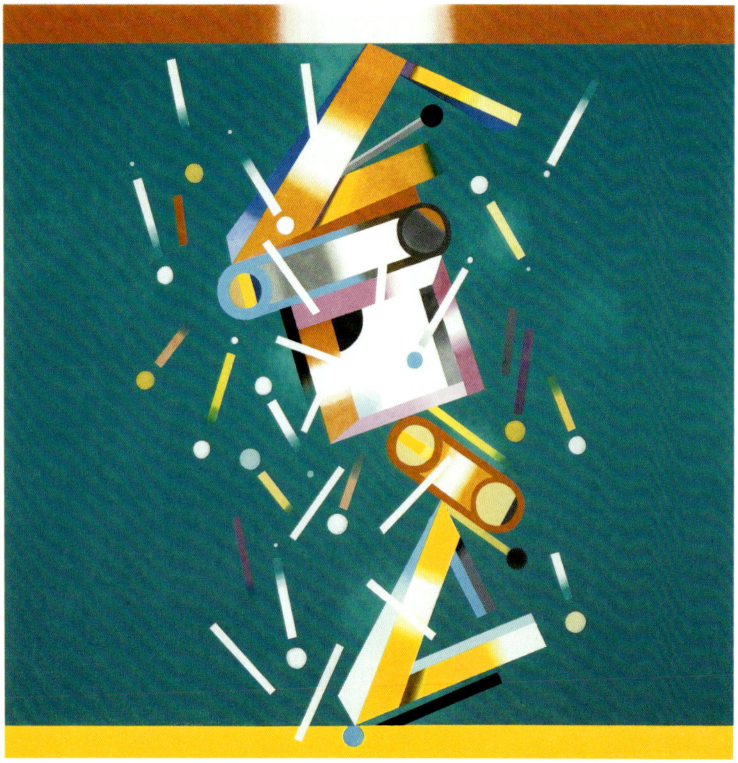

Cascade on Green 1997

Oil on canvas
91 x 91 cm

substantial and can be disconcerting at first. Yet the same appetite is sensed throughout and, though the expressive character of each composite image is distinct, there is a general sense of joy in creation, of the artist marvelling at what can be done and may yet be to do.

A particular instance of a surprising development – a major step, more radical in some respects than the leaps he can make between individual paintings – was his turn to making reliefs, in the early 1970s. Answering Alan Bowness's enquiry about using 'extra elements', he said that

> *It came from doing some collage drawings in 1971 and '72, I tend to use things I find lying about, wherever I'm working. As I was working at Chelsea I found a lot of pins and paper clips and things like that, which I started using just because they were there.*

In a painting of 1967, *Diagram No.2* (not illustrated), he had already, he said, 'used the pins' — black lines looking like pins holding down a form like a specimen in a museum. In 1974 he used real pins, .e.g. in *Pins, White above Blue*, ill. p.45. This small painting is on board, and Smith has pushed twenty-four pins at various angles into a white rectangle on the left. They are emphatically three-dimensional, in reality and effect. A somewhat larger rectangle on the right is occupied by painted forms, three flat discs and two flat angled bands, next to which are similar bands painted three-dimensionally to look like metal tubing, also a T-junction of two tubes. Little discs indicate their sections. An occasional

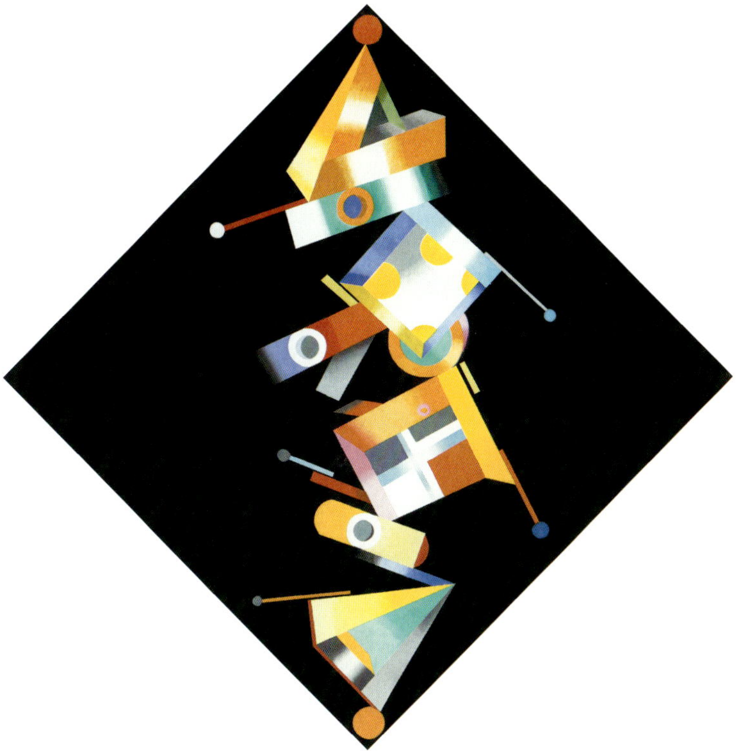

Cascade on Black (Diamond) 1997

Oil on canvas
91 x 91 cm

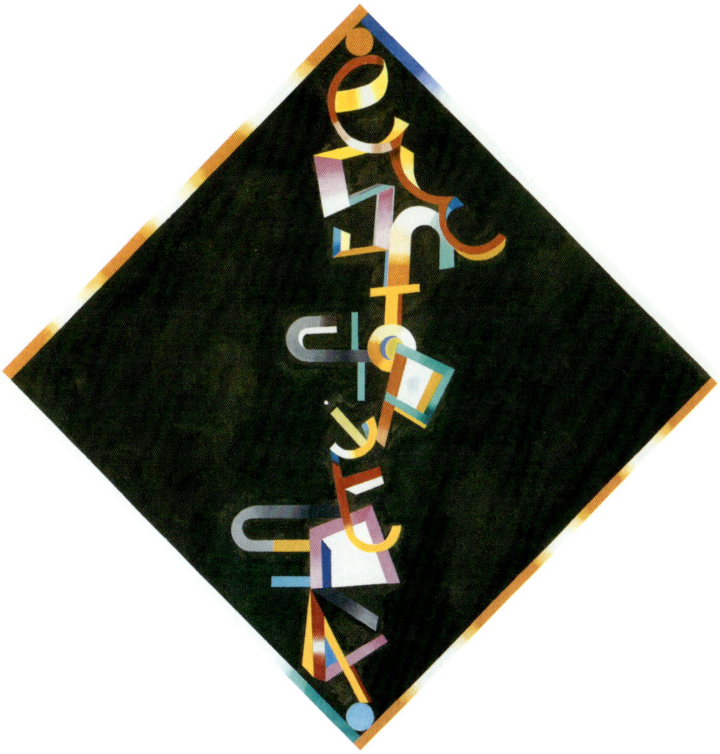

Self Portrait (Diamond) 1997

Oil on canvas
91 x 91 cm

precedent can be found in Smith's earlier paintings (e.g. *Sound Graph*, 1973); none the less this introduction of forms painted to appear three-dimensional is a remarkable departure, reminding us that an artist can break his own rules.

In about 1956-57 he had turned away from painting scenes taken from the real world. In about 1960 he had ceased using thickened paint to give material presence to immaterial events in his paintings. His *Painted Relief* of 1963 had not only consisted of boards of some thickness mounted on top of each other but had used one of its painted bands to give a powerful suggestion of recession by means of perspective. By the mid-1960s he was working without any three-dimensional devices beyond that of sometimes letting forms overlap, suggesting time-sequence as well as a modicum of space. He was using oil paint neatly, without drawing any extra meaning from his use of it. One might have said that he was purifying painting and concentrating on the basics of deploying marks on a surface. He told Bowness that he was avoiding having visible brushmarks in his paintings, but that he gets deep sensual satisfaction from manipulating oil paint which, unlike acrylic, dries slowly. His titles too were becoming even more abstract. They were necessary as a means of identifying works but he was reluctant to let them announce their nature, hint at any kind of message. Often they would state the number of elements in a picture, as in *Thirty-One plus Ten* (1971-72) or *Thirty Disturbances on Blue* (1974), and again the process seems to be one of purification. Yet other titles of those years help to focus the viewer's attention on particular qualities in the composition and, in broad terms, how they might be received. There are many instances; one taken at random is *Four Sounds. Two Silences* (1974), where the title ascribes a kind of meaning to two sorts of form. *11 Activities, 9 Major 2 Minor* (1973), ill. p.47, refers to nine strong multicoloured elements dispersed over the surface and two relatively small and more linear devices, also multicoloured. The major elements appear ambiguously three-dimensional, projecting or receding; each of them consists of a rectangle to which are attached extensions which invite spatial reading. In *120 Major 105 Minor* (1972), ill. p. 42, a hundred and twenty little clusters of coloured marks are neatly assembled in eight rows of fifteen. The hundred and five minor elements are perhaps to be found among them, possibly characterized by colour. In that case the major/minor indication in itself becomes ambiguous since it suggests keys in music as well as relative importance or size. Leaving this unexplained is a way of holding the viewer's attention, always a problem in abstract art.

From this to incorporating painted forms that represent three-dimensional forms by means of illusionism, and also material objects, whether pins or paper-clips or paper, remains a major step of a permissive, undogmatic

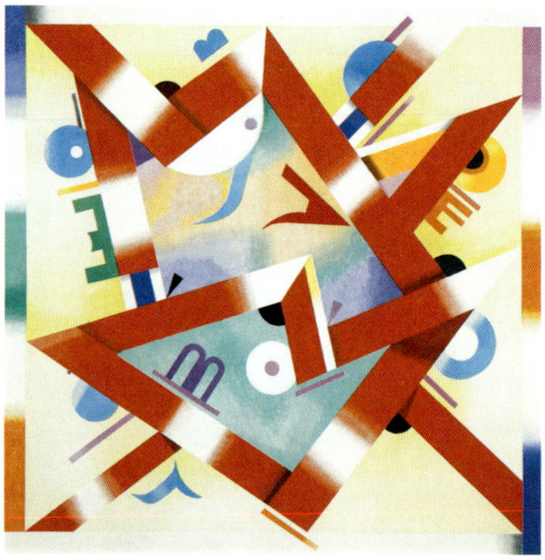

Jamboree I 1996

Oil on canvas
106 x 106 cm

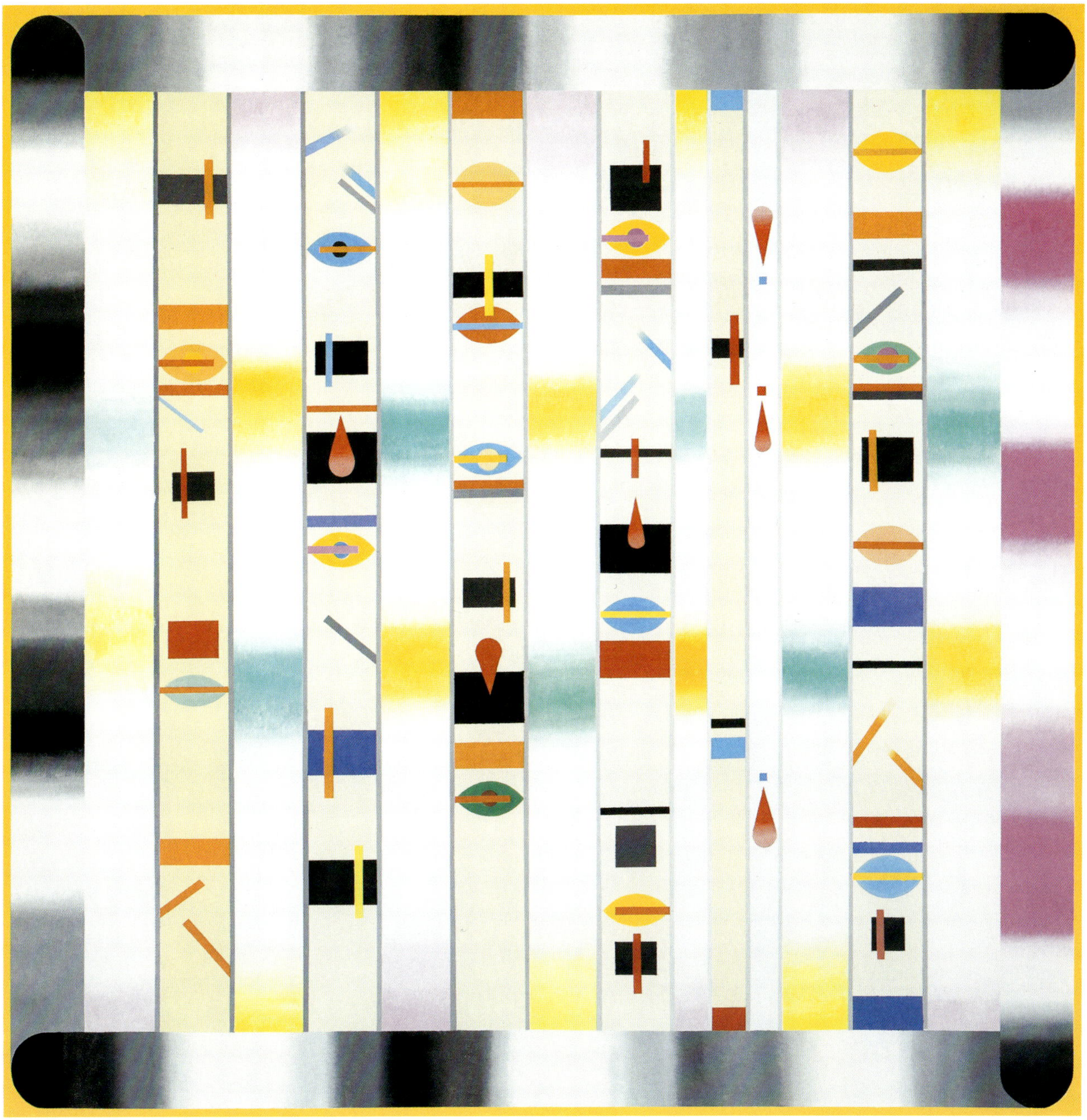

Vertical Inventions 1997

Oil on canvas
152.5 x 152.5 cm

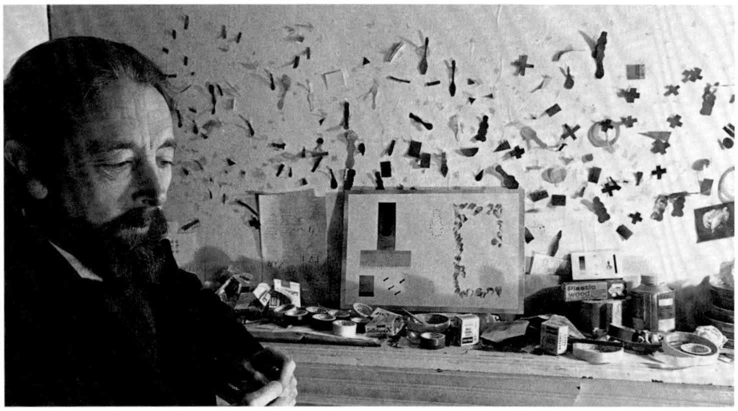

Jack Smith, Studio, Leytonstone, London 1967
Photograph: Jorge Lewinski

sort. We can learn to respond to the economy and restrictions Smith demonstrates; it is oddly difficult at the same time to accept that what he imposes on himself he can also relax or jettison. Self-contradiction is as laudable a means of continuing as any other.

A photograph of 1967 shows a small part of his studio at the time he was living in Leytonstone. On the mantelpiece is a variety of clutter, all to do with making paintings: cans and boxes, rolls of tape, a brush. There is also a small painting, on board, perhaps twelve by eighteen inches, and, nearby, a much smaller painting, propped up. On the wall is a swarm of forms cut out of coloured paper, attached lightly to the white wall, perhaps with bits of 'bluetack', rectangular and rounded forms of many sorts, many of which we can find also as painted forms in his pictures. Painters' use of pieces of paper or cloth to test and prepare their compositional ideas has a long history. Jack Smith must have used cut-out paper shapes to plan his pictures more or less from the day he started incorporating in them discrete but repeating signs. What we see in the photograph is part of the kit of signs he was using then. If we go to his studio today, we see another kit. When he works, he can attach and re-attach his selection from the kit, as well as add to it, constructing his composition gradually. This tells us that he does not work to a system but invites change by keeping possibilities open. When he paints them in, he has to determine the colour of each sign, which may or may not relate to the colour of the paper shape: painted colour is by no means the same as coloured paper.

Smith's exhibition at the Arts Council's Serpentine Gallery, in January-February 1978, was as perfect as any exhibition can be. Its title was *Jack Smith: The Written and the Diagrammatic Paintings and Drawings 1965-1977*. It showed seventy-four paintings (including three pictorial reliefs in deep frames) and twenty drawings in a variety of media; some of each included collage and other extraneous materials (paper-clips, cotton wool); there was no sculpture. The scale of the gallery, the light in it and its location in Kensington Gardens made this the ideal space for showing Smith's at this stage particularly subtle, understated art. For many people, though, the work lacked emotional rhetoric. Though it was intuitive in origin and at least partly playful, it was mistaken for demonstrations of theorems, just as earlier Smith's paintings had been, and still are, mistaken for demonstrations of social protest. The sheer quantity of work on show may have made it difficult to connect with it, though the gallery's spaces and free admission invited patient looking and repeated visits. But each Smith painting benefits from exclusive attention, whereas quantity tempts one to move on. The modest but efficient catalogue included selected Smith texts and twenty illustrations. Even today, it speaks of amazing productivity in a positive, inventive spirit.

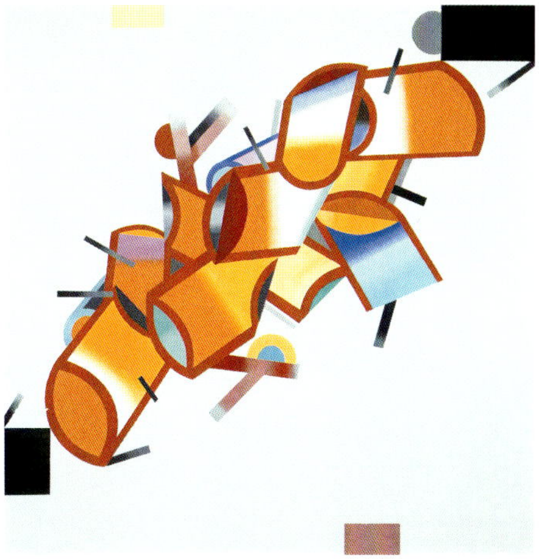

Cascade 4 1998

Oil on canvas
91 x 91 cm

Jack Smith was head of painting at Chelsea School of Art until the summer of 1979. Earlier that year he and Susan had moved to the south coast, to a house in what is now Brighton-and-Hove. He commuted to London for teaching and administration at Chelsea, but that autumn he accepted a part-time teaching post at the Brighton School of Art (now the fine art department of Brighton University). He worked there for ten years, but above all he painted at home, in an upstairs room. This has a typical bay-window and faces west; it is full of light most days. The sea front is a stroll away. As the years pass, the animation that goes with this English seaside town, its life, its amusements, its decorative forms, have entered Smith's art – a very different awareness from that which led to his dramatic accounts of the northern sea of the 1950s. In addition, he claims that the light of Brighton is just about the best England has to offer, as good as that of St Ives. He and Susan arrange their life style around painting; the environment helps them in this concentration, with London accessible but another place. He showed with Fischer Fine Art in London in 1981 and 1983 and at the Mayor Gallery in 1987; since 1990 he has shown regularly at Flowers East.

The Mayor Gallery show was primarily of his designs and models for two ballets. Bryan Robertson, an advisor to the Royal Opera House on ballet and interested in the work of the Rambert Dance Company, had in 1986 proposed Jack Smith as designer for a ballet, *Carmen Arcadiae Mechanicae Perpetuum* to music by Harrison Birtwistle, choreographed by Ashley Page. Smith welcomed the commission and was stimulated by the work it called for: the involvement with the many specialists required by an undertaking of this sort, the deft realization of his proposals by the company's scene constructors and dressmakers, the experience of seeing his designs on the stage as backdrop and in the costumes worn by dancers. He had determined on a black background with strong colours as forms on it and as moving forms in front of it. Lighting could fade in and out; filters could enhance, modulate and diminish the power of particular colours, ill. p.73. In 1987 the Royal Ballet Company asked Ashley Page to choreograph the ballet *Pursuit* to the music of Colin Matthews, and Page brought in Smith as designer, this time, of two backdrops as well as costumes. Jack Smith had not known Colin Matthews' music before, and responded to its complexity with brightly coloured designs more complicated than those he had used for the Rambert Dance Company, and now to be seen under brilliant light. Both productions were warmly welcomed.

These ventures were very satisfying. Meeting the two composers and working with two compositions led Smith that year to paint abstract portraits of Birtwistle and Matthews, reflecting not on their physical presence but on their personalities as revealed in their music. Both are square pictures, thirty six by thirty six inches. The Birtwistle image (ill. p.63) is on a white ground. On it are three clusters of activity, the central one including a red parallelogram. Because of its placing and the much smaller forms swarming over it, and because of subtle changes of tone within it, this suggests recession. The Matthews picture (ill. p.64) is more concentrated but just as complex when one attempts to read its forms and relationships. Its ground is a vivid orange. This is dominated by an almost square form outlined in broad black. It again suggests space, even movement in space. Its colour is uneven, a bluish green that changes from pale to mid-tone and hints that we are looking through the black frame into space. There are hints, too, that this frame is three-dimensional in some parts, though not regularly so. It is linked to the right edge of the painting by another black band around which various activities take place. Below is a row of four white rectangles with central grey-black marks on them, a little like bullet holes; because of blue bands attached to those on the right, we cannot decide whether or not these rectangles are equal in size. In 1988 Smith painted another portrait of this sort, thirty inches square. It has a non-referential title, *Scattered*, but there is also a subtitle, *Portrait of AP, Choreographer* (ill. p. 71). It is on a pale orange ground. Here too, a red parallelogram may signal recession, perhaps that of a stage on which there are patches of light and standing letter-forms, but close-by there are patches of blue and other letter-forms that deny any easy, one-off reading. Angled bands, mostly black but shot with other colours, dominate the lower half of the picture. Between these two centres is a right-angled white triangle, two of its corners touched with light blue. It is a stabilizing element in this complex, yet seems itself delicate and vulnerable. There are similarities between these three paintings, but also major

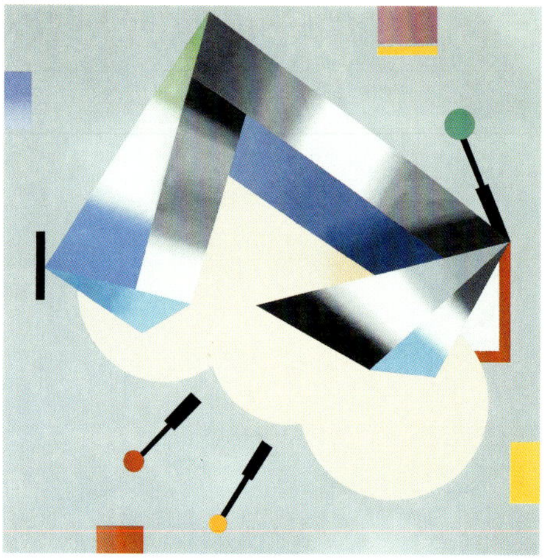

Touching on Grey 1998

Oil on canvas
76 x 76 cm

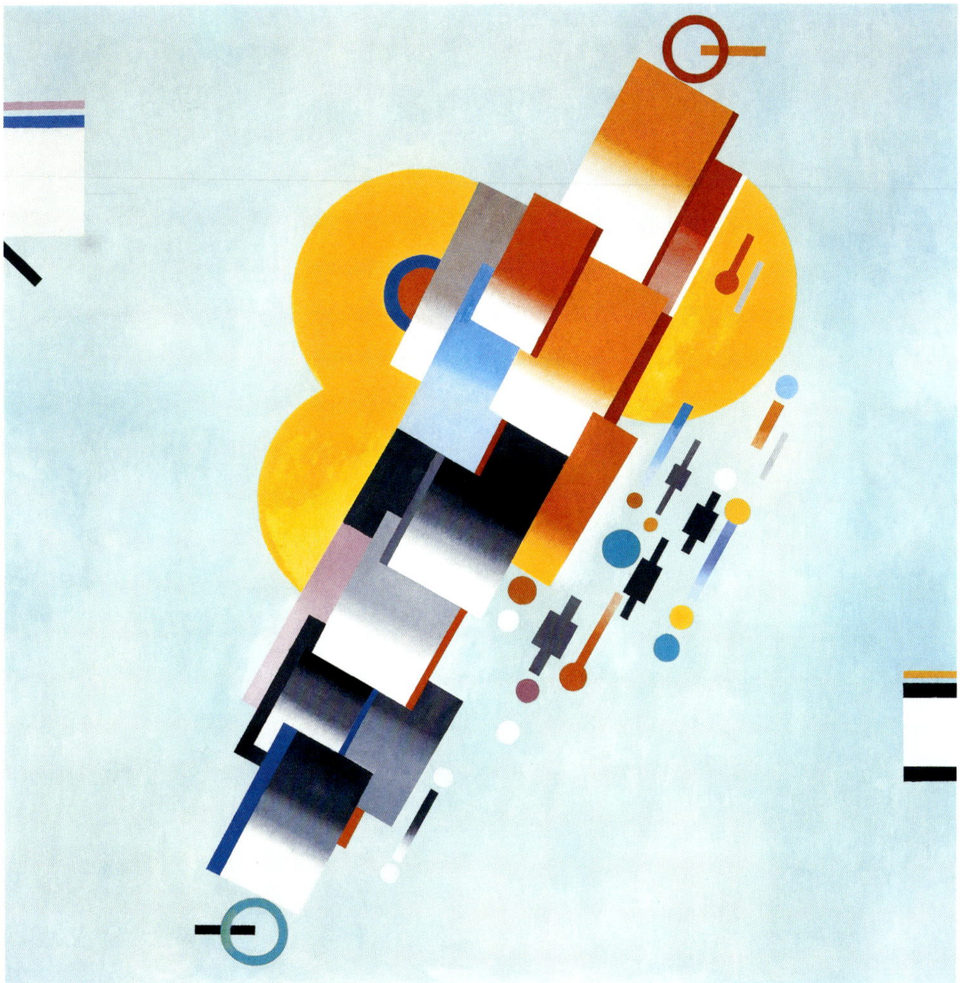

Cascade on Green. Touching 1998

Oil on canvas
106 x 106 cm

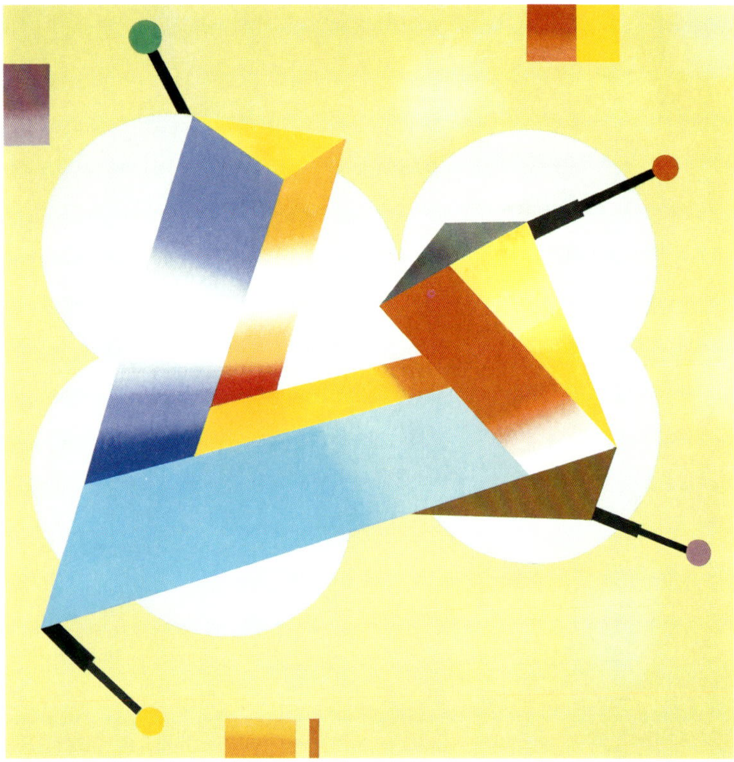

Floating World 1998

Oil on canvas
76 x 76 cm

differences. Again one wonders at the inventiveness and the expanding utility of the language Smith developed for himself.

It would be convenient to suggest that the stage designs and these three paintings, of 1987-88, are milestones in Smith's progress. They are not. The problem is to find anything to pick on in mapping his development. The 1970s, 1980s and the 1990s have been unbelievably fecund for him, though the phrase might mislead one into thinking that, having arrived at his maturity and chosen field of action, Jack Smith can just let the paintings happen. They vary continually. New motifs come in, representing new ideas; some stay, some are used just once. Whatever general statement one makes about them must soon be abandoned. All the forms are abstract? Yes, but some of them come full of associations while others remain exactly what they are: abstract forms. A disc can be a lot of things from a full-stop to the sun. Are letter-forms abstract? In *Inside. Outside Sensation* (1981), ill. p.56, we find two letters, fading away on the right: either 'ar' or 'an'. The letters 'ar' could stand for *Architectural Review*, which used these lower case initials as its logo. There is nothing unusually architectural about the composition. This is arranged in three horizontal bands, the central of which is black and exhibits five cloud-like shapes in white. They are not *very* like clouds but they do not suggest anything else. At some points they fade into the black ground, which brings suggestions of space, time and movement. Smaller forms address these five and reappear in other parts of the picture. Its total

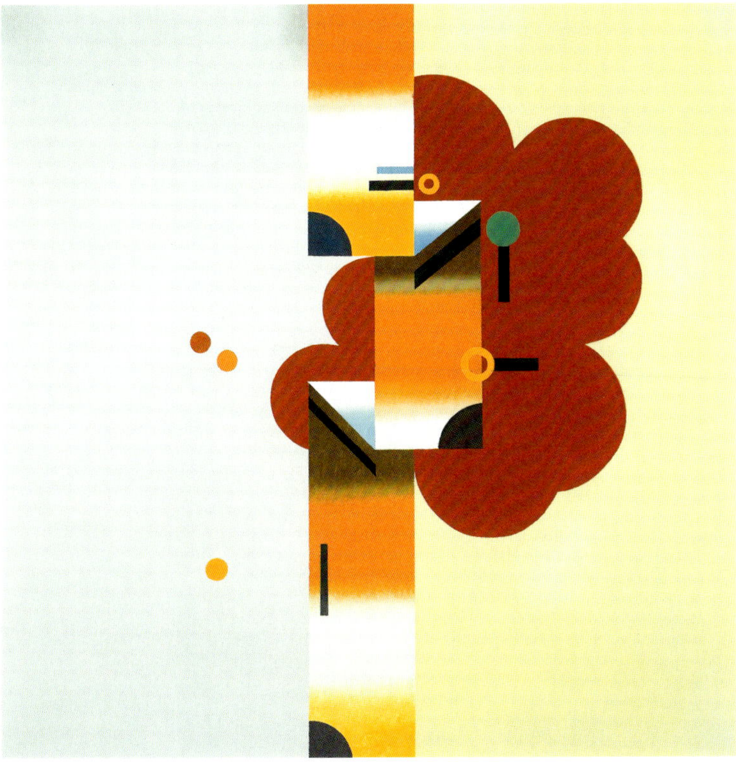

Vertical Invention 1998

Oil on canvas
91 x 91 cm

character is unique in Smith's work yet entirely representative of it in that its organization and some of the visual events in it are decidedly quirky.

This is particularly difficult to discuss and assess away from the originals. In effect, Jack Smith works on a painting within temporary limits of language or style, set by what he has been working on but at times also springing from conscious decisions, as we shall see. As he works, he may feel moved to introduce alien motifs. These do not speak the same language and can seem ironical, like an aside, or disruptive, like the wrong notes in Mozart. Occasionally they are blatant; more often they are discreet.

In many of Smith's paintings there is so much to assimilate that we seem to be reading several languages at once, even when the surface is not crowded. Two paintings of 1987 use many of the elements we found in the two composer portraits. *Musical Painting*, ill. p.66, has three parallelograms that could be tilted rectangles but they exist within a dominant form, almost square but standing on two corners and shrunk in the lower part, stretched above so that there is, again, a hint of perspective and movement. Smaller forms move across these, and attach themselves here and there with what feels like total freedom. A white ground feels pinned down by little discs in three corners; in the fourth, top left, are two squares, black and red, that make one think of El Lissitzky's famous book *About Two Squares* of 1920. Similar elements make up *Sounds and Silences* (ill. p.68), though grouped quite differently and on a positive

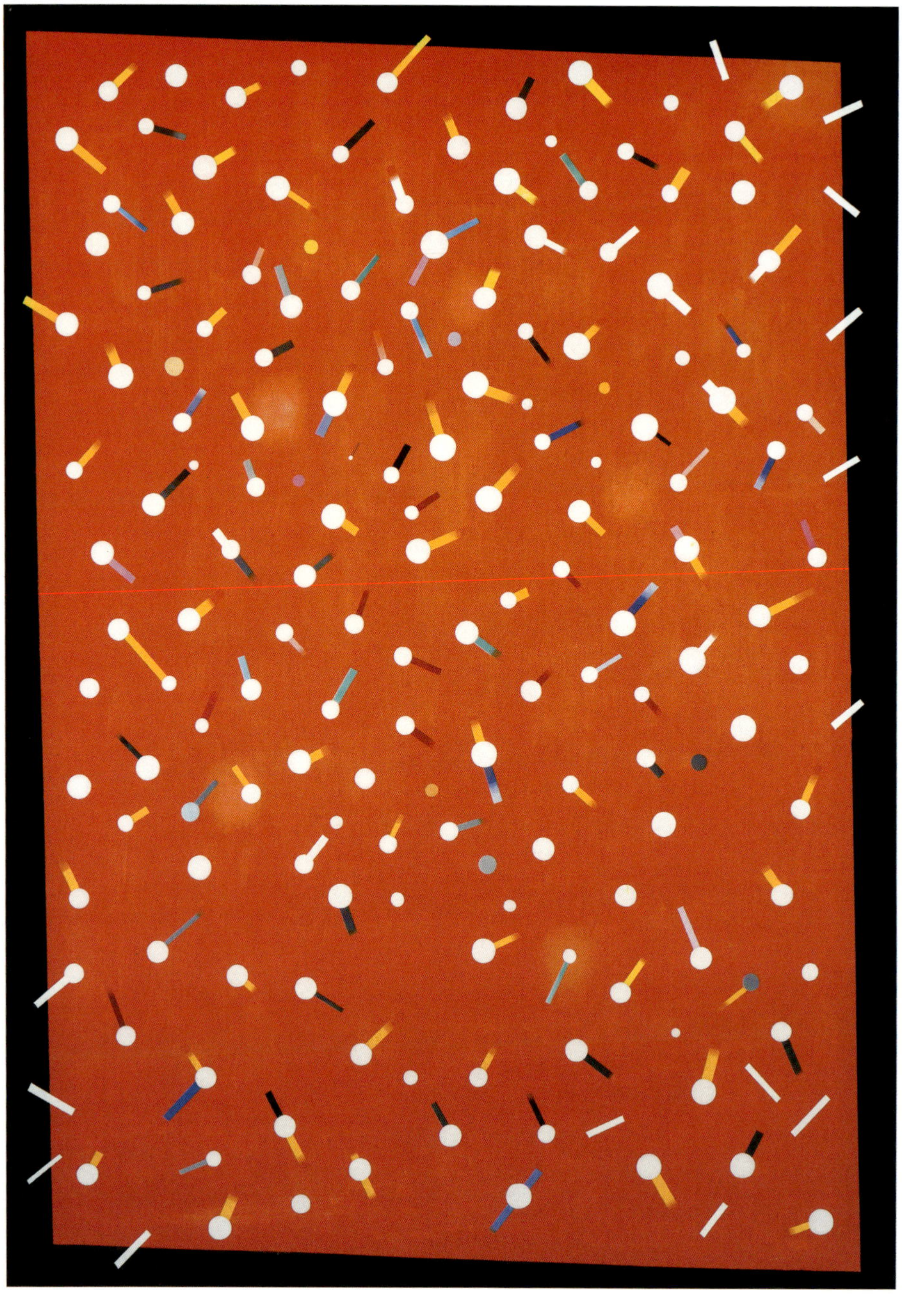

One Six Zero 1998

Oil on canvas
213.5 x 152.5 cm

orange ground, but the main distinction between these two pictures is that of size, the latter being fifty-six times the size of the former.

In others we find great economy and concentration. *Zig Zag 6* (1982), ill. p.57, has two ground colours, yellow above, blue below, and black zig-zag lines making a noisy horizon between them, beset by rounded forms that change colour and cling to the lines like barnacles. There are other things, calling for other words, perhaps the oddest being half a pale ring, right of centre, that could be the end of a tube emerging out of the blue ground. The blue ground of *Light and Sound* (1982), ill. p.61, is traversed by an isosceles triangle whose base is the entire left edge of the picture and whose apex touches the middle of the right edge. The triangle is white on the left, becomes yellow, but ends in a fiercely red tip. Even without this there would be a strong sense of movement across the picture, but that sharp red end makes for thrust. About half way along the triangle is a stack of lines and bands, with and without interjacent discs and other lines and colours that seem to move in and out of sight. Together they make a vertical stratum within the triangle, but also beyond it because the red spots drift beyond its confines and seem closer to us than the rest. A linear form within this stratum almost makes a number, but to my reading the oddest elements in the picture are the two lines springing from the corners that hold the triangle's base. They seem important; they go nowhere at no particular angle; they look like mistakes yet are fine and firm.

The most evident step Jack Smith took in his work during the 1970s was to give all possible power to colour. After the calm, refined and reticent character of most of the Serpentine Gallery's exhibits he decided to employ colours at their fullest. As he points out, colour in English paintings is often muted to work tonally and adjusted to echo aspects of nature. Colour became something for him to lay out in large, carefully worked areas, but also to disport in bands and sometimes to modulate by shooting it through with other colours which may or may not add a three-dimensional effect. We must not assume that this move was unprecedented within his own work. In the early 1970s, and in the early 1960s too, Smith at times used colour brightly and loudly, to what I think of as brass-band effect. A clear case was the *Painted Relief* of 1963, discussed before. Another is *Sounds & Silences on Black* (1971), ill. p.41. Black often means gloom. Here, as elsewhere in Smith's work, it is the occasion for colour and light. He painted the ground very densely, for evenness and to avoid shine (on occasion he has used acrylic black in paintings otherwise worked in oils), and painted luminous colours onto it. Rectilinear lines make something like a plan in the middle of the picture, housing hard-edged forms within it that seem three-dimensional, as well as other signs. There are three rings, marked

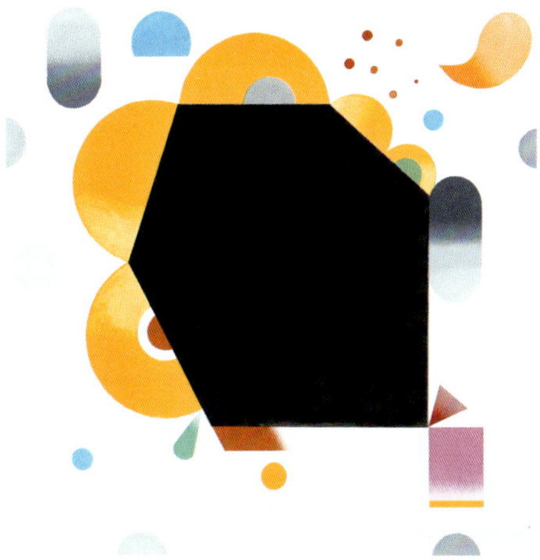

Beyond the Abyss 1998

Oil on canvas
91 x 91 cm

with little touches of grey, that may be hoping to find their way into three white angular U-shaped bays, all open at the top, as in a game. A violet band frames this design, and outside this there is another framing device of bands and corner squares. Everywhere there is colour, enhanced to almost neon brightness by the black setting.

A new format emerges in Jack Smith's painting in the early 1980s, to reappear at intervals to this day: the square picture hung by one corner, the diamond shape. There is a history of it in Modernism and in heraldry and commemorative tablets. See, for example, those dark diamond boards hung high up on the piers of Dutch Reformed churches, making their presence felt in the church interiors painted by, particularly, Pieter Saenredam. Mondrian made significant use of the format from 1918 on, intermittently, until his very last, unfinished painting, *Victory Boogie-Woogie* (1943-44). John Milner points out that as a structural device the diamond form had played a controlling role in several of Mondrian's earlier pictures, and he relates it to Mondrian's keen interest in the work of Vermeer.[34] Jack Smith's admiration for Vermeer and for Mondrian has already been mentioned. The diagonal black and white tiled floors pictured so tellingly in several Vermeers may have given Smith a taste for their extraordinary offering of clarity with complexity. The diamond format was used occasionally by other De Stijl artists, and then also by artists contributing to the broad Constructive art tendencies of the 1920s and after, including Domela, Vordemberge-Gildewart and Max Bill. Mondrian asked that his diamond paintings be hung higher than normal, with their bottom corner at eye level, so that one would look up at them, and that is how we see them in some studio photographs of his. Malevich had his white-on-white paintings of around 1918-19 exhibited close to the ceiling. Smith's use of the diamond format does not imply a spiritualizing programme, but he makes original and full use of the special dynamics the form yields.

Sounds (Fractured) 3. (1982), ill. p.58, is a fully-fledged and telling example of the sort. We see a white ground on which straight black lines, meeting – and sometimes not meeting – to make acute angles, come close to inscribing a large eight-pointed star. Attached to these lines are many curved elements, parts of discs, some flat and monochrome, others with fading colours that

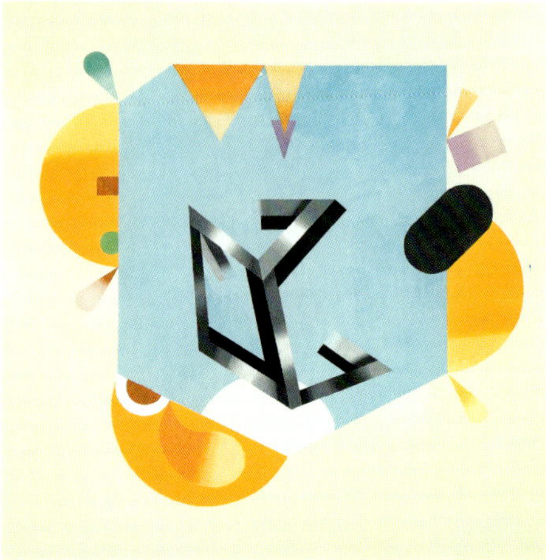

Floating World. Inside. Outside 1998

Oil on canvas
91 x 91 cm

34. See John Milner, *Mondrian*, London 1992, especially pages 143-49, 195 and 222-25. In Mondrian's *Composition with Yellow Lines* (1933), yellow vertical and horizontal bands look as though they could meet to form one square, rather larger than the diagonal canvas, and that is how one imagines them – only to find that they cannot unite in this way, being of different widths and thus possibly differently located in space. This may be a foretaste of that quirkiness which becomes so marked in the work of Mondrian's last years in New York.

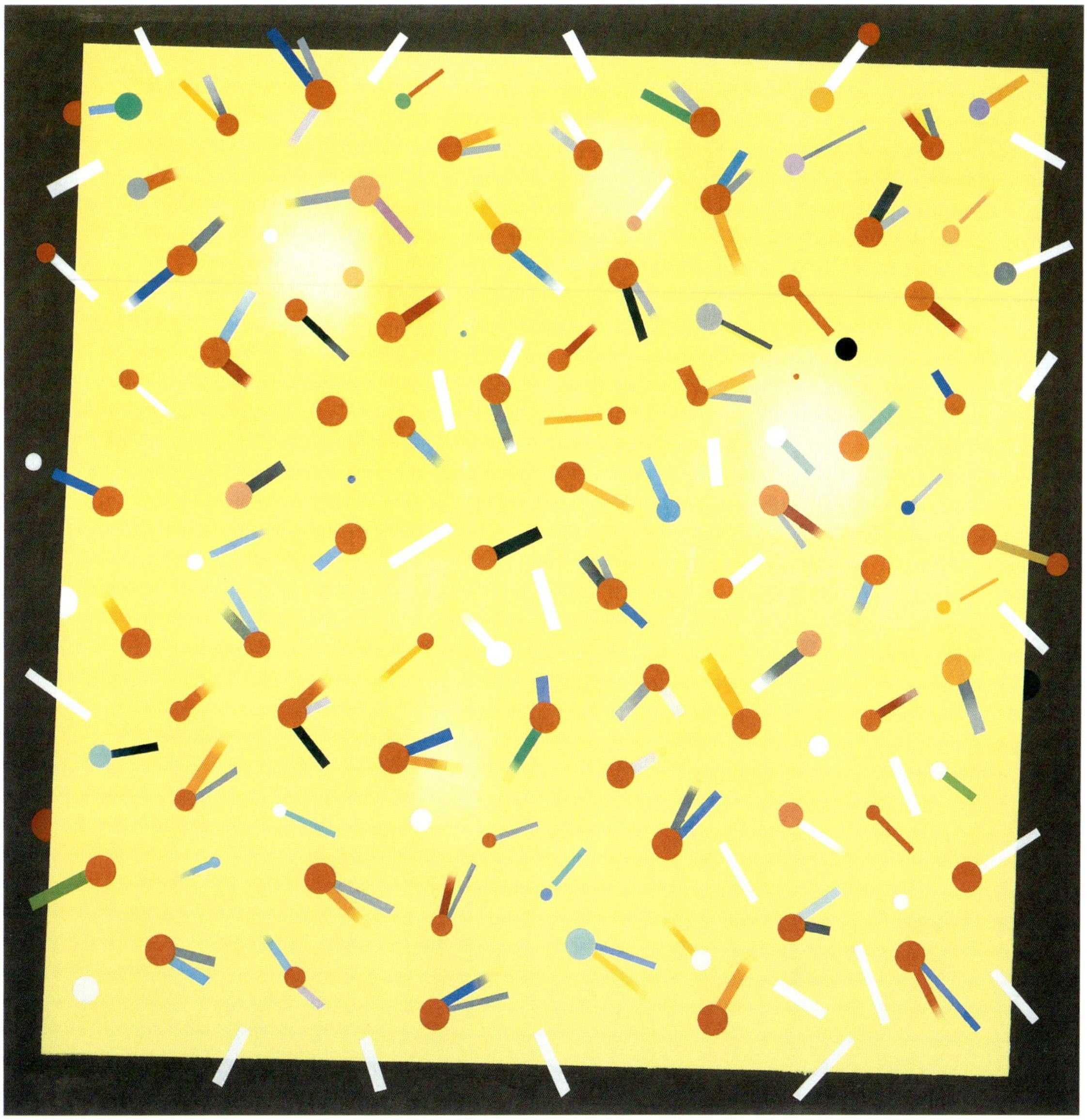

One Zero Five 1998

Oil on canvas
122 x 122 cm

imply space, one multicoloured. There are also many small elements, little rectangles and dots, finer lines etc., and a firm red disc in what is sensed as, and almost is, the geometrical centre of the picture. It is flanked by two independent clusters, one in blue, almost a piece of writing, the other a meeting of little forms in blue, black and yellow. Our eyes are teased this way and that. Perceptual processes keep trying to complete what is here fragmented and bring pictorial logic to arrangements bordering on the chaotic. It is the neatness and clarity of it all that forces this sense of noncoherence on us. And then, at (so to speak) seven o'clock, we notice a little red line (one among several such red lines) with thinner red and yellow lines fluttering from it. It says: don't expect to make order out of this — it is life, it is happiness, it is painting.

The essential point is that all this, the physical material and the visual outcome, is in the painter's hands. He controls every part. Directed by his spirited imagination, he injects disjunctive elements and contradictory devices into art that could seem authoritarian or merely programmatic without them. He does not work to prove his power, but to speak of diversity, of surprise, of the contrariness often involved in being alive. Some of the most dramatic of Smith's diagonal paintings belong to the 1990s. They all exhibit this vivacity.

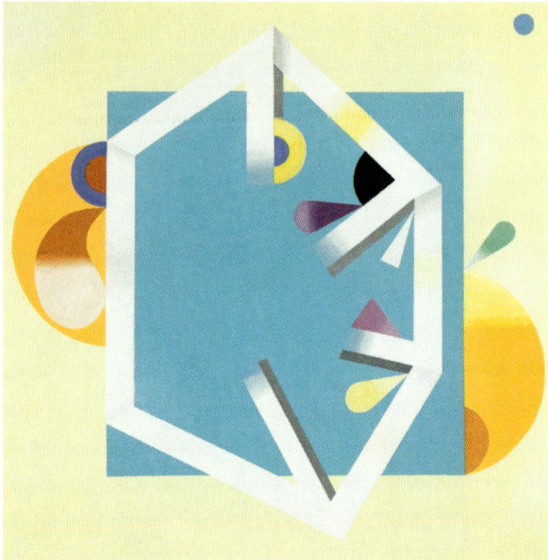

Inside. Outside 1998

Oil on canvas
76 x 76 cm

Since 1990, Jack Smith has been showing regularly in London at Flowers East. His first exhibition there, in January-February 1990, consisted of work selected from his output of the preceding five years, including the abstract portraits already mentioned and some exceptionally tough paintings with 'sound' and 'light' in their titles. *Sound of Light (Early one Morning) I* (1988), ill. p.72, makes powerful use of broad black bands, shaped a little like fat paper-clips and placed along the four edges of the canvas. They contain colours, firm sometimes, more often melting into white or into each other. The black bands themselves have greyish highlights on them that deny their flatness. So there is a lot of rhythm and wave motion around the composition, all of it enhanced by the sharp-edged blue square lodged within the area left by the clips, in the lower left corner. This is as firm as can be against its white ground, and makes everything else, in spite of first impressions, feel insubstantial. Similar black bands and shapes occupy much of *Sound and Light* (1987), ill. p.65, the central area as well as the sides, on a yellow ground that turns out to be not even but variegated. Here too, some colours fade, some stay firm, and there are a few clear but small forms to set against this malleability. The firmest element is the square that ends one clip shape, bottom right, insisting on flatness and permanence, and almost making us not notice that in seven places the black bands weave over and under each other to deny both flatness and strength.

Bryan Robertson wrote his foreword for the catalogue with evident enjoyment. Smith, he wrote, 'is painting some of the most radiant and compulsively watchable pictures of my lifetime in this country ... Such high spirits in such an energetic series of balancing acts and aerial bombardment are rare in British art'. He spoke of 'elusive reverberations' and 'lots of sudden doubletakes', and referred to Malevich, as if he had 'started to fly kites', and to Stuart Davies and Calder. European non-Expressionist abstract art tends to be 'staid and poker-faced'; here is wit and endless formal invention, catching 'some of the jaunty, playful sense of fun and brightly lit gusto of the seaside: the sharpness, clarity of contour, and waving, acrobatic, semaphore-like vivacity of the marine prospect'. One of the paintings in the show was actually titled *Faisons une Folie 2,* ill. p.70, and incorporates those letters in it in an almost legible manner.

The catalogue for Smith's 1991 show included a text by the artist Larry Berryman. It opens challengingly: 'It is thirty years since the first manned orbital flight and still no artist in space', no one, that is, with the eyes and the communicative urge to share such experiences with us. But then, perhaps, it might be foolish to risk an artist: 'Imagination fuels and launches its own rockets'. He recommends Jack Smith's work as an important contribution to 'the central achievement of twentieth century art, the lingua franca of abstraction'. Smith especially demonstrates that this is ' – in green-speak – infinitely renewable', and the role, *vis-à-vis* us as audience of his wit. Berryman compares his acute spatial sense to 'the practised timing of a great comedian', and suggests that even in England, exuberance should at long last be welcomed as a virtue greater than moderation, as William Blake had recommended. 'But he who kisses the Joy as it flies / Lives in Eternity's sunrise'.

The work in this second show was again selected from about five years' production, but inclined to the more diagrammatic aspects of it. The first illustration in the catalogue is of a large 'collage drawing' in diamond format, titled *Areas of Energy* (1986), ill. p.67. In spite of its multiplicity of firm shapes and colours, including black, this is light in weight of colour and tone, and full of light. Long, fine lines are paired to indicate two long channels with bends and corners, and our eyes travel along these endlessly, drawn away sometimes by adjacent formal events but returning again to see where they lead. This exhibition also included a group of what Smith calls 'painted objects', assembled sculptures made mostly of found ingredients which he painted and painted upon. These are far removed from the almost surrealistic and somewhat ominous white plaster sculpture he made in 1964 (*Inside and Outside No.1*).

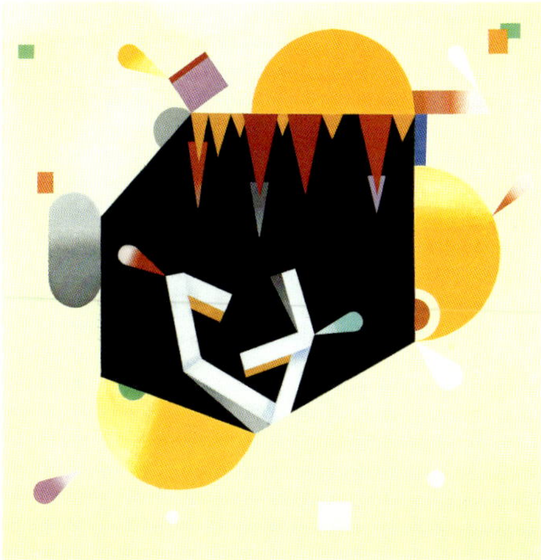

Visual Invention on Yellow 1998

Oil on canvas
91 x 91 cm

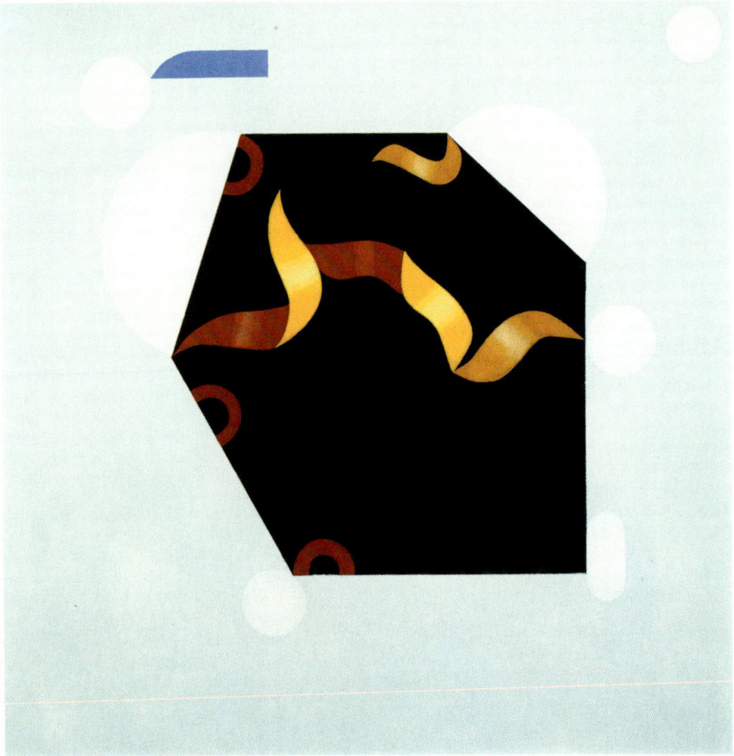

Slow Movement I 1999

Oil on canvas
91 x 91 cm

Now colour determines the character of each part as much as form, and the groupings tend to play down solidity and weight.

Jack Smith's 1992 exhibition was all of work from 1990 onwards, and was again full of strong colour and lively goings-on on the pictorial stage. Even so, *Ta Ra Ra* (1991), ill. p.81, is exceptional. It is a painting in Smith's own tradition of fairground and circus entertainments, all *con brio*, up-front and straightforward until you start questioning what it consists of. The manner in which it is painted generally confirms flatness, though there are highlights on some forms that bring them bending forward, and here and there forms overlap in ways that imply layering and space. The ground, a greyish pale pink, holds back and is not interfered with. There are many small and medium-sized forms in bright colours, many of them turning this way or that, or, like the three red fat apostrophes, seeming to leap forward. There are letter-forms that approximate to the letters of the title. There are also four more or less square forms, planted orthogonally and thus exercising a great deal of authority as stabilizers amid the free-for-all. If we rely on them for this, however, they breed doubts as to where they are in space, and whether or not they are of one family. What is certain is that they contrast with the rest and so enhance the general vivacity just as Smith's black grounds can enhance colours.

Paul Overy's essay, in the 1992 catalogue, examines Smith's procedures, referring to Kandinsky's and Mondrian's art and writings, and to semiotic theory. He speaks of Smith's 'system' and 'codes', and quotes Roman Jakobson's argument that our desire to read images as representing things we know turns abstract paintings into 'puzzle pictures'. This desire is well established – for example, by our habit of seeing living creatures in trees, clouds, etc. – but any attempt to read Smith's 'sign system' as a code or sequence of codes is blocked, as Overy admits, by 'contradictory codes' though it is 'internally consistent'. I find that it is consistent only if received as entirely concrete: each form, whether we call it a sign and see it as part of a language or not, is only itself and its meaning and action is exclusively pictorial. We may also read them analogically – a yellow disc might suggest the sun – but their existence is, in my view, entirely factual in pictorial terms; any other reading, when it can be made, is extraneous. 'Code' implies that each element consistently stands for something else; 'system' that they are used logically, in accord with inherent rules. In my view, Jack Smith's art is free of such constraints and does not call for interpretation, but, like sound in music, acts directly on our sensibilities. It is when, as here, we need to use words to describe or in some way explicate what happens in his pictures that we are forced to express ourselves analogically. Our language invites this, sometimes forces it. If I write that forms in a picture 'swarm', I invoke images of a multitude of creatures moving together. But this does not mean that Smith's crowded forms mean bees or starlings or a herd of buffalo. Reading abstract compositions via such similes ignores the painter's freedom to invent forms and the relationships that suggest actions. As Smith himself reminds us, the only profitable analogy is with music: his paintings employ many of the dynamics of music. Some of their titles suggest analogies, for ease of identification more than to invite us to interpret them. They are not intended to reveal a coded meaning, and they follow after, rather than precede, inventing the image.

This becomes clearer than ever in Smith's work since 1991. These almost ten years have found him in full production, inventing freely as well as developing new pictorial themes through variations pursued over years. Sampling this production will have to serve to indicate its fullness and freshness. *Jamboree I* (1996), ill. p.94, has something of the same presence as *Ta Ra Ra* though its squareness makes for firmer containment. A border painted just inside the frame should add to that, but is disrupted, not held, by colour. The letters of the title are there too, and broad orange bands angled this way and that, at once strong and inconstant. Where they meet or cross we seem to see shadows! Surely these belong to an older language created for representational purposes. Has not that dreadful thing, illusion, been wholly overcome? So wholly, in fact, that Jack Smith can play with it, just as in the areas

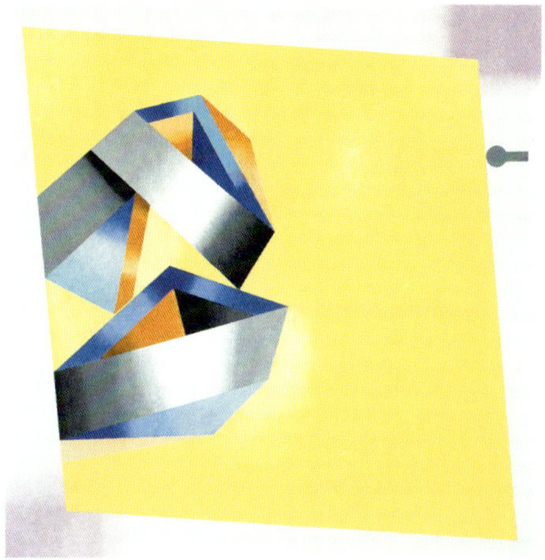

Dialogue 4 1998

Oil on canvas
76 x 76 cm

framed by his red bands here he can produce mottled and multiple mists sweetly tinted in the manner of Kandinsky. In other words, the sensory effects of his forms and their modulation, to which we automatically attribute meanings derived from our general experience, *are* his facts and his meaning. Highlights on orange bands cannot but suggest some movement forwards and back even though we know that what we see is flat paint. Forms can look as though they are overlapped by other forms and thus must be behind these. Visual facts and material facts are often at odds in art. Painted differently, *Jamboree* could be a stable, authoritarian design; painted the way it is, every certainty is undermined.

In 1996 Jack Smith embarked on the *Cascade* series. It is characterized by relatively small but strong forms of one family apparently moving across the canvas. At first, they are combinations of parallel lines and circles, hinting at tubes but also countering any three-dimensionality. These come in swarms and move, though ambiguously. In *Cascade on Grey* (1996), ill. p.88, they are mostly red and are placed diagonally. Smaller lines and spots alongside them encourage the sense of movement — but are they swarming up to the left top corner or down from it? In *Cascade No.2*, ill. p.88, we have to read them, mostly in blue and black, as descending centrally from the top, where they appear from behind an orange band, to the bottom where they project over a yellow band. They also seem to be dispersing freely. A more regimented platoon of the same forms comes straight down the centre of the canvas in *Cascade No.3* (1996, not illustrated). *Cascade on Black. Balancing and Touching* (1996), ill. p.90, uses a largely different array of forms, and the title says what many of them are doing. They occupy mostly the middle of the canvas from top to bottom – nothing touches the lateral borders – but there is no clear indication of up or down movement. Instead, the whole arrangement is poised on a little blue disc: fickle Fortune used to be shown as a woman standing on a sphere in Renaissance emblems. The black ground gives extra brilliance to Smith's bright colours. In 1997 Smith made a similar composition with colours that produce a strikingly different sort of presence: *Cascade on Green*, ill. p.92. He also painted a diamond format *Cascade on Black (Diamond)*, ill p.93, with fewer and larger forms that still seem precarious, and thus temporary, in their arrangements. The forms themselves, aided by occasional shadows, hint at three-dimensionality. The *Cascades* continue into 1998, mostly as diagonal or off-vertical groupings of brightly coloured, or in one case modulated grey 'metallic' forms, ill. p. 91. Close to the series but differently titled is another forty-two-inch diamond painting of 1997 *Self-Portrait (Diamond)*, ill. p.93, in which bright, disruptive

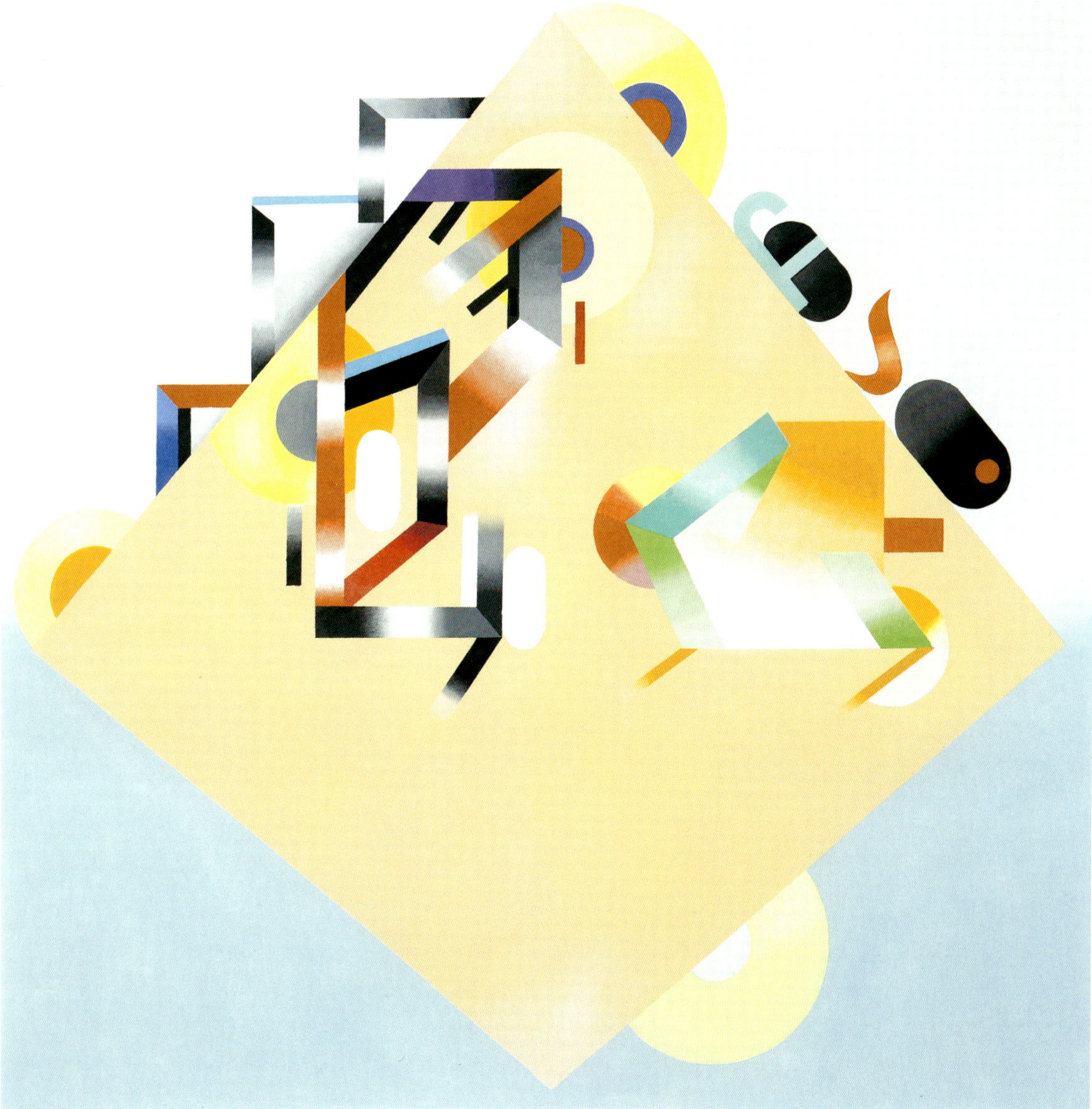

Visual Invention (Fractured) 1999

Oil on canvas
122 x 122 cm

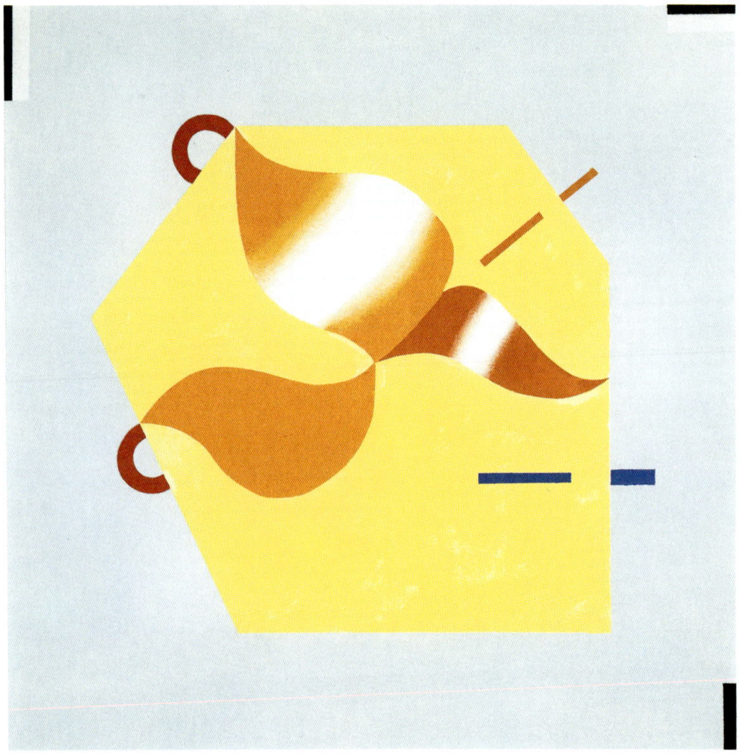

Slow Movement 2 1999

Oil on canvas
76 x 76 cm

colours on a black ground half deliver, half prevent our reading of letters that make up the painter's name.

Several other series invite discussion. *Visual Invention* and *Vertical Invention* with and without other indications serve as titles for works using similar devices but sometimes quite different arrangements: see, for example, *Vertical Inventions* (1997), ill. p.95, with its rather delicate signs and colour shifts in vertical channels, framed by a broad but entirely inconstant order. A six-sided shape, placed centrally, always asymmetrical but variously proportioned, provides continuity in a series that sometimes uses the *Visual Invention* formula as title and belongs to 1998-99. *Visual Invention on Yellow* (1998), ill. p.107, is one of the first. The shape is black but has forms inside it as well as adhering to its outside, so that the old *Inside/Outside* terminology would fit too. Sharp and jagged forms are silhouetted against the black; outside it, on the pale yellow ground, are large and small semi-circles, squares etc. There are minor implications of space and movement, least ambiguously in the two overlapping rectangles top right. White forms, brilliant on the black, are scarcely discernible on the yellow. The same black shape dominates *Beyond the Abyss* (1998), ill. p.103, but here the shape stands on its longest side and is solid (or hollow) black. Against it cluster, and around it float, large and small rounded forms, a variegated rectangle and a fat comma, all on white and accentuating the blackness of the black. The title invites but also refutes interpretations in terms

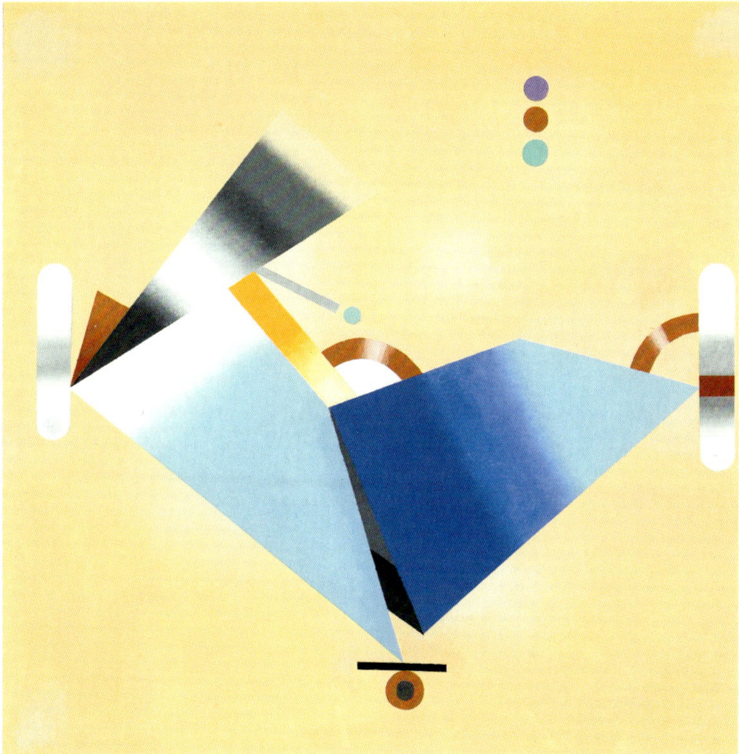

Touching (side to side) 1999

Oil on canvas
76 x 76 cm

of mood. The same shape, also in black, holds court in *Slow Movement 1* (1999), ill. p.108. Inside it are half-rings in red and what seem to be fluttering ribbons, irresistibly three-dimensional in effect. So the black is read as a space. Outside, on a pale grey ground, we see one firm blue form and a number of white circles and half-circles, ghostlike amid the grey. The same shape, similarly placed but yellow, reappears in other variations with pale grounds. In *Slow Movement 2* (1999), ill. p.112, it seems to be pinned down by blue and red strips; on its left sides a half-ring in red, and another more-than-half ring, imply an overlap and again raise the yellow shape a little off the grey ground. This seems as though held down by elements in three of the corners, black and white, again black and white, and just black.

Another series, *Floating World*, ill. p.80, started in 1992, and climaxed in 1998 with such pictures as *Floating World, Inside. Outside*, ill. p.104. An irregular hexagon, related to the others, here in light blue, contains some forms, has others clinging to its sides, and seems held down by a short black band that lies on it and on the pale yellow ground. Inside the blue, spacious shape, floats a metallic form, that seems alien to the rest, all highlit grey-to-black bands or bars, sharply angled, a potential aggressor in a generally serene world. The key word for another series, also begun in 1992, is *Touching*. It draws attention to the places where forms just touch each other, often points against straight sides, as though to say 'look, no overlaps', yet overlaps occur in the same pictures, as well as tones that speak of space. In *Touching (side to side)* (1999), ill. p.113, there are many such touchings, as well as three-dimensional effects in forms large and small. The whole arrangement teeters on a disc and exceptionally *avoids* touching any of the four sides of the canvas. In *Touching on Grey* (1998), ill. p.98, what could seem a relatively top-heavy arrangement of angled bands and triangles, implying solids, floats over over/underlapping circles that could be clouds on the grey ground, while firm rectangles are lodged like keystones against the picture's four edges.

Two exceptionally large paintings must be drawn attention to, not least because they cannot be reproduced successfully. *Summer Sensation* (1995), ill. p.87, is a serene though busy scene, a complex but neat array of small discs and other clear forms, as well as a few pink blotches, on a yellow ground which itself has pale blotches in it. Sunshine dominates, the more so for the firm bands, black and white plus patches of colour, that frame the composition. Very effective, too, is the blue line along the bottom, answered by a red line at the top. Above the blue line is an empty expanse of yellow before the discs etc. start. This lifts the composition and makes it float. Differences in the scale of the forms, abetted by the slight patchiness in the yellow and the lurking pinks, give what at first seems a flat, all-over arrangement a curious liveliness and depth. Smith used rather similar ingredients in two paintings of 1998, *One Zero Five*, ill. p.105, and *One Six Zero*, ill. p.102: small formal units, a prominent but blotched ground-colour, yellow and red respectively, now set into a black border or background. The little units, usually small discs plus one or more lines, recall the real pins Smith used in the 1970s and the pin-like forms he had painted before then. Here they seem to be angled in all directions and the effect is very lively, with forward and backwards tensions. It is striking in both paintings that the 'pins' do not keep out of the black areas. In *One Zero Five* two red discs in the black area on the left appear from behind the yellow field and thereby push it forward: what had seemed a luminous space in which the forms could move about, some near, some further away, suddenly announces itself to be a yellow membrane. That the yellow area here and the red area in *One Six Zero* are both parallelograms – in effect, slightly tilted rectangles – heightens their spatial ambiguities and instability. As so often in Smith's work, what seems a very limited programme reveals its visual and thus also sensational richness gradually, as we become intimate with it.

The exceptionally large *Summer Sensation* of 1995 was a special venture, following the sort of inner imperative Kandinsky and Goethe spoke of. In 1980 Jack Smith had set out to paint an even larger canvas, eight by twelve feet. He painted this in acrylics, knowing that it would have to be rolled for storage once

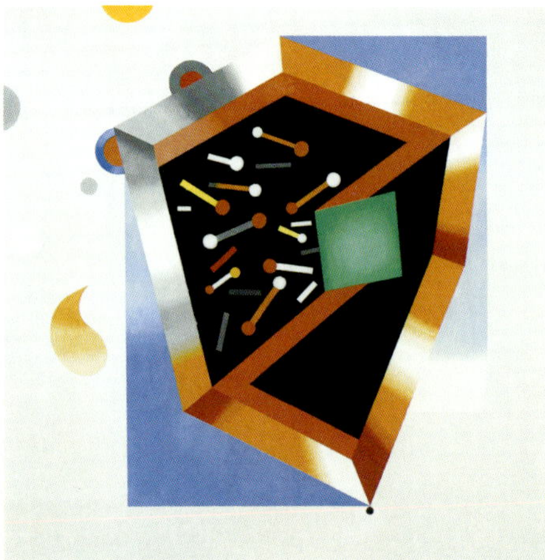

Balancing Within. Without 1999

Oil on canvas
106 x 106 cm

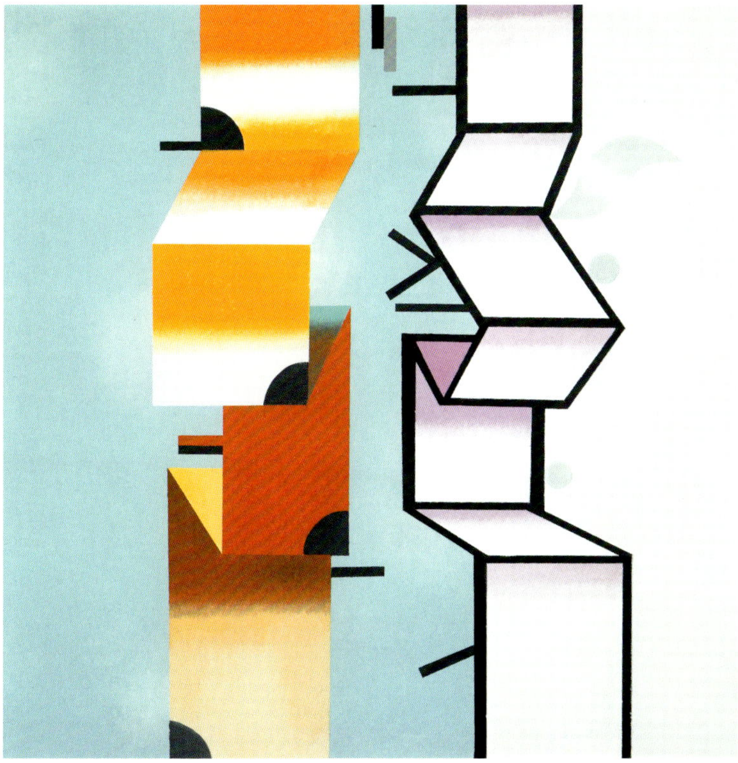

Dialogue. Fandango 1999/2000

Oil on canvas
91 x 91 cm

it was finished: acrylic paint is less liable to crack. Recently it has been unrolled and stretched, and found to be in perfect condition. It is *Bridge No.3*, ill. p.52, in many ways a contrast to the hedonistic *Summer Sensation*. Where that, not only because of its title, signals warmth and high spirits, *Bridge No.3* looks a more reticent, almost scholarly composition. We see a great quantity of forms and patches on a white ground. Small, linear forms, somewhat akin to shorthand signs, are in neat rows. There are also grey squares that fade in and out and do not quite follow the same horizontal ordering but generally seem to drift upwards as we read the picture left to right. They appear, most of them, to be transparent; we are left uncertain whether to read them as in front of, or behind, the linear forms. These vary infinitely. Blue lines, just above and just below the array, make us more aware that the forms and patches at the top and bottom seem to disappear out of sight — as though what we saw on this large canvas was only a section of a larger document, continuing top and bottom, like a partly unrolled scroll. None of these details is likely to strike one at first glance, just as *Summer Sensation* does not reveal itself all at once. Here, for example, strong, relatively large discs along the top counteract weight and recession. In *Bridge No.3*, a few small spots appear in the top right area to add to the spatial play there.

Again, using words to draw attention to what happens in Jack Smith's paintings makes for hard reading. At the same time words can point at only some of their visual energies and general characteristics. What one tends not to say, in the attempt not to impose too much on the reader — especially in the way of emotional responses that will in part be personal but not, I am sure, unsharable – is the pleasure and the thrills the paintings (but not the words) provide. Jack Smith's paintings vary in their presence, from the openly dramatic and forceful to the more surreptitious ones, slighter at first encounter but somehow insidious. They are always more complex than they announce, and in different ways. One hesitates to speak of art done with such care and deliberation as spilling out from the artist's fertile imagination, yet that is how it is: slowly, patiently, they emerge, and tomorrow there will be more, born out of this dedicated, generous, commitment. I find *Summer Sensation* brilliant and joyous, again and again, *Bridge No.3* more and more enchanting in its cryptic, reserved way, as I stay with it.

Jack Smith's 1996 show of *New Paintings* included *Summer Sensation* and much smaller variations on it, as well as Cascades and a number of paintings of the *Various Activities* sort, with and without letter-forms in them. The catalogue of this vivid show used Smith's own words: his 1965 statement at the front, and the newer, of 1995 (both already mentioned) at the back. In the first he spoke about the need for complexity and of 'letting [a painting] have visual space and eye dance'; in the second he spoke of an internal logic 'which needs to be discovered'. In a sense, he is still discovering it: 'Abstract painting is still in its infancy; there is so much to explore'. The adventure continues, irresistibly.

right
Jack Smith, Studio, Brighton 1991
Photograph: George Newson

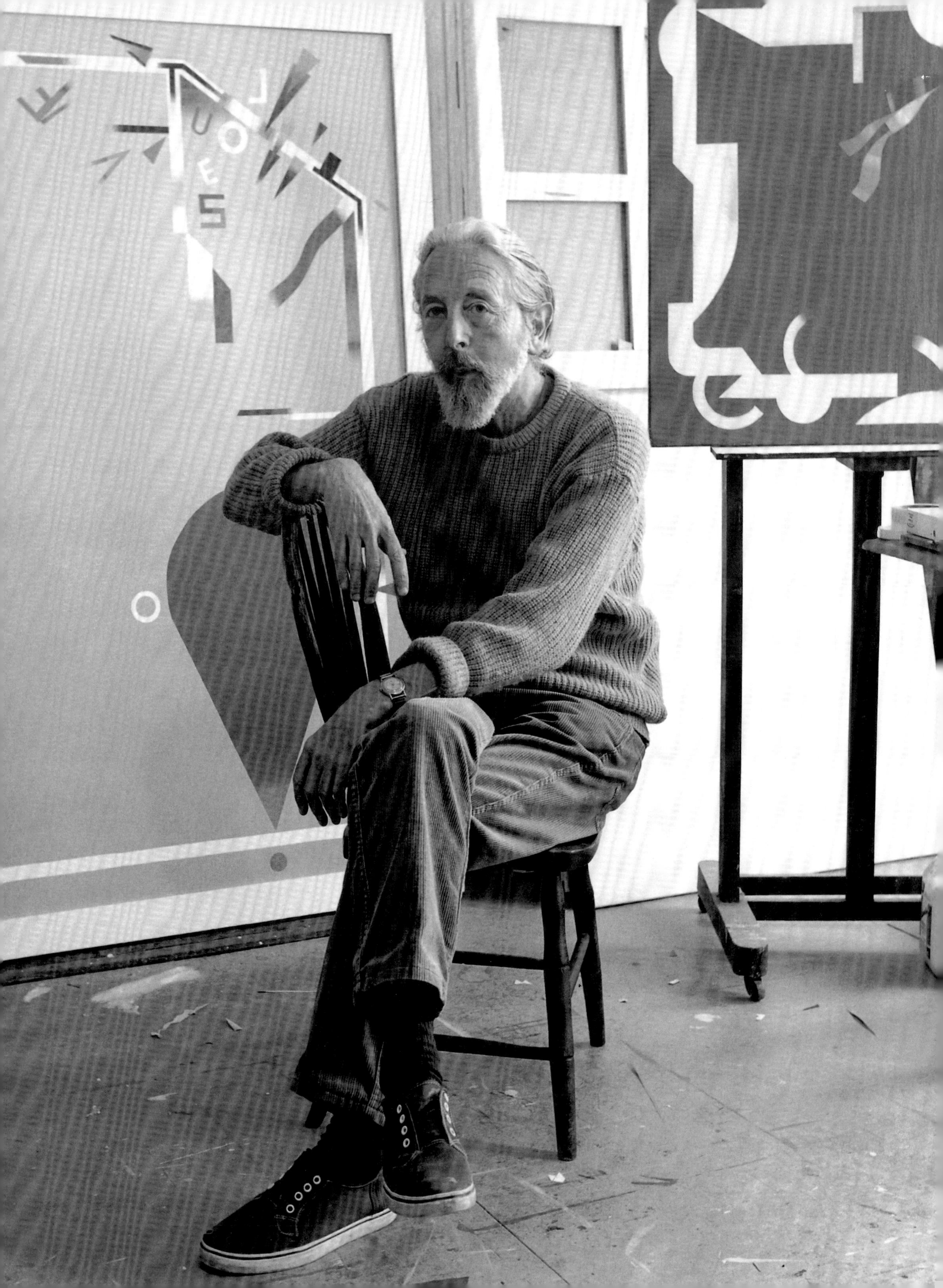

BIOGRAPHY

1928	Born, Sheffield
1944/46	Sheffield College of Art
1948/50	St.Martin's School of Art
1950/53	Royal College of Art

ONE PERSON EXHIBITIONS

1952/3/4/6/8	Beaux Arts Gallery, London
1958/62/63	Catherine Viviano Gallery, New York
1959	Retrospective, Whitechapel Art Gallery, London
1960/63	Matthiesen Gallery, London
1961	Midland Group Gallery, Nottingham
1965	Grosvenor Gallery, London
1968	Marlborough Fine Art, London
1968	Konsthallen, Gothenburg, Sweden
1969	Hull University
1970	Bear Lane Gallery, Oxford
1971	Whitechapel Art Gallery, London
1974	Redfern Gallery, London
1975	Ray Hughes Gallery, Brisbane
1976	Redfern Gallery, London
1977	Retrospective organised by Sunderland Art Centre toured to Mappin Gallery, Sheffield; Hatton Gallery, University of Newcastle; Ikon Gallery, Birmingham; Northampton Art Gallery Kettle's Yard, Cambridge
1978	Serpentine Gallery, London
1981/83	Fischer Fine Art, London
1987	The Mayor Gallery, London
1988	Studio 5, Chippenham
1990	Flowers East, London
1991	Flowers East, London
1992	Flowers East, London
1996	Flowers East, London
2000	Flowers East, London

GROUP EXHIBITIONS

1954	*British Painting and Sculpture*, Whitechapel Art Gallery, London
1955/8/61/3	*Pittsburgh International*, Carnegie Institute
1956	*Venice Biennale* (touring to Munich)
1957	*Six Young Painters*, Arts Council
	John Moores Liverpool Exhibition (1st prize)
1960	*Guggenheim International* (National prize)
1963	*British Painting in the Sixties*, Tate Gallery, London
	Premio Lissone, Milan
1964	*Englische Kunst der Gegenwart*, Stadtische Kunstgalerie, Bochum
1965	*Stuyvesant Foundation: A Collection in the Making*, Whitechapel Art Gallery, London
1966	*London under Forty*, Galleria Milano, Milan
1967	*Aspects of New British Art*, touring Australia and New Zealand
1974	*British Painting*, Hayward Gallery, London
1975	Sunderland Arts Centre
1983	*British Painting*, Museo Municipal, Madrid
1994	*Forster, Smith and Sutton*, Flowers East at London Fields, London
	British Abstract Art, Part I, Painting, Flowers East, London
1995	*The Twenty Fifth Anniversary Exhibition*, Flowers East at London Fields, London
1996	*British Abstract Art, Part III, Works on Paper*, Flowers East, London
	Angela Flowers Gallery (Ireland) Inc., Co. Cork
1997	*Angela Flowers Gallery 1997*, Flowers East at London Fields, London
	New Abstract Paintings, Riverside Studios, London
1998	*Angela Flowers Gallery at Riverside Studios*, London
	Small is Beautiful: Part XVI, Music, Flowers East at London Fields, London

1999	*Ten New Abstract Paintings*, Flowers East at London Fields, London
	Small is Beautiful: Part 1, Abstract, Flowers West, Santa Monica, California
2000	*Angela Flowers Gallery 30th Anniversary Exhibition*, Flowers East, London and Flowers West, Santa Monica, California
	Artists' Choice, Flowers East, London

PUBLIC COLLECTIONS

Arts Council
Auckland City Art Gallery, New Zealand
Berlin National Gallery
British Council
Cardiff Art Gallery
Contemporary Art Society
City Art Gallery, Manchester
City Art Gallery, Plymouth
Ferens Art Gallery, Hull
Graves Art Gallery, Sheffield
Gothenburg Museum, Sweden
Government Art Collection
Guggenheim Museum, New York
Hove Museum of Art, Hove, Sussex
Ipswich Museums & Gallery
Kingston upon Thames Polytechnic
Leicester City Art Gallery
Leeds City Art Gallery
Manchester City Art Gallery
National Westminster Bank
Scottish National Gallery of Modern Art, Edinburgh
S.E. Arts Collection, Towner Art Gallery, Eastbourne
Swindon Art Gallery, Swindon, Wiltshire
Tate Gallery, London
The Art Gallery of South Australia, Adelaide
The Art Gallery of New South Wales, Sydney
The National Gallery of Victoria, Melbourne
Victoria and Albert Museum, London
Walker Art Gallery, Liverpool
Whitworth Art Gallery, Manchester
Welsh Contemporary Art Society

COSTUME AND SET DESIGN

1986	*Carmen Arcadiae Mechanicae Perpetuum*, Ballet Rambert. Music Harrison Birtwistle
1987	*Pursuit*, Royal Ballet. Music Colin Matthews

BIBLIOGRAPHY

1958 Graham Ackroyd, Jack Smith: The Inward Eye, *The Painter and Sculptor*, Autumn

1959 Mark Roskill, Catalogue Introduction, Whitechapel Art Gallery, London

1963 David Sylvester, Catalogue Introduction, Matthiesen Gallery

1965 Jack Smith, *Notes on Painting*, London Magazine, March

Charles S. Spencer, *Movement and Sound in New Paintings*, Studio International

1968 Mark Glazebrook, London Magazine, June

1969 Jack Smith, *Contribution to Letterforms in the Arts*, Journal of Typographic Reseach

1977 Alan Bowness, Helder Macedo, Jack Smith, *Jack Smith Paintings and Drawings 1949-1976*, Ceolfrith Press, Sunderland

1981 Paul Overy, Catalogue Introduction, Fischer Fine Art

1987 Nigel Reynolds, The Daily Telegraph, 19 June

1992 *Viewpoints*, Arts Review, June

1994 John McEwen, Sunday Telegraph, 27 February

ACKNOWLEDGEMENTS

Any close account of a living artist's work depends first and foremost on close contact with the artist. Having long admired Jack Smith's work, I had no doubt that he would be good to work with, and so it was. We both live in Brighton-and-Hove, so that Jack and Sue Smith bore lots of visits from me and he put up with something like an Inquisition. I am grateful to them both for their patience and hospitality. Jack and I spent many hours looking through his work, in his house and at his London gallery; I was already attuned to it but my responses became more complete as familiarity with it deepened. Angela and Matthew Flowers, of Flowers East, commissioned this book, and I am grateful to them for giving me this opportunity to study and report on the work of a fascinating and important British artist. They charged Kate Leese with bringing the book, the text and many illustrations, into being; she has been an admirable collaborator in every way, careful, steadfast and supportive. Linda Saunders brought to sub-editing the text her rare gift for engaging sympathetically with the tone and purpose of a script while watching out for every sort of clumsiness and obscurity. If faults remain, they do so in spite of her care, and of Kate's and Jack's; they are mine. My hope is that this book, the result of our combined efforts, will be followed by other studies and lead to much greater awareness of Jack Smith's art. Many collectors and collections have supplied images and information. I am especially grateful to Isobel Johnstone and to Jill Constantine for giving me access to Jack Smith's paintings, and for lending me slides and photographs of them, in the Arts Council Collection.

Norbert Lynton

First published in Great Britain in 2000 by
Momentum, P.O. Box 12752, London E8 3UA

ISBN (paper) 1 902945 07 7
ISBN (cased) 1 902945 08 5

A catalogue record for this book is available from the British Library

Designed and coordinated by Peter Gladwin and Kate Leese

Printed in London by Specialblue Ltd

Jack Smith is represented by Angela Flowers Gallery

Flowers East
199 -205 Richmond Road
London E8 3NJ
Telephone: 020 8985 3333 Facsimile: 020 8985 0067
e-mail: gallery@flowerseast.com

www.flowerseast.com